A BASIC BAHÁ'Í DICTIONARY

A BASIC BAHÁ'Í DICTIONARY

General Editor
Wendi Momen

GR

GEORGE RONALD
OXFORD

GEORGE RONALD, Publisher
46 High Street, Kidlington, Oxford OX5 2DN

British Library Cataloguing in Publication Data

Momen, Wendi
A Basic Baha'i dictionary
1. Bahism
I. Title
297'.89

ISBN 0-85398-230-9
ISBN 0-85398-231-7 Pbk

Printed in England by Billing & Sons Ltd., Worcester

Acknowledgements

A debt of gratitude is due to those who contributed to this book: Dorothy Heller, W. M. Heller, May Ballerio, Mark Hofman and Moojan Momen.

We wish to thank all those who provided the many black-and-white photographs, in particular the Audio-Visual Department of the Bahá'í World Centre, the UN International Labour Organization, and the Save the Children Fund.

Introduction

Born in the middle of the last century, the Bahá'í Faith is now one of the most widely spread religions in the world, with adherents in virtually every country, territory and island. The teachings of Bahá'u'lláh are becoming more well known and the literature of the Bahá'í Faith more readily available. With this emergence from obscurity has come the need to explain some of the terminology and concepts of the Bahá'í Faith, particularly those found in the Bahá'í Writings and generally used by Bahá'ís.

A Basic Bahá'í Dictionary is a non-specialist's introduction to the Bahá'í Faith and to Bahá'í literature. It is intended neither to be comprehensive nor to provide a deep understanding of the Bahá'í Faith, which can only come through reading and reflecting on the Writings of Bahá'u'lláh, 'Abdu'l-Bahá and Shoghi Effendi. Rather, the *Dictionary* offers brief explanations of many of the concepts of the Bahá'í Faith, defines words found in Bahá'í literature, provides a glossary of several Persian and Arabic words, gives a short introduction to some of the more well-known figures and events from Bahá'í history, and presents a broad outline of the administrative structure, organization and practices of thc Bahá'ís. It does not attempt to provide a guide to the pronunciation of any terms.

The *Dictionary* is alphabetized word by word, ignoring the connecting letters of '-i-' and 'y-i-' in Persian and Arabic names. The connecting word 'ibn' is also ignored except where it is capitalized. Those entries which consist of whole phrases, such as the 'elimination of extremes of wealth and poverty', are generally listed by key words, in this case 'wealth'.

The origins of foreign terms are indicated thus: Ar (Arabic), Pers (Persian) and Turk (Turkish).

Wendi Momen

A

'abá [Ar] A loose outer garment or cloak, open in front, worn by Iranian men.

'Abbás Effendi The name by which 'Abdu'l-Bahá was known outside the Bahá'í community.
See also 'Abdu'l-Bahá.

'Abbás-i-Núrí, Mírzá *See* Buzurg-i-Vazír, Mírzá.

'Abbúd, Ilyás A wealthy Christian merchant of 'Akká who owned a home on the edge of what is now called Genoa Square. He was a patron of the Greek Orthodox Church of St George. Bahá'u'lláh and His family lived in the house of 'Údí Khammár which was attached to 'Abbúd's house. Such were the charges of impiety, atheism, terrorism and heresy which were levelled against the Holy Family that 'Abbúd reinforced the partition that separated his house from their dwelling. Eventually, however, he was won over as a friend and offered a room in his house for the use of 'Abdu'l-Bahá and Munírih Khánum. Later he rented the whole house to the Holy Family. 'Abbúd died in 1878.
See also House of 'Abbúd *and* Khammár, 'Údí.

'Abdu'dh-Dhikr [Ar] Servant of the Remembrance. A designation of the Báb.

n 'abá, worn by Mírzá
ɔu'l-Faḍl

Ilyás 'Abbúd

Sulṭán 'Abdu'l-'Azíz

'Abdu'l-'Azíz Sulṭán of the Ottoman Turkish Empire (ruled 1861–76) who banished Bahá'u'lláh from Constantinople (Istanbul) to Adrianople (Edirne) in 1863, and finally to 'Akká in 1868. The Sulṭán's decree condemned Bahá'u'lláh and His companions to permanent banishment and ordered that they be strictly confined and forbidden to associate with each other or with the local inhabitants. Bahá'u'lláh is reported to have said that in banishing Him without reason to the Most Great Prison ('Akká), 'Abdu'l-'Azíz's tyranny was worse than Náṣiri'd-Dín Sháh's.[1] Bahá'u'lláh addressed the Sulṭán in two Tablets including the *Súriy-i-Mulúk* (Tablet to the Kings), but he did not respond. 'Abdu'l-'Azíz was deposed and assassinated in 1876.

'Abdu'l-Bahá Eldest surviving son of Bahá'u'lláh and His designated successor. Named 'Abbás after his grandfather, 'Abdu'l-Bahá was known as 'Abbás Effendi outside the Bahá'í community. Bahá'u'lláh also gave Him the titles Ghuṣn-i-A'ẓam (the Most Great Branch), Sirru'lláh (Mystery of God) and Áqá (the Master). He chose the name 'Abdu'l-Bahá (Servant of Bahá) for Himself after the passing of Bahá'u'lláh.

'Abdu'l-Bahá was born in Ṭihrán, Iran, on 23 May 1844. While still a child, He recognized His Father's station even before it had been openly revealed. He shared Bahá'u'lláh's banishment and exile and often served as His Father's deputy when dealing with officials and the public. Bahá'u'lláh described the station of 'Abdu'l-Bahá in the *Súriy-i-Ghuṣn* (Tablet of the Branch). In the *Kitáb-i-'Ahdí* (Book of the Covenant), He named 'Abdu'l-Bahá as His successor and the authorized Interpreter of His Writings.

'[T]hough essentially human and holding a station radically and fundamentally different from that occupied by Bahá'u'lláh and His Forerunner,' Shoghi Effendi has explained, 'Abdu'l-Bahá was 'the perfect Exemplar of His Faith . . . endowed with superhuman knowledge, and to be regarded as the stainless mirror reflecting His light.'[2] While not regarding 'Abdu'l-Bahá as a prophet, Bahá'ís show special respect to His unique station by capitalizing pronouns referring to Him.

In about 1873 'Abdu'l-Bahá married Munírih Khánum. Of their nine children, four daughters lived to adulthood. His eldest daughter Ḍiyá'íyyih was the mother of Shoghi Effendi.

In 1901 Sulṭán 'Abdu'l-Ḥamíd II again ordered 'Abdu'l-Bahá confined to 'Akká but in 1908 He was set free after the Young Turks' revolution. It was 'Abdu'l-Bahá who, at the instruction of Bahá'u'lláh, saw to the transfer of the Báb's remains to the Holy Land and their interment in a permanent shrine on Mount Carmel in 1909.

In 1911 He began His historic journeys to Europe and North

America to proclaim His Father's message, returning to the Holy Land in 1913. Renowned outside the Bahá'í community for His humanitarian work, 'Abdu'l-Bahá was knighted in 1920 by the British government for his efforts for the relief of hunger in Palestine during World War I.

Among the achievements of the ministry of 'Abdu'l-Bahá were the spread of the Bahá'í Faith to the West and Australia; the building of the first Mashriqu'l-Adhkár in 'Ishqábád and the beginning of the Mother Temple of the West in Wilmette, Illinois, USA; and the establishment of the first institutions of the Bahá'í Administrative Order.

'Abdu'l-Bahá

'Abdu'l-Bahá

During His lifetime, 'Abdu'l-Bahá wrote many books and Tablets, interpreting and elucidating the Writings of Bahá'u'lláh. Among His books published in English are *The Secret of Divine Civilization, Memorials of the Faithful* and *A Traveller's Narrative*. In addition, the texts of many of His talks and Tablets have been collected and published in volumes such as *Tablets of 'Abdu'l-Bahá, Tablets of the Divine Plan, The Promulgation of Universal Peace, Some Answered Questions* and *Paris Talks*.

In His Will and Testament, 'Abdu'l-Bahá named His grandson, Shoghi Effendi, to succeed Him as Guardian of the Bahá'í Faith. 'Abdu'l-Bahá died in Haifa on 28 November 1921, and is buried in a vault of the Shrine of the Báb.

See also Munírih Khánum, Shoghi Effendi, Shrine of 'Abdu'l-Bahá *and* Will and Testament of 'Abdu'l-Bahá.

Sulṭán 'Abdu'l-Ḥamíd II

'Abdu'l-Ḥamíd II Sulṭán of the Ottoman Turkish Empire (ruled 1876–1909). As a result of the plotting of Mírzá Muḥammad-'Alí, in 1901 'Abdu'l-Ḥamíd restricted 'Abdu'l-Bahá's freedom, confining Him and His family within the city walls of 'Akká. Later the Sulṭán sent two commissions of inquiry to investigate false charges made against 'Abdu'l-Bahá by Covenant-breakers, and for a time 'Abdu'l-Bahá was in great danger. However, with the Young Turks' revolution in 1908, all religious and political prisoners in the Ottoman Empire were freed and the Sulṭán was overthrown the following year. He died in 1918.

'Abdu'l-Vahháb-i-Shírází A shopkeeper of Shíráz who, as a youth, dreamed of the appearance of the Imám 'Alí. With him in the dream was Mullá 'Alíy-i-Basṭámí, one of the Letters of the Living who was sent to Iraq. On awakening, 'Abdu'l-Vahháb saw Mullá 'Alíy-i-Basṭámí passing and followed him. Mullá 'Alí tried to persuade the young man to return to his shop but to no avail. 'Abdu'l-Vahháb's father overtook them, ordered his son to return home and beat Mullá 'Alí. On their return to Shíráz, 'Abdu'l-Vahháb related his dream to his father, who was overcome with regret for his actions. Later 'Abdu'l-Vahháb moved to Káẓimayn near Baghdád where in 1851 he encountered Bahá'u'lláh who was visiting the sacred shrines there. His dearest wish was now to travel back to Iran in the company of Bahá'u'lláh, but Bahá'u'lláh persuaded him to stay where he was and gave him money to enlarge and extend his trade. 'Abdu'l-Vahháb followed Bahá'u'lláh to Ṭihrán, where he was caught up in the persecution of the Bábís that followed the attempt on the life of the Sháh. Found giving praise to his Lord in the market-place, he was thrown into the Síyáh-Chál and chained to Bahá'u'lláh. One night he dreamed that he was soaring into a space of infinite vastness and beauty. Bahá'u'lláh told him that that day he would sacrifice himself for the Cause. In the morning the gaoler called for 'Abdu'l-Vahháb. He threw off his chains, sprang to his feet and embraced each of his fellow prisoners. Because he had no shoes, Bahá'u'lláh gave him His own. 'Abdu'l-Vahháb kissed the knees of Bahá'u'lláh, then sang and danced all the way to his execution. His executioner later returned to the cell praising the spirit 'Abdu'l-Vahháb had shown at the hour of his death.[3]

See also 'Alíy-i-Basṭámí, Mullá.

'Abdu'lláh Pásh͟há Governor of 'Akká from 1819 to 1831, succeeding Sulaymán Pásh͟há, his father-in-law. 'An ambitious and acquisitive young man',[4] he inherited extensive lands outside of 'Akká, including land at al-Bahja and Mazra'ih, and he took over Sulaymán's large property now known as the Bayḍún estate. He built a third mansion at the tip of Carmel, now forming part of the foundation of the lighthouse there. He used as his Governorate buildings in the northwest corner of 'Akká which had been built around 1810 by his father and which incorporated Crusader buildings in its structure.

One commentator writes, ''Abdu'lláh Pásh͟há, throughout his stormy days as a ruler of the area, had elevated ideas of his own merits, even going so far as to announce publicly . . . that he fulfilled in himself the conditions of the true Caliph.'[5]

The Egyptians invaded Palestine in 1831 and took 'Akká in 1832. 'Abdu'lláh Pásh͟há surrendered and was taken to Egypt. In 1840 the area reverted to Turkish rule and 'Abdu'lláh was freed by Egypt. He returned to Palestine and sold the Stella Maris monastery back to the monks. He then went to Constantinople, and eventually to the Ḥijáz where he died.

Several of the residences that once belonged to 'Abdu'lláh Pásh͟há were occupied by Bahá'u'lláh and His family: the Mansion of Mazra'ih; the original structure of the Mansion of Bahjí, which he built in 1821; and the Governorate in 'Akká.

See also House of 'Abdu'lláh Pásh͟há, Bahjí *and* Mazra'ih.

Abhá [Ar] Superlative of 'Bahá' (Glory), meaning 'Most Glorious'.

Abhá Beauty Bahá'u'lláh.

Abhá Kingdom The 'next world'; the spiritual realm beyond the grave into which the soul passes after death.

abjad (From the four letters of the Arabic alphabet 'A', 'B', 'J' and 'D') The ancient Arabic system of allocating a numerical value to letters of the alphabet, so that numbers may be represented by letters, and not to be confused with numerology (the study of the occult meaning of numbers). Shoghi Effendi explained in a letter written on his behalf: ‘In the Semitic languages – both Arabic and Hebrew – every letter of the alphabet had a numerical value, so instead of using figures to denote numbers they used letters and compounds of letters. Thus every word had both a literal meaning and also a numerical value. This practice is no more in use but during the time of Bahá’u’lláh and the Báb it was quite in vogue among the educated classes, and we find it very much used in the Bayán. As the word Bahá also stood for the number nine it could be used interchangeably with it.’[6] The letters and their values are:

a,á,’	b	j	d	h	v,ú	z	ḥ	ṭ	y,í
ا ء	ب	ج	د	ه	و	ز	ح	ط	ی
1	2	3	4	5	6	7	8	9	10

k	l	m	n	s	‘	f	ṣ
ک	ل	م	ن	س	ع	ف	ص
20	30	40	50	60	70	80	90

q	r	sh	t	th	kh	dh	ḍ	ẓ	gh
ق	ر	ش	ت	ث	خ	ذ	ض	ظ	غ
100	200	300	400	500	600	700	800	900	1000

ablutions Washing of the face and hands before reciting the obligatory prayers.[7] Although stated as a law in the *Kitáb-i-Aqdas*, the performance of ablutions is not yet required in the West.

Abraham Considered to be the Father of the Jewish people. Bahá’u-’lláh was descended from Abraham through his wife Keturah. Abraham is referred to in Bahá’í scriptures as the ‘Friend of God’ and the ‘Father of the Faithful’.

Abu’l-Faḍl-i-Gulpáygání, Mírzá The most outstanding scholar of the Bahá’í Faith. Born in 1844 in Gulpáygán, Iran, to a family of Muslim religious scholars, at thirty Mírzá Abu’l-Faḍl was the master teacher of a Ṭihrán religious seminary. After years of rejecting the Bahá’í Faith, he was moved to study it after an encounter with a humble Bahá’í blacksmith. In 1876 Abu’l-Faḍl became a Bahá’í and devoted the rest of his life to teaching, travelling and writing about the Bahá’í Faith. In

Cairo he was the centre of Bahá'í activity. In 1901 'Abdu'l-Bahá sent him to America where he spent nearly four years, making a lasting mark on the American Bahá'í community. Among the books he wrote which have been translated into English are *The Bahá'í Proofs, The Brilliant Proof, Miracles and Metaphors* and *Letters and Essays, 1886–1913*. Mírzá Abu'l-Faḍl died in Cairo in 1914. Shoghi Effendi named him one of the nineteen Apostles of Bahá'u'lláh.

Abu'l-Ḥasan-i-Ardikání, Mullá (Ḥájí Amín, Amín-i-Iláhí) A Hand of the Cause and an Apostle of Bahá'u'lláh, Abu'l-Ḥasan became a Bábí shortly after the martyrdom of the Báb. When Bahá'u'lláh declared His mission, Abu'l-Ḥasan accepted immediately and travelled throughout Iran teaching other Bábís of the advent of Bahá'u'lláh. Eventually he became the assistant of Ḥájí Sháh-Muḥammad Manshadí, Amínu'l-Bayán, who was Trustee of the Ḥuqúqu'lláh. Abu'l-Ḥasan earned his living by trading and by writing letters for those were were unable to write, while at the same time he collected the Ḥuqúqu'lláh and any letters the believers wanted sent to Bahá'u'lláh and distributed Tablets revealed by Bahá'u'lláh. He visited 'Akká whilst Bahá'u'lláh was still a prisoner in the citadel and was the first Bahá'í from the outside world to be able to meet Bahá'u'lláh in 'Akká (in the public baths). On the death of Ḥájí Sháh-Muḥammad Manshadí in 1880, Abu'l-Ḥasan was appointed Trustee (Amín) of the Ḥuqúqu'lláh. In 1891 he was imprisoned for three years in Ṭihrán and Qazvín. He continued his travels during the life of 'Abdu'l-Bahá, visiting Haifa and 'Akká on several occasions. He died in 1928 and was posthumously named a Hand of the Cause by Shoghi Effendi.

Right Mírzá Abu'l-Faḍl-i-Gulpáygání

Far right Ḥájí Amín

Abú-Ṭálib, Mullá A master mason who came to the Holy Land from Baku, Ádharbáyján before the passing of Bahá'u'lláh. He had original responsibility, under the supervision of 'Abdu'l-Bahá, for the construction of the Shrine of the Báb, and two doors of the Shrine are named for his two sons, 'Alí-Ashraf and Áqá Bálá. Abú-Ṭálib originally bought the area of the Ashraf Garden and gave the property to his son 'Alí-Ashraf who later donated it to the Faith.[8]

See also Ashraf Garden.

Acre *See* 'Akká.

'Ád Traditionally, a fourth generation descendant of Noah, whose people 'inhabited a large tract of country in Southern Arabia . . . His people, who are said to be of a tall race, were idolators and aggressive people . . . God chose Húd to be a prophet to the people of 'Ád.'[9] The majority of the people of 'Ád rejected the teachings of Húd and they were destroyed by a calamity.

See also Húd, Ṣáliḥ *and* Thámud.

Adam The first Manifestation of God to appear on earth in recorded religious history. His dispensation began the Adamic Cycle.

Adam is also considered to be a collective term for the whole of mankind, as in Genesis 5:1–2: 'In the day that God created man, in the likeness of God made he him; Male and female created he them; and blessed them, and called their name Adam, in the day when they were created.'

'Abdu'l-Bahá has explained that the Biblical story of Adam and Eve is symbolic: 'Therefore this story of Adam and Eve who ate from the tree, and their expulsion from Paradise, must be thought of simply as a symbol. It contains divine mysteries and universal meanings, and it is capable of marvellous explanations . . . We will explain one of them, and we will say: Adam signifies the spirit of Adam, and Eve his soul. For in some passages in the Holy Books where women are mentioned, they represent the soul of man. The tree of good and evil signifies the human world . . . The meaning of the serpent is attachment to the human world. This attachment of the spirit to the human world led the soul and spirit of Adam from the world of freedom to the world of bondage, and caused him to turn from the Kingdom of Unity to the human world. When the soul and spirit of Adam entered the human world, he came out from the paradise of freedom and fell into the world of bondage. From the height of purity and absolute goodness, he entered into the world of good and evil . . . This is one of the meanings of the Biblical story of Adam.'[10]

Adamic Cycle The period of time, approximately six thousand years, beginning with the revelation of Adam and ending with the Declaration of the Báb. Also called the 'Prophetic Era', the Adamic Cycle included a series of successive divine revelations which gave rise to the religions of Hinduism, Buddhism, Zoroastrianism, Judaism, Christianity and Islam. The Declaration of the Báb in 1844 marked the end of the Adamic Cycle and the beginning of the 'Bahá'í Cycle' or 'Era of Fulfilment'.

See also progressive revelation, universal cycle *and* Universal Manifestation.

adhán [Ar] Announcement. The Muslim call to prayer, made by the muezzin from the minaret of the mosque before each of the five times of obligatory prayer.

See also mu'adhdhin.

Ádharbáyján Mountainous province in the northwest of Iran where the Báb was imprisoned. The provincial capital is Tabríz.

See also Máh-Kú *and* Chihríq.

Adíb *See* Ḥasan-i-Adíb, Mírzá.

administration Colloquial term used by Bahá'ís to refer to the whole administrative structure of the Bahá'í Faith. Also often used to refer only to the elected part of this structure.

See also Administrative Order, Bahá'í.

Administrative Order, Bahá'í The structure of Bahá'í institutions, conceived by Bahá'u'lláh, formally established by 'Abdu'l-Bahá in His Will and Testament, and cxpanded during the guardianship of Shoghi Effendi. Its 'twin pillars' are the Universal House of Justice and the Guardianship.

The Bahá'í Administrative Order includes the local and national spiritual assemblies (in future to be called Houses of Justice) and the Universal House of Justice, the Guardianship and the institution of the Hands of the Cause. Shoghi Effendi described the Bahá'í Administrative Order 'not only as the nucleus but the very pattern of the New World Order destined to embrace in the fullness of time the whole of mankind',[11] and as 'the sole framework'[12] of the future Bahá'í Commonwealth.

Combining the best features of various secular forms of government without their drawbacks, the Bahá'í Administrative Order is unique in religious history in its structure and origin. Its establishment by the Founder Himself, and the clear provisions set down for its continuation into the future, safeguard it against division and the formation of sects.

Bahá'í administration, Shoghi Effendi has emphasized, is 'an instrument and not a substitute for the Faith of Bahá'u'lláh, . . . a channel through which His promised blessings may flow' and which 'should guard against such rigidity as would clog and fetter the liberating forces released by His Revelation.'[13]

See also World Order of Bahá'u'lláh.

administrative rights The rights belonging to all members enrolled in the Bahá'í community. These include the right to vote in Bahá'í elections, which is, at present, limited to members aged twenty-one and older, as well as other rights including attendance at the Nineteen Day Feast, serving on Bahá'í administrative bodies, the right to a Bahá'í marriage ceremony and to contribute to the Bahá'í Fund. When a believer persistently and flagrantly breaks Bahá'í law, the national spiritual assembly may, after repeated warnings, remove some or all of these administrative rights. Rights may be restored when the person shows repentance and corrects his behaviour.

Adrianople (Edirne) A city in European Turkey to which Bahá'u'lláh was exiled from Constantinople (Istanbul) in 1863 and where He lived for five years. While in Adrianople He proclaimed His message to the kings and rulers of the earth, and it was there He suffered the rebellion of Mírzá Yaḥyá. Among the many Tablets Bahá'u'lláh revealed in Adrianople are the *Súriy-i-Mulúk*, the *Lawḥ-i-Sulṭán*, the *Súriy-i-Ghuṣn*, both the Arabic and the Persian Tablet of Aḥmad and the prayers for fasting. Of the revelations He received in Adrianople Bahá'u'lláh has written: 'In those days the equivalent of all that hath been sent down aforetime unto the Prophets hath been revealed.'[14]

Adrianople

Advent of Divine Justice, The A volume by Shoghi Effendi written as a letter to the Bahá'ís of the United States and Canada in 1938. In it, against the background of the events preceding World War II, he calls upon the Bahá'ís of North America to arise to establish the World Order of Bahá'u'lláh. He describes the opportunities and responsibilities facing the Bahá'ís of North America, their mission and the tasks they are to carry out, and outlines as standards the 'essential spiritual requirements'[15] for success: a high sense of moral rectitude, absolute chastity and freedom from racial prejudice, which he terms 'the most vital and challenging issue confronting the Bahá'í community at the present stage of its evolution'.[16] He calls upon the American Bahá'ís to arise to pioneer and to attain the goals of the Seven Year Plan (1937–44), cites passages from Bahá'u'lláh about the tests ahead of the community and outlines the future role of the American nation in helping to bring about universal peace.

Afnán [Ar] Twigs (of the Sacred Lote-Tree). The descendants of the two brothers of the Báb's wife and of the Báb's maternal uncles.

ages of the Bahá'í Era Broad divisions of the Bahá'í Era corresponding to stages in the development and growth of the Bahá'í Faith. The first century of the Bahá'í Era (1844–1944) may be said to comprise the Heroic, Primitive or Apostolic Age as well as the initial stages of the Formative, Transitional or Iron Age, which is the present Age. The future will see the Golden Age, which will witness the establishment of the Kingdom of God on earth.

See also Formative Age, Golden Age *and* Heroic Age.

Aghṣán [Ar] (plural of 'ghuṣn') Branches (of the Sacred Lote-Tree). The family of Bahá'u'lláh, specifically His sons and His descendants. 'Abdu'l-Bahá was designated 'the Most Great Branch' (Ghuṣn-i-A'ẓam), preceding Mírzá Muḥammad-'Alí, 'the Greater Branch' (Ghuṣn-i-Akbar).

AH Anno Hejirae (in the year of the Hijra). Used to signify a date in the Muslim calendar. The Muslim calendar is based on lunar years which in most years are 13 days shorter than solar years. The beginning of this calendar is AD 622, the year of the Hijra (Hejira), the flight of the Prophet Muḥammad from Mecca to Medina.

Ahlu'l-Kitáb *See* People of the Book.

Aḥmad, Tablet of Bahá'u'lláh revealed two Tablets known by this name. The most well known is the Arabic Tablet of Aḥmad, which was revealed around 1865 for a faithful believer from Yazd. A simple, pure and truthful man, Aḥmad travelled throughout Persia telling the Bábís about the coming of Bahá'u'lláh. He would carry with him the original Tablet in Bahá'u'lláh's handwriting and in old age he 'spent most of his time reading the Holy Writings, especially his own Tablet which he chanted very often.'[17] The Tablet of Aḥmad is often read in times of trouble. In it, Bahá'u'lláh promises that 'Should one who is in affliction or grief read this Tablet with absolute sincerity, God will dispel his sadness, solve his difficulties and remove his afflictions.'[18]

A second, more lengthy, Tablet of Aḥmád was revealed by Bahá'u'lláh in Persian for Ḥájí Mírzá Aḥmad of Káshán 'in order to guide him to the path of faith and belief'.[19] However, Ḥájí Mírzá Aḥmad was unfaithful to Bahá'u'lláh, who eventually expelled him from His presence. Almost two-thirds of this Tablet have been translated into English by Shoghi Effendi and appear in *Gleanings from the Writings of Bahá'u'lláh*.[20]

Aḥmad-i-Aḥsá'í, Shaykh Founder of the Shaykhí School, whose doctrines prepared the way for the Báb. Shaykh Aḥmad was born in 1743 in Aḥsá in Arabia. He was a respected interpreter of Islamic doctrine in the Shí'ih holy cities of Najaf and Karbilá, where he was named a mujtahid. Shaykh Aḥmad attracted many disciples, although his teachings differed from accepted Shí'ih beliefs. He taught that such concepts as resurrection, Muḥammad's Night Journey to heaven, and the signs expected with the coming of the Qá'im, should be interpreted metaphorically and spiritually, rather than literally as physical events. Shaykh Aḥmad was certain that the time of the coming of the long-awaited Qá'im was near.

Shaykh Aḥmad travelled to Persia, where in Yazd Siyyid Káẓim-i-Rashtí became his disciple and designated successor. On a pilgrimage to Mecca and Medina in 1828, Shaykh Aḥmad died at the age of eighty-one and was buried near the tomb of Muḥammad in Medina.

See also Shaykhí *and* Káẓim-i-Rashtí, Siyyid.

Aḥmad Big Tawfíq The 'sagacious and humane governor' in 'Akká who, in response to a request for permission to render Bahá'u'lláh some service, restored the aqueduct into 'Akká which for some thirty years had been allowed to fall into disuse.[21]

See also aqueduct of Sulaymán.

akbar [Ar] Comparative of 'kabir' (great), meaning 'greater', 'greatest'.

Ákhúnd, Ḥájí *See* 'Alí-Akbar-i-Shahmírzádí.

'Akká Arabic name for the port city of Akko (known in ancient times as Accho, in the late classical period as Ptolemais, and in the crusader era as St Jean d'Acre), located on the coast of what is now Israel, near Haifa. In the nineteenth century, as a prison-city or penal colony of the Turkish Empire, it was a place so foul that it was said a bird flying over 'Akká would drop dead from the stench. In 1868 Bahá'u'lláh was banished to 'Akká, which, on His arrival, He named the Most Great Prison. For the first two years He and His family were imprisoned in the prison barracks. It was during this period that Bahá'u'lláh suffered the tragic death of his son Mírzá Mihdí, and it was here that Bahá'u'lláh revealed a number of Tablets to rulers including the *Lawḥ-i-Ra'ís* to 'Alí Pá<u>sh</u>á, His second Tablet to Napoleon III, and Tablets to Czar Alexander II, Queen Victoria and Pope Pius IX. In 1870 the barracks were needed for housing soldiers, and Bahá'u'lláh was allowed to live in better quarters within the city, first the Houses of Malik, <u>Kh</u>avvám and Rábi'ih; then, the House of 'Údí <u>Kh</u>ammár and the adjacent House of 'Abbúd. In 1877 Bahá'u'lláh left 'Akká for Mazra'ih.

After Bahá'u'lláh moved to Mazra'ih, 'Abdu'l-Bahá remained in 'Akká with the other members of the Holy Family. In 1896, after the passing of Bahá'u'lláh, the Holy Family moved from the House of 'Abbúd to the House of 'Abdu'lláh Pá<u>sh</u>á. It was in this house that Shoghi Effendi was born in 1897. The first Western pilgrims visited 'Abdu'l-Bahá in 'Akká in 1898–9. 'Abdu'l-Bahá was reincarcerated in 'Akká from 1901 until His release in 1908. In 1907 He began moving the Holy Family from 'Akká to Haifa and in 1910 He Himself left 'Akká for His new home at the foot of Mount Carmel.

See also House of 'Abbúd, House of 'Abdu'lláh Pá<u>sh</u>á, House of 'Údí <u>Kh</u>ammár *and* Most Great Prison.

An aerial view of 'Akká

'Alá' [Ar] Loftiness. The nineteenth month of the Bahá'í year (from sunset 1 March to sunset 20 March). The Fast occurs during this month.

alcohol *See* drugs and alcohol *and* wine.

'Alí, Ḥájí Mírzá Siyyid The maternal uncle of the Báb who brought up the Báb after His father died. He was known as Khál-i-A'ẓam (the Most Great Uncle). Ḥájí Mírzá Siyyid 'Alí was a leading merchant of Shíráz and the first, after the Letters of the Living, to embrace the Bábí Faith in that city. He devoted the rest of his life to serving his nephew. After visiting the Báb in Chihríq, he went to Ṭihrán where he was arrested in 1850. With great eloquence he refused to recant his faith, was beheaded, and became known as one of the Seven Martyrs of Ṭihrán.

'Alí ibn Abí Ṭalib Cousin and son-in-law of the Prophet Muḥammad; to Shí'ih Muslims, the Prophet's chosen successor and first of the Twelve Imáms.

'Alí-Akbar-i-Shahmírzádí (Ḥájí Ákhúnd) Hand of the Cause born in Shahmírzád in about 1842, the son of a mullá. He attended religious colleges in Mashhad and in about 1861 he encountered the Bábís and became a Bábí. When news of his conversion spread, the religious students rose against him and forced him to leave town. He eventually settled in Ṭihrán where he became so well known as a Bahá'í that whenever there was an outburst against the Bahá'ís he would wrap himself in his 'abá and wait for the guards to come and arrest him. He died in Ṭihrán on 4 March 1910.

'Alí-Akbar-i-Shahmírzádí, Ḥájí Ákhúnd

'Alíy-i-Basṭámí, Mullá Letter of the Living who was directed by the Báb to go to Iraq to teach among the Shaykhís. His presentation of a copy of the Báb's *Qayyúmu'l-Asmá'* to one of the leading exponents of Shí'ih Islam, Shaykh Muḥammad Ḥasan-i-Najafí, led to a violent debate and eventually to his arrest and transfer to prison in Baghdád. A court of inquiry was held in January 1846 where the Sunnís argued for the death penalty on grounds of heresy while the Shí'ihs argued for banishment or imprisonment. He was eventually transferred to Istanbul where he was apparently sentenced to labour in the docks. He died in prison near the end of 1846, thus making him the first Bábí martyr.

'Alí-Muḥammad, Siyyid Given name of the Báb.

'Alí Páshá, Muḥammad Amín (1815–71) Grand Vizier of Turkey who helped bring about Bahá'u'lláh's banishment from Baghdád to Constantinople (Istanbul) and thence to Adrianople (Edirne) and eventually to 'Akká. Bahá'u'lláh addressed the *Súriy-i-Ra'ís* and *Lawḥ-i-Ra'ís* to 'Alí Páshá, rebuking him for his cruelty.

'Álim [Ar] One who possesses knowledge ('ilm); a learned scholar.
See also 'ulamá.

Alláh [Ar] God. Originally the name by which Muḥammad designated the one God.

Alláh-u-Abhá [Ar] God is Most Glorious, God is All-Glorious. A form of the Greatest Name, used as a greeting among Bahá'ís. It replaced 'Alláh-u-Akbar' (God is Most Great), the greeting of Islam, during the years Bahá'u'lláh lived in Adrianople, although the Báb had approved both of these greetings as well as 'Alláh-u-Ajmal' (God is Most Beauteous). Shoghi Effendi directed that 'Alláh-u-Abhá' should not be said at the end of prayers and advised not to use it indiscriminately in public in the West lest it give the impression of the Faith being a strange Oriental sect.

Alláh-u-Akbar [Ar] God is Most Great. Islamic invocation.

amanuensis Secretary; one who writes from dictation or copies manuscripts.

In Bahá'í history it refers to the person who wrote down the words of revelation as they were spoken by Bahá'u'lláh and the Báb. Siyyid Ḥusayn-i-Yazdí, one of the Letters of the Living, was the Báb's amanuensis in Máh-Kú and Chihríq. Mírzá Áqá Ján was for many years the amanuensis of Bahá'u'lláh.

Hand of the Cause

Amatu'l-Bahá Rúḥíyyih Khánum

Amatu'l-Bahá Rúḥíyyih Khánum Born Mary Sutherland Maxwell, to May Bolles Maxwell and Sutherland Maxwell. In 1937 she became the wife of Shoghi Effendi, the Guardian of the Bahá'í Faith. Their marriage 'cemented' the 'union of East and West proclaimed by [the] Bahá'í Faith'.[22] Appointed by the Guardian as liaison between the International Bahá'í Council and the Guardian, she was named a Hand of the Cause of God in 1952. She served as the Guardian's secretary during his lifetime. Since his death, she has written his biography, *The Priceless Pearl* (1969) and has undertaken extensive journeys, giving public lectures and visiting villagers and tribal peoples in many parts of the world. She resides in the House of 'Abdu'l-Bahá in Haifa and is a member of the International Teaching Centre.

Amín, Ḥájí *See* Abu'l-Ḥasan-i-Ardikání, Mullá.

Amín-i-Iláhí *See* Abu'l-Ḥasan-i-Ardikání, Mullá.

Amír [Ar, Pers] Prince, governor, commander, lord.

Ancient Beauty, the A title of Bahá'u'lláh.

Ancient of Days, the God.

Angel of Mount Carmel, the *See* Ḥaydar-'Alí, Ḥájí Mírzá.

Anís *See* Muḥammad-'Alíy-i-Zunúzí.

Anísá [Ar] Tree of Life. In the Writings of Bahá'u'lláh it is associated with the Covenant in such passages as: 'The Lord, the All-Glorified, hath, beneath the shade of the Tree of Anísá (Tree of Life), made a new Covenant and established a great Testament . . .'[23]

Antichrist of the Bábí Revelation *See* Áqásí, Ḥájí Mírzá.

Antichrist of the Bahá'í Revelation *See* Muḥammad-i-Iṣfahání, Siyyid.

Apostles of Bahá'u'lláh Nineteen outstanding early Bahá'ís designated by Shoghi Effendi as Apostles of Bahá'u'lláh. They are:

1 Mírzá Músá (Kalím), the brother of Bahá'u'lláh
2 Mírzá Buzurg (Badí')
3 Siyyid Ḥasan (Sulṭánu'sh-Shuhadá')
4 Mullá Abu'l-Ḥasan (Amín)
5 Mírzá Abu'l-Faḍl-i-Gulpáygání
6 Mírzá 'Alí-Muḥammad (Varqá)
7 Mírzá Maḥmúd Furúghí
8 Mullá 'Alí-Akbar (Ḥájí Ákhúnd)
9 Mullá Muḥammad (Nabíl-i-Akbar)
10 Ḥájí Mírzá Muḥammad-Taqí (Vakílu'd-Dawlih)
11 Mírzá Muḥammad-Taqí (Ibn-i-Abhar)
12 Mulla Muḥammad (Nabíl-i-A'ẓam)
13 Shaykh Káẓim (Samandar)
14 Mírzá Muḥammad Muṣṭafá
15 Mírzá Ḥusayn (Mishkín-Qalam)
16 Mírzá Ḥasan (Adíb)
17 Shaykh Muḥammad-'Alí
18 Mullá Zaynu'l-'Ábidín (Zaynu'l-Muqarrabín)
19 Mírzá 'Alí-Muḥammad (Ibn-i-Aṣdaq)

Apostles of Bahá'u'lláh

Apostles of Bahá'u'lláh

Mírzá Áqá Ján

Apostolic Age *See* Heroic Age.

áqá [Turk, Pers] Sir, though generally used to mean 'master'. Áqá was the title given specifically to 'Abdu'l-Bahá by Bahá'u'lláh, in which context it is rendered into English as 'the Master'. In modern usage, when affixed to a surname it means 'Mister'.

Áqá Ján, Mírzá The amanuensis of Bahá'u'lláh. As a youth of sixteen he met Bahá'u'lláh in Karbilá and there became the first to whom Bahá'u'lláh gave a glimpse of His station, years before His public declaration. For forty years Mírzá Áqá Ján served Bahá'u'lláh as amanuensis and personal attendant, and was given the title Khádim'u-'lláh (Servant of God). Bahá'u'lláh often addressed him as 'Abd-i-Ḥáḍir (Servant in Attendance). But after the passing of Bahá'u'lláh, Mírzá Áqá Ján broke the Covenant and turned against 'Abdu'l-Bahá. He died in 1901.

Áqáy-i-Kalím *See* Músá, Mírzá.

Áqásí, Ḥájí Mírzá Grand Vizier of Persia under Muḥammad Sháh and called by Shoghi Effendi the 'Antichrist of the Bábí Dispensation'. Described as cruel and treacherous, affecting religious piety although intolerant and bigoted, his misrule of Persia brought the country to the edge of ruin. Jealous fear for his own power and position led him to prevent the meeting of Muḥammad Sháh and the Báb. He ordered the Báb imprisoned in Máh-Kú and later in Chihríq. Ḥájí Mírzá Áqásí was also a bitter enemy of Mírzá Buzurg, the father of Bahá'u'lláh, although for a time he admired Bahá'u'lláh. However, his mind became poisoned against Him and he obtained an order from Muḥammad Sháh for Bahá'u'lláh's arrest, intending to kill Him. His plan was frustrated by the death of the Sháh and Ḥájí Mírzá Áqásí fell from power soon afterwards. He died poor and abandoned in Karbilá in 1849.

Ḥájí Mírzá Aqásí, Grand Vizier to Muḥammad Sháh

aqdas [Ar] Comparative of 'quddús' (very holy), meaning 'most holy'.
See also Kitáb-i-Aqdas.

aqueduct of Sulaymán An aqueduct carrying water to 'Akká built by Sulaymán Pá<u>sh</u>á in about 1815 to replace an earlier one destroyed by Napoleon. By the time of the arrival of Bahá'u'lláh in 'Akká in 1868 this aqueduct had fallen into disrepair. When Aḥmad Big Tawfíq became Pá<u>sh</u>á of the city he became attracted to the Faith through his association with 'Abdu'l-Bahá and his perusal of Bahá'í literature. He asked whether there was anything he could do for Bahá'u'lláh and the suggestion was made to him that he repair the aqueduct – this he immediately arose to do. One portion of the aqueduct bisects the Bahá'í property at Mazra'ih and a second segment runs through Bahjí. Both sections are preserved as historic mementoes of settings recalling Bahá'u'lláh's life.[24]
See also Aḥmad Big Tawfíq.

The aqueduct of Sulaymán, at a point just above Bahjí. Through the arches may be seen the Crimson Hill, referred to by Bahá'u'lláh

Arc An arc cut into Mount Carmel along which the international administrative buildings of the Bahá'í Faith are being built. In the Tablet of Carmel, Bahá'u'lláh, addressing Carmel, proclaimed, 'Ere long will God sail His Ark upon Thee, and will manifest the people of Bahá who have been mentioned in the Book of Names.'[25] Shoghi Effendi interpreted this not only symbolically but literally to mean that the various institutions associated with the development of the Faith would actually have a physical presence on Mount Carmel.

Shoghi Effendi 'began the construction of the Administrative Centre of the Faith, to comprise five buildings in a harmonious style of architecture, standing on a far-flung Arc centering on the Monuments of the Greatest Holy Leaf, her Mother and Brother. The first of these five buildings, the International Archives, was completed in the beloved Guardian's lifetime. The second, the Seat of the Universal House of Justice, now stands at the apex of the Arc.'[26] In 1987 the Universal House of Justice called for the erection of the remaining three buildings: the Seat of the International Teaching Centre, the Centre for the Study of the Sacred Texts; and the International Bahá'í Library, along with an extension to the International Archives Building and the creation of nineteen monumental terraces surrounding the nearby Shrine of the Báb. The completion of the buildings on the Arc is linked to the beginning of the Lesser Peace.

See also Ark *and* Tablet of Carmel.

Aerial view of the Bahá'í properties on Mount Carmel before the building of the Seat of the House of Justice. The Arc is clearly shown on the left centre

A model of the Arc on Mount Carmel. From left to right: International Library, Seat of the International Teaching Centre, Seat of the Universal House of Justice, Centre for the Study of the Sacred Texts and International Archives

Arch-breaker of the Covenant *See* Muḥammad-'Alí, Mírzá.

Archives, Bahá'í International The collection of personal relics of Bahá'u'lláh, the Báb and 'Abdu'l-Bahá, the portraits of both the Báb and Bahá'u'lláh, original manuscripts and Tablets in the handwriting of Bahá'u'lláh and the Báb, and other items associated with the Faith which are housed in the first building to be completed on the Arc of Mount Carmel. Before the completion of the International Archives building in 1957 these mementoes were housed in three rooms adjoining the Shrine of the Báb (the 'Major' Archives) and, later, also in a small house in the gardens near the monument to the Greatest Holy Leaf (the 'Minor' Archives). Shoghi Effendi announced his decision to build the International Archives building in 1952 and by

1954 work was under way. Shoghi Effendi himself approved the Parthenon-like design, and it was while he was staying in London to purchase furnishings for the newly-completed building that he passed away. The furnishing was completed by his widow, Rúḥíyyih Khánum. An extension to the present building forms part of the plans for the development of the Arc on Mount Carmel. Bahá'í pilgrims visit the Archives building once during their pilgrimage.

Bahá'í International Archives

Ark 'In the Bahá'í Writings the term "Ark" is often used to signify the Cause of God, or the Covenant, and Bahá'u'lláh, the Holy Mariner. For example, the Báb in the Qayyúmu'l-Asmá' has lauded the community of the Most Great Name, the Bahá'ís, as the companions of the Crimson-coloured Ark.'[27]

In the Tablet of Carmel Bahá'u'lláh declares, 'Ere long will God sail His Ark upon thee, and will manifest the people of Bahá who have been mentioned in the Book of Names.'[28] In this context, Shoghi Effendi has said that the Ark refers to the law of God[29] and that the 'sailing of His Ark' refers to the establishment of the Universal House of Justice.[30]

See also Arc, Tablet of Carmel *and* Universal House of Justice.

Ark, Crimson The Covenant. In the *Kitáb-i-Aqdas* Bahá'u'lláh writes of the companions of the Crimson Ark which God has prepared for the people of Bahá.
See also Covenant of Bahá'u'lláh.

Funeral procession of 'Abdu'l-Bahá, 29 November 1921

Ascension of 'Abdu'l-Bahá Bahá'í Holy Day commemorating the passing of 'Abdu'l-Bahá, who died in the early hours of 28 November 1921 in Haifa. His tomb is on Mount Carmel, in a vault within the Shrine of the Báb. The anniversary of His Ascension is observed at 1:00 a.m. Suspension of work is not obligatory on this Holy Day.
See also 'Abdu'l-Bahá *and* Shrine of 'Abdu'l-Bahá.

Ascension of Bahá'u'lláh Bahá'í Holy Day commemorating the anniversary of the passing of Bahá'u'lláh, which occurred in the early hours of the morning of 29 May 1892 at Bahjí. This solemn anniversary is observed at 3:00 a.m., often by the reading or chanting of the Tablet of Visitation. Work is suspended on this Holy Day.
See also Bahá'u'lláh *and* Shrine of Bahá'u'lláh.

As͟hraf, Áqá Siyyid A Bahá'í martyr whose steadfastness, as well as that of his mother, known as Umm-i-As͟hraf (Mother of As͟hraf), was often praised by Bahá'u'lláh. As͟hraf, the son of a martyr, was born in the besieged fort of Zanján. He was arrested as a Bábí, sentenced to death and brutally beaten, yet refused to recant his faith. His mother was brought to the prison to persuade him to recant in order to save his life, but instead she told her son that she would disown him if he denied his belief. Áqá Siyyid Ashraf was martyred in 1870.

Ashraf Garden A large garden immediately adjacent to the Riḍván and Firdaws Gardens in the Holy Land. Originally the property of Mullá Abú-Ṭálib, the garden was given to his son 'Alí-Ashraf who later donated it to the Faith. The present custodians of all three gardens live on this property.
See also Abú-Ṭálib, Mullá.

Ásiyih Khánum *See* Navváb.

Asmá' [Ar] Names. The ninth month of the Bahá'í year (from sunset 19 August to sunset 7 September).

assembly *See* local spiritual assembly *and* national spiritual assembly.

Assistants to the Auxiliary Boards Members of the appointed arm of the Administrative Order who help with the work of Auxiliary Board Members. An Assistant's work may either be general, though usually more limited geographically than that of the Auxiliary Board Member he serves, or he may be assigned a particular function, such as working with youth or encouraging the education of children. Unlike other members of the appointed arm, Assistants may simultaneously serve on the elected arm as members of local or national spiritual assemblies or their committees.
See also Administrative Order, Bahá'í, *and* Auxiliary Board.

attar of roses An essential oil of rose often used by 'Abdu'l-Bahá to anoint the believers. Although it has no particular Bahá'í significance, Eastern believers occasionally follow this custom.

attributes of God Those qualities such as love, mercy, justice and trustworthiness through which man can come to know something of the nature of God. God reveals Himself through His attributes. Further, each created thing has been made the bearer of one of the signs or attributes of God, 'so that the whole of creation mirrors forth the beauty of God.'[31] Human beings alone among creation have been made the bearers of all the divine attributes, and therefore may be said to be made in the 'image' of God. It is one of man's purposes in this life to acquire and refine these attributes and virtues. However, the chief locus of divine attributes in this world are the Manifestations of God who exemplify most perfectly all God's attributes. Many Bahá'í prayers end with a list of some of the attributes, or names, of God.[32]

See also God *and* Manifestation.

Auxiliary Board An institution created by Shoghi Effendi in 1954 to assist the Hands of the Cause of God. In 1968 the Auxiliary Boards were placed under the direction of the Continental Boards of Counsellors, who appoint Auxiliary Board Members from among the Bahá'ís living in their geographical zone. In 1973 the Universal House of Justice allowed the Continental Boards to authorize Auxiliary Board Members to appoint Assistants. Each zone has two Auxiliary Boards. The Protection Boards protect the Faith from attack by external enemies and Covenant-breakers, encourage believers to deepen their knowledge of and loyalty to the Covenant and promote unity in Bahá'í communities. The Propagation Boards promote teaching work, assist in the achievement of the goals of teaching plans and encourage contribution to the funds. The Auxiliary Board Members and their Assistants work directly with individuals, groups and local spiritual assemblies. They do not make administrative decisions or judgements, but offer advice and counsel. Auxiliary Board Members are eligible for any elective office but if elected to a local or national spiritual assembly must choose between accepting the post and remaining on the Board. If elected to the Universal House of Justice, the Auxiliary Board Member ceases to be a member of the Board.

Auxiliary Board Members of India gather for their eighth annual conference in January 1985

An Ayyám-i-Há gathering in Grenada, West Indies

Ayyám-i-Há Literally, Days of Há (i.e. the letter Há, which in the abjad system has the numerical value of 5). Intercalary Days. The four days (five in leap year) before the last month of the Bahá'í year, 'Alá', which is the month of fasting. Bahá'u'lláh designated the Intercalary Days as Ayyám-i-Há in the *Kitáb-i-Aqdas* and specified when they should be observed; thc Báb had left this undefined. The Ayyám-i-Há are devoted to spiritual preparation for the fast, hospitality, feasting, charity and gift giving.

Azal *See* Yaḥyá, Mírzá.

Azalí A follower of Mírzá Yaḥyá, Ṣubḥ-i-Azal.

A'ẓam [Ar] Most Great (or Greatest). It is translated as 'universal' in 'Universal House of Justice'.

'Aẓamat [Ar] Grandeur. The fourth month of the Bahá'í year (from sunset 16 May to sunset 4 June).

B

B and E Be. The English equivalent of the Arabic 'k' and 'n' (kun). Refers to the act of creation, from the Qur'án 3:42: 'When He decreeth a thing, He only saith, "Be", and it is.'

Bá and Há [Ar] The English transliteration of the Arabic 'b' and 'h', meaning 'Bahá'.

Báb, the Gate. The title assumed by Siyyid 'Alí-Muḥammad, the Forerunner of Bahá'u'lláh, and Prophet-Founder of the Bábí Faith.

Born in Shíráz on 20 October 1819, Siyyid 'Alí-Muḥammad was raised by His uncle Ḥájí Mírzá Siyyid 'Alí, a merchant. As a child, He showed uncommon wisdom, although He received little formal schooling. He became a merchant and earned a high reputation for fairness. In 1842 He married Khadíjih-Bagum and they had one son, Aḥmad, who died in infancy. Siyyid 'Alí-Muḥammad declared Himself to be the Báb, or 'Gate of God', on 23 May 1844, to the Shaykhí disciple Mullá Ḥusayn-i-Bushrú'í, the first of eighteen individuals who sought and discovered the Báb and who are known as the Letters of the Living.

The Báb proclaimed Himself to be the Promised One of Islam, the Qá'im, and said that the Mission of His Dispensation was to alert the people to the imminent advent of another Prophet, 'Him Whom God shall make manifest'.

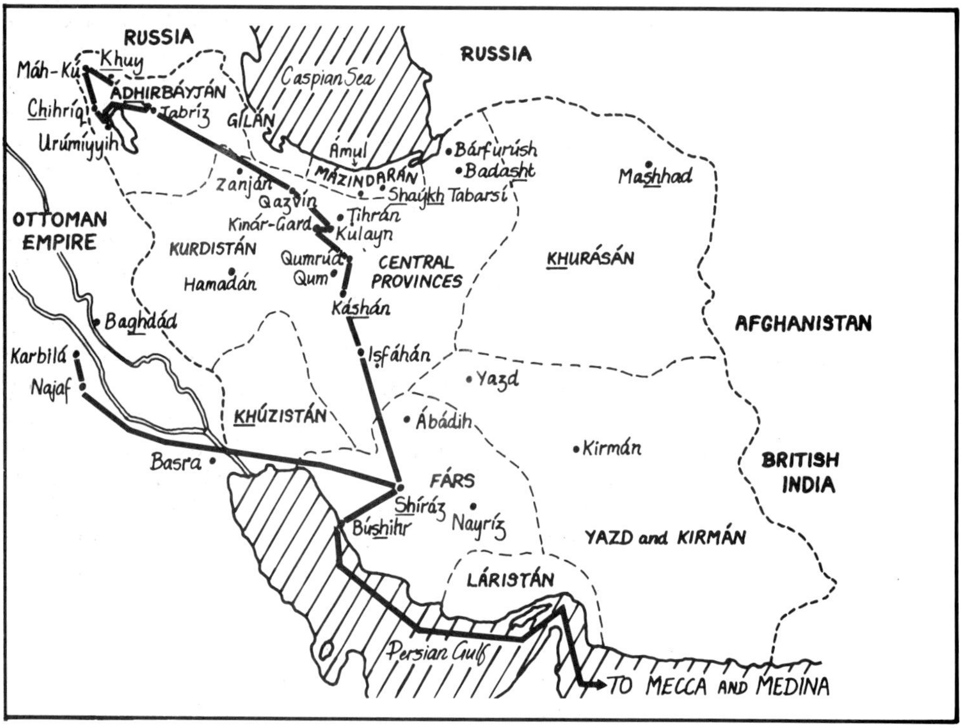

Map showing the journeys of the Báb

Interior of the Shrine of the Báb

As the Báb gained followers, His doctrines inflamed the Shí'ih clergy, who determined to stamp out the new faith. Muḥammad Sháh's Grand Vizier, Ḥájí Mírzá Áqásí, imprisoned the Báb in the fortress of Máh-Kú, then, when sympathy for Him spread there, moved Him to Chihríq. In 1848 the Báb was subjected to a trial before the Muslim divines of Tabríz and punishment by bastinado. While the Báb was imprisoned, a group of Bábís met at the Conference of Badasht. It was here that Ṭáhirih boldly exemplified the break with Islám by appearing unveiled in public and that Bahá'u'lláh demonstrated His leadership.

The Báb's followers were subjected to brutal persecution and massacres by the fanatical Shí'ih clergy, along with the forces of the Persian government throughout the country, notably in Mázindarán at the fort of Shaykh Ṭabarsí, Zanján, Nayríz and Ṭihrán. In 1850 Mírzá Taqí Khán, Grand Vizier of the new Sháh, Náṣiri'd-Dín, ordered the Báb executed. On 9 July 1850 the Báb was brought before a firing squad in the barracks square of Tabríz, along with a young follower. When the smoke cleared, the crowd was amazed that the Báb was nowhere to be seen. He was located in the room He had occupied, finishing a conversation with His amanuensis. The commander of the Armenian regiment, Sám Khán, refused to fire a second time and another regiment had to be found. This time their bullets killed the

Báb. His remains were hidden by His followers and in 1899 transferred to Palestine where in 1909 'Abdu'l-Bahá Himself interred them in the sepulchre on Mount Carmel known as the Shrine of the Báb.

Among the most important of the Báb's Writings are the *Qayyúmu'l-Asmá'*, the Persian and Arabic *Bayán, Dalá'il-i-Sab'ih* and the *Kitáb-i-Asmá'*.

Bahá'ís revere the Báb as the Forerunner or Herald of Bahá'u'lláh, but also as a Manifestation of God in His own right, considering His Writings to be Holy Scripture. The beginning of the Bahá'í Era is dated from the day of His Declaration. The Declaration of the Báb, His birth and the day of His Martyrdom are observed as Bahá'í Holy Days on which work is suspended.

See also Declaration of the Báb; Ḥusayn-i-Bushrú'í, Mullá; Martyrdom of the Báb; *and* Shrine of the Báb.

Báb, House of the *See* House of the Báb.

Bábí A follower of the Báb; of or pertaining to His revelation. The name Bábí continued to be applied to the followers of Bahá'u'lláh for several years after His declaration as the One whose advent had been foretold by the Báb. But during the later years of Bahá'u'lláh's residence in Adrianople His followers became known as Bahá'ís.

The Bábís suffered terrible persecution at the hands of the Muslim clergy and the government of Iran, particularly after the attempt on the life of the Sháh by two Bábís in 1852. Over 20,000 Bábís died as martyrs for the Cause of the Báb.

Bábí Dispensation The period when the Báb's teachings prevailed, beginning on the eve of 23 May 1844 and ending at the Declaration of Bahá'u'lláh at Riḍván 1863.

See also dispensation.

Bábu'l-Báb *See* Ḥusayn-i-Bushrú'í, Mullá.

Bábu'lláh [Ar] The Gate of God; one of the titles of the Báb.

baby naming ceremony A ceremony described in a letter written by 'Abdu'l-Bahá to an individual and published in *Tablets of 'Abdu'l-Bahá*, but which is not obligatory. 'Abdu'l-Bahá wrote: 'Thou hast asked regarding the naming of children: When thou wishest to name a babe, prepare a meeting therefor; chant the verses and communes, and supplicate and implore the Threshold of Oneness and beg the attainment of guidance for the babe and wish confirmated firmness and constancy; then give the name and enjoy beverage and sweetmeat. This is spiritual baptism.'[1]

Shoghi Effendi further clarified this in 1938: 'Regarding your question whether there is any special ceremony which the believers should perform when they wish to "name" a baby: the Teachings do not provide for any ceremony whatever on such occasions. We have no "baptismal service" in the Cause . . . There could be no objection, however, for the friends to come together on such happy occasions, provided they do not hold an official public ceremony, and provided also they strictly avoid any uniformity and rigidity in all such practices.'[2]

backbiting Saying mean or spiteful things about a person behind his back.

Backbiting and calumny are forbidden by Bahá'u'lláh in the *Kitáb-i-Aqdas* and backbiting is described by Him as 'grievous error . . . inasmuch as backbiting quencheth the light of the heart, and extinguisheth the life of the soul.'[3]

'Abdu'l-Bahá wrote of the effects of backbiting on the Bahá'í community: 'If any soul speak ill of an absent one, the only result will clearly be this: he will dampen the zeal of the friends and tend to make them indifferent. For backbiting is divisive, it is the leading cause among the friends of a disposition to withdraw.'[4] He goes on to say how backbiting can be stopped: 'If any individual should speak ill of one who is absent, it is incumbent on his hearers, in a spiritual and friendly manner, to stop him, and say in effect: would this detraction serve any useful purpose?'[5]

See also calumny.

Badasht, Conference of The Báb called a gathering of eighty-one of His followers in the early summer of 1848 in the hamlet of Badasht. The primary purpose of the conference was 'to implement the revelation of the Bayán by a sudden, a complete and dramatic break with the past – with its order, its ecclesiasticism, its traditions, and ceremonials.' A second, subsidiary purpose was 'to consider the means of emancipating the Báb from His cruel confinement in Chihríq. The first was eminently successful; the second was destined from the outset to fail.'[6] During the conference Mírzá Ḥusayn 'Alí (later to become Bahá'u'lláh) gave each participant a new name, designating Himself as 'Bahá', entitling the last Letter of the Living 'Quddús' and giving the title 'Ṭáhirih' to Qurratu'l-'Ayn.

During the twenty-two-day conference various arguments and counter-arguments were put forward and differences of view and approach arose between Ṭáhirih and Quddús. Eventually Ṭáhirih made a sudden and symbolic gesture which made it clear to all that a new Dispensation had begun: she appeared before the assembled Bábís unveiled, her face uncovered for all to see. This caused consternation among many of the men, some of whom fled in horror while one tried to cut his throat. H. M. Balyuzi writes of this occasion, 'At Badasht the faint-hearted fell away. And when those who had remained steadfast left the hamlet it was to go out into a world, for them, greatly changed. That change was in a sense a reflection of the transformation they had experienced. They were determined to assert their freedom from the fetters of the past.'[7]

See also Quddús *and* Ṭáhirih.

Badí‘ Unique, wonderful. The title given by Bahá'u'lláh to Áqá Buzurg-i-Níshápúrí, the 17-year-old youth who carried the *Lawḥ-i-Sulṭán* to Náṣiri'd-Dín Sháh.

Though he had been known as a rebellious youth, Áqá Buzurg was touched when Nabíl related to him verses in which Bahá'u'lláh described His sufferings. He walked from Mosul to 'Akká to see Bahá'u'lláh, arriving in 1869. His two audiences with Bahá'u'lláh completely transformed the young man. Though many had sought the honour of carrying Bahá'u'lláh's Tablet to the Sháh, Bahá'u'lláh entrusted it to Áqá Buzurg, whom Bahá'u'lláh named Badí‘. When Badí‘ returned to Persia and delivered the Tablet to the Sháh, he was tortured by bastinado and branding and finally put to death. Bahá'u'lláh often extolled his heroism, stating in a Tablet that Badí‘'s station was so high that it was beyond description and giving him the title Fakhru'sh-Shuhadá' (Pride of Martyrs). Shoghi Effendi named him an Apostle of Bahá'u'lláh.

Badí‘

Badí‘ being tortured

Badí' calendar *See* calendar, Bahá'í.

Baghdád The city in Iraq to which Bahá'u'lláh went when he was exiled from Persia in 1853 and where He lived until 1863, except for the period between 1854 and 1856 which He spent in the mountains of Sulaymániyyih. It was just before His departure from Baghdád, during the period now celebrated as the Festival of Riḍván (21 April–2 May), that Bahá'u'lláh declared Himself to be the One promised by the Báb. Among the Tablets and Books revealed by Bahá'u'lláh in Baghdád are *The Hidden Words*, the *Kitáb-i-Íqán, The Seven Valleys, The Four Valleys* and the *Tablet of the Holy Mariner*.

See also Declaration of Bahá'u'lláh *and* Riḍván, Garden of.

Baghdád

Baghdád House *See* House of Bahá'u'lláh in Baghdád.

Bagum (also, Bigum) [Turk] The feminine form of 'Big'. A lady of rank; a title of respect, placed after a woman's name.

Bahá [Ar] Glory. The Greatest Name. A title by which Bahá'u'lláh is designated. Also, the first month of the Bahá'í year (from sunset 20 March to sunset 8 April).

Bahá'í A follower of Bahá'u'lláh. Of or pertaining to Bahá'u'lláh's revelation. The designation 'Bahá'í' began to be applied to the followers of Bahá'u'lláh during the later years of Bahá'u'lláh's residence in Adrianople. By 1988 there were some four million Bahá'ís in the world.

A group of Bahá'ís in Adrianople. 'Abdu'l-Bahá is sitting in the centre, with the Purest Branch to His left

African Bahá'ís

Western Bahá'ís with 'Abdu'l-Bahá

Bahá'í Centre *See* Ḥaẓíratu'l-Quds.

Bahá'í Commonwealth *See* World Commonwealth.

Bahá'í Cycle A period of time beginning with the Declaration of the Báb, including the Bahá'í Dispensation (the Bahá'í Era) and extending beyond it into the future, to include the dispensations of future Manifestations of God who shall be under the shadow of Bahá'u'lláh. In a letter interpreting a Zoroastrian prophecy, 'Abdu'l-Bahá described the Bahá'í Cycle as lasting 'at least five hundred thousand years'.[8] The Bahá'í Cycle is also called by Shoghi Effendi the 'Era of Fulfilment', which succeeded the 'Prophetic Era' or 'Adamic Cycle'.

See also progressive revelation.

Bahá'í Era The period of the Bahá'í dispensation beginning with the Declaration of the Báb on 23 May 1844, and ending with the appearance of a new Manifestation of God at some date in the future. The Bahá'í Era is promised by Bahá'u'lláh to last no less than a thousand years. The opening of the Bahá'í Era marks the end of the Prophetic Era (Adamic Cycle) and the beginning of the Era of Fulfilment or Bahá'í Cycle.

Shoghi Effendi has identified three phases or 'Ages' of the Bahá'í Era. These are the Apostolic, Heroic or Primitive Age (1-77 BE/AD 1844–1921), which began with the Declaration of the Báb and included three epochs comprising the Bábí dispensation and the ministries of

Bahá'u'lláh and 'Abdu'l-Bahá; the Transitional, Formative or Iron Age (77 BE–/AD 1921–), which began with the passing of 'Abdu'l-Bahá and includes the time in which we live now; and the Golden Age, which shall see the achievement of world civilization and the Most Great Peace.

Some of the Bahá'ís attending the International Esperanto Conference in Warsaw in 1987

Bahá'í Esperanto League An international organization with members in forty countries, whose goals are to facilitate communication among Bahá'í Esperantists, to represent the Bahá'í Faith at the annual Congresses of the Universal Esperanto Association and at other gatherings of Esperantists, to translate Bahá'í literature into Esperanto, and to teach the Bahá'í Faith among the Esperantists. Established in 1973, it publishes a bimonthly newsletter, *Belmonda Letero*.

Bahá'í Faith Religion founded by Bahá'u'lláh.

Bahá'í International Community The official name of the worldwide Bahá'í community in its relations with the outside world. That community 'represents a cross-section of humanity, the four million adherents coming from virtually every nationality, racial or ethnic group, religious background, culture and social class.

Representatives of five national spiritual assemblies and the members of the Geneva and New York offices of the Bahá'í International Community at their meeting in Washington DC in February 1988

'Under the guidance of the Universal House of Justice, its governing authority, the Bahá'í International Community comprises 148 national affiliates (the National Spiritual Assemblies). At the international level it operates through branches specialized for different aspects of its work. At the present time these are three in number: the Secretariat, located at the World Centre of the Faith in Israel; the United Nations Office, based in New York City with a branch in Geneva; and the Office of Public Information, with its headquarters in Israel and a bureau in New York. Both the United Nations Office and the Office of Public Information have representatives in a number of major centres of the world.'[9]

Bahá'í International Community

The relationship of the world Bahá'í community to the United Nations began in 1948 when the eight National Spiritual Assemblies then existing were recognized collectively by the UN Office of Public Information as an international non-governmental organization (NGO) under the name 'Bahá'í International Community'. Today, the Bahá'í International Community is accredited in consultative status with the United Nations Economic and Social Council (ECOSOC) and with the United Nations Children's Fund (UNICEF). It also has a working relationship with the UN Environment Programme (UNEP), the Centre for Human Settlements, the Centre for Human Rights, the Centre for Social Development and Humanitarian Affairs, the Department of Disarmament Affairs and the Peace Studies Unit, the UN Regional Commissions, and other members of the UN system. It is continually increasing its contact with several of the UN specialized agencies such as the World Food Council (WFC), the World Health Organization (WHO), the UN Educational, Scientific and Cultural Organization (UNESCO) and the Food and Agricultural Organization (FAO).

In addition, the Bahá'í International Community has representation with the South Pacific Commission and has kept in close touch with the European Parliament and the Council of Europe during the recent persecutions of the Bahá'ís in Iran. It works closely with other non-governmental organizations at the UN, through membership in many NGO/UN committees in New York, Geneva, Vienna and Santiago.

Believing that the United Nations represents a major effort in the unification of the planet, Bahá'ís have supported its work in every way possible. During its participation in conferences, congresses and seminars the United Nations Office makes contributions to those aims of the United Nations that are kindred to the teachings of the Bahá'í Faith, such as the status of women and particularly their role in the achievement of world peace; economic justice and cooperation; racial equality; religious tolerance; universal education; minority rights; human rights generally; crime prevention; the control of narcotic drugs; the welfare of children and the family; the movement towards disarmament; and the protection of the environment.

In 1987 the Bahá'í International Community became the sixth major religion to join the World Wide Fund for Nature in its initiative for the Conservation of Nature and the Environment.

The Office of Public Information was appointed in 1986. It gathers and prepares information about the Bahá'í Faith and coordinates its dissemination to international and national entities, prominent persons, leaders of thought, the mass media and the general public. It seeks to foster a climate of understanding about the aims and achievements of the Bahá'í Faith and to correct misinformation. It also works with national Bahá'í information agencies to help them mobilize their energies in support of international objectives.

Bahá'í principles *See* principles.

Bahá'í Temple Unity A national organization created in Chicago in March 1909 at a convention of thirty-nine delegates representing thirty-six cities called in pursuance of instructions received from 'Abdu'l-Bahá. The Bahá'í Temple Unity was incorporated as a religious corporation in the state of Illinois and was invested with full authority to hold title to the property of the Temple and to provide ways and means for its construction. This national body was superseded in 1925 by the National Spiritual Assembly of the United States and Canada.
See also national spiritual assembly *and* Mashriqu'l-Adhkár.

Bahá'u'lláh Prophet-Founder of the Bahá'í Faith and the Manifestation of God for this Day. He was born Mírzá Ḥusayn-'Alí on 12 November 1817 to a noble family of Núr in Mázindarán, Iran. His mother was Khadíjih Khánum and his father Mírzá Buzurg-i-Vazír, a courtier. Bahá'u'lláh was a descendant of the last Sassanian king, Yazdigird III.

He became a follower of the Báb in 1844 at the age of twenty-seven, when the Báb sent Mullá Ḥusayn to tell Him of the new Revelation. Although Bahá'u'lláh and the Báb never met, they corresponded. As Mírzá Ḥusayn-'Alí, Bahá'u'lláh became known as a Bábí leader, and His leadership was especially shown at the Conference of Badasht, after which He was known by the name of Bahá. Bahá'u'lláh suffered from the persecution waged against the Bábís at the time and was made to endure imprisonment and the bastinado.

After an attempt on the Sháh's life by two misguided Bábís, in 1853 Bahá'u'lláh was imprisoned for four months in an underground prison known as the Síyáh-Chál in Ṭihrán. It was there He first received a revelation, through a dream of a Maid of Heaven, that He was the One promised by the Báb.

Bahá'u'lláh was released from prison but banished from Iran. He chose to go to Baghdád accompanied by some members of His family

Nineteenth-century 'Akká

and companions. After their arrival in Baghdád the community of believers was disrupted by the actions of Mírzá Yaḥyá, Bahá'u'lláh's disloyal brother. Bahá'u'lláh departed for a period of solitary retreat in the mountains of Sulaymániyyih until He was persuaded to return in March 1856.

Upon His return He became the recognized spiritual leader of the Bábís. His influence spread and the Persian government persuaded the Ottoman Sulṭán 'Abdu'l-'Azíz to banish Bahá'u'lláh further. On the eve of His departure from Baghdád for Constantinople, in the Garden of Riḍván, in April–May 1863, Bahá'u'lláh declared to His followers that He was the Promised One foretold by the Báb. The Riḍván Festival is celebrated as the holiest and most significant of Bahá'í Holy Days.

Mount Carmel as it was in the time of Bahá'u'lláh

Bahá'u'lláh departed for Constantinople and soon afterwards was banished to Adrianople where He publicly proclaimed His Mission, addressing His proclamation to the kings and rulers of the earth and calling on them to establish world peace, justice and unity.

Because of the disloyal Mírzá Yaḥyá's plotting against Bahá'u'lláh, the Turkish authorities condemned Bahá'u'lláh to perpetual imprisonment in the prison-city of 'Akká.

There He was at first subjected to strict confinement for two years in the barracks, during which time He suffered the death of His son Mírzá Mihdí. In spite of the hardship and isolation, from 'Akká He continued

The entrance to the barracks where Bahá'u'lláh entered the prison

His proclamation to the rulers of the earth and the revelation of the foundation-principles which would bring about a new world order of society founded on the unity of mankind, equality and justice.

Bahá'u'lláh and His family, including His Son, 'Abdu'l-Bahá, were moved to a succession of houses in the city, notably the houses of 'Údí Khammár, where Bahá'u'lláh revealed the *Kitáb-i-Aqdas*, His Book of Laws, and the House of 'Abbúd. In 1877 Bahá'u'lláh took up residence in the Mansion of Mazra'ih for two years, and then moved to the Mansion of Bahjí where He ascended at the age of seventy-four on 29 May 1892. In His Will, the 'Book of My Covenant', Bahá'u'lláh named His eldest son, 'Abdu'l-Bahá, as His successor and authorized Interpreter of His Teachings.

Bahá'u'lláh's Writings are considered by Bahá'ís to be revelation from God and some 15,000 of His Tablets have so far been collected. His major works include The Most Holy Book (*Kitáb-i-Aqdas*), *The Hidden Words* (*Kalimát-i-Maknúnih*), *The Book of Certitude* (*Kitáb-i-Íqán*), *The Seven Valleys, The Four Valleys*, the Súrih of the Kings (*Súriy-i-Mulúk*), the Tablets to the kings and rulers, the Tablet of the Branch (*Súriy-i-Ghuṣn*), The Tablet of Wisdom (*Lawḥ-i-Ḥikmat*), The Tablet of the Proof (*Lawḥ-i-Burhán*), The Tablet of the World (*Lawḥ-i-Dunyá*), The Words of Paradise (*Kalimát-i-Firdawsíyyih*), Glad-Tidings (*Bishárát*), Ornaments (*Ṭarázát*), Effulgences (*Tajallíyát*), Splendours (*Ishráqát*), The Tablet of Carmel (*Lawḥ-i-Karmil*) and *Epistle to the Son of the Wolf.*

Bahíyyih Khánum (also, Bahá'íyyih Khánum) The Greatest Holy Leaf, daughter of Bahá'u'lláh, sister of 'Abdu'l-Bahá. Designated by Shoghi Effendi as 'the outstanding heroine of the Bahá'í Dispensation', she was born in 1846 in Ṭihrán. She accompanied Bahá'u'lláh on every stage of His exiles. When a young girl she decided to devote herself to the service of the Faith of her Father; therefore she never married. Following the passing of Bahá'u'lláh, she stood by her brother, 'Abdu'l-Bahá, and assisted Him greatly at the time when the activities of the Covenant-breakers were at their height. Perhaps her greatest hour of service was after the passing of 'Abdu'l-Bahá when Shoghi Effendi, overwhelmed by the responsibilities thrust upon him, decided to leave the affairs of the Cause in the hands of Bahíyyih Khánum while he retired to recuperate and contemplate the tasks ahead.

The Greatest Holy Leaf, Bahíyyih Khánum

Of her character Shoghi Effendi has written: 'A purity of life that reflected itself in even the minutest details of her daily occupations and activities; a tenderness of heart that obliterated every distinction of creed, class and colour; a resignation and serenity that evoked to the mind the calm and heroic fortitude of the Báb; a natural fondness of flowers and children that was so characteristic of Bahá'u'lláh; an unaffected simplicity of manners; an extreme sociability which made her accessible to all; a generosity, a love, at once disinterested and undiscriminating, that reflected so clearly the attributes of 'Abdu'l-Bahá's character; a sweetness of temper; a cheerfulness that no amount of sorrow could becloud; a quiet and unassuming disposition that served to enhance a thousandfold the prestige of her exalted rank; a forgiving nature that instantly disarmed the most unyielding enemy – these rank among the outstanding attributes of a saintly life which history will acknowledge as having been endowed with a celestial potency that few of the heroes of the past possessed.'[10]

The Greatest Holy Leaf passed away on 15 July 1932 and is buried under a shrine in the Monument Gardens on Mount Carmel.

Bahjí Place of Delight. The site on the plain of 'Akká which gives its name to the Mansion which was the last residence of Bahá'u'lláh. Originally built by 'Abdu'lláh Páshá in 1821, it was later restored and expanded by 'Údí Khammár, who completed it in 1870. The Mansion of Bahjí became empty in 1879 when the Khammár family fled an epidemic disease, probably bubonic plague. Bahá'u'lláh took up residence in the Mansion in 1879 and while living there revealed His final major volume, *Epistle to the Son of the Wolf*, as well as the Tablets of *Ishráqát, Bishárát, Ṭarázát, Tajallíyát, Kalimát-i-Firdawsíyyih, Lawḥ-i-Aqdas, Lawḥ-i-Dunyá,* and *Lawḥ-i-Maqṣúd,* writings which Shoghi Effendi described as 'among the choicest fruits which His mind has yielded [and which] mark the consummation of His forty-year-long ministry'.[11]

It was in the Mansion of Bahjí in 1890 that Bahá'u'lláh received the Cambridge orientalist E. G. Browne. On 29 May 1892 Bahá'u'lláh passed away and was interred in the small house adjacent to the Mansion. This small house became His Shrine, the holiest spot on earth, and the Qiblih of the Bahá'í Faith.

However, in the years that followed, the Mansion was occupied by Covenant-breakers and allowed to decay. In 1929 Shoghi Effendi regained custody of the building and started the work of restoration.

In the early 1950s, with the acquisition of surrounding land, Shoghi Effendi began a programme of beautification including the setting out of extensive gardens surrounding the Mansion. The northwestern quadrant which encloses the Shrine of Bahá'u'lláh itself is called the Ḥaram-i-Aqdas (Most Holy Sanctuary or Precincts).

The Mansion of Bahjí

Baní-Háshim The sons of Háshim, great-grandfather of Muḥammad. The family from which Muḥammad descended.

Baqíyyatu'lláh [Ar] Remnant of God. A title of the Twelfth Imám. It is applied to both the Báb and Bahá'u'lláh.

barracks *See* 'Akká.

The bastinado

bastinado Punishment or torture by beating with a wooden rod on the soles of the feet. The bastinado was inflicted upon the Báb by the Shaykhu'l-Islám of Tabríz, Mírzá 'Alí-Aṣghar, after the Báb's trial by the divines in that city. Bahá'u'lláh suffered the bastinado in Ámul, after He had been arrested on His way to the fort of Shaykh Ṭabarsí and had been interrogated by the divines. Bahá'u'lláh had intervened to spare His companions the punishment, requesting that He alone receive it.

Bayán [Ar] Explanation, exposition or utterance.

The Persian *Bayán* is the major doctrinal work of the Báb, which Shoghi Effendi has described as a 'monumental repository of the laws and precepts of the new Dispensation and the treasury enshrining most of the Báb's references and tributes to, as well as His warning regarding, "*Him Whom God will make manifest*".[12] Revealed in the fortress of Máh-Kú, the Persian *Bayán* comprises some 8000 verses and is divided into nine sections called Váḥids, of nineteen chapters each, except for the last Váḥid which has ten chapters. The book, Shoghi Effendi has written, 'should be regarded primarily as a eulogy of the Promised One rather than a code of laws and ordinances designed to be a permanent guide to future generations.'[13] In the third Váḥid the Báb specifically refers to the name of the Promised One and anticipates His World Order: 'Well is it with him who fixeth his gaze upon the Order of Bahá'u'lláh, and rendereth thanks unto his Lord. For He will assuredly be made manifest. God hath indeed irrevocably ordained it in the *Bayán*.'[14] This statement, according to Shoghi Effendi, 'deserves to rank as one of the most significant statements recorded in any of the Báb's writings'.[15]

The Arabic *Bayán* is a 'smaller and less weighty' work of the Báb, revealed in the fort of C_h_ihríq during the last months of His life.[16]

The term Bayán also refers to the Revelation of the Báb as set down in His Writings.

Bayt-i-A'ẓam [Ar] The Most Great House.
See also House of Bahá'u'lláh in Baghdád.

Baytu'l-'Adl-i-A'ẓam [Ar] *See* Universal House of Justice.

Baytu'l-Ma'múr [Ar] *See* Frequented Fane.

begging Begging and giving to beggars is forbidden in the *Kitáb-i-Aqdas*. Bahá'u'lláh has made engaging in some kind of useful work obligatory. 'Waste not your time in idleness and sloth,' He writes. 'Occupy yourselves with that which profiteth yourselves and others . . . The most despised of men in the sight of God are those who sit idly and beg.' The *Kitáb-i-Aqdas* also states, however, that if a person is unable to earn a living, the House of Justice and the wealthy must provide for him, and the rich are exhorted to engage in charity to the needy.

believers Term commonly used by Bahá'ís to refer to themselves.

Beloved of Martyrs *See* King of Martyrs and Beloved of Martyrs.

Big [Turk] A title placed after a man's name, meaning 'lord' or 'prince'.

Bis_h_árát (Glad-Tidings) A Tablet of Bahá'u'lláh revealed in 'Akká, containing fifteen passages on subjects including the abolition of ordinances and practices of the past such as holy war, monastic seclusion, and the confession of sins; statements on the establishment of a universal auxiliary language and the Lesser Peace; work as worship; the role of the House of Justice; and the 'majesty of kingship'.

Black Pit *See* Síyáh-Chál.

Black Standard The flag of which Muḥammad said, 'Should your eyes behold the Black Standards proceeding from Khurásán, hasten ye towards them, even though ye should have to crawl over the snow, inasmuch as they proclaim the advent of the promised Mihdí, the Vicegerent of God.'[17] Quddús had been arrested in Mázindarán, and Mullá Ḥusayn was instructed by the Báb to go to his aid with the Black Standard unfurled before him. Many Bábís accompanied him, with more joining on the way. They found many new supporters as they raised the call of the New Day, but they also met with much hostility. It was this march under the Black Standard which marked the beginning of the episode at Fort Shaykh Ṭabarsí.

See also Ḥusayn, Mullá; Quddús; *and* Ṭabarsí, Fort of Shaykh.

Blessed Beauty, the (Jamál-i-Mubárak) Bahá'u'lláh. A title sometimes applied to Him by Bahá'ís.

Book of Certitude *See Kitáb-i-Íqán.*

Book of My Covenant *See Kitáb-i-'Ahdí.*

Book of Names *See Kitáb-i-Asmá'.*

Branches *See* Aghṣán.

Breakwell, Thomas The first English Bahá'í. Thomas Breakwell held a responsible post in a cotton mill in the south of the United States. He was introduced to the Faith by May Bolles (Maxwell) while visiting Paris on holiday in 1901. He later travelled to 'Akká to visit 'Abdu'l-Bahá. 'He told 'Abdu'l-Bahá the nature of his profession, that his work was worthwhile and his earnings were considerable, but he added that now he had misgivings because the organization that he served was buttressed by child labour. 'Abdu'l-Bahá advised him: "Cable your resignation." He did. He went back to Paris and made it his home.'[18] Breakwell, who was battling against advanced consumption, wrote regularly to 'Abdu'l-Bahá. One day, although no news had been sent to 'Abdu'l-Bahá, He said to his secretary, 'Breakwell has passed away. I am grieved, very grieved. I have written a prayer of visitation for him.'[19] 'Abdu'l-Bahá's lengthy and moving eulogy reveals the esteem

Thomas Breakwell

with which he was regarded. Shoghi Effendi called him a 'luminary in the firmament of the Faith of Bahá'u'lláh'.[20]

Browne, Edward G. The Cambridge orientalist who studied and wrote about the Bábí and Bahá'í Faiths and who met Bahá'u'lláh in 1890 at Bahjí. Browne wrote: 'The face of him on whom I gazed I can never forget, though I cannot describe it. Those piercing eyes seemed to read one's very soul; power and authority sat on that ample brow; while the deep lines on the forehead and face implied an age which the jet-black hair and beard flowing down in indistinguishable luxuriance almost to the waist seemed to belie. No need to ask in whose presence I stood, as I bowed myself before one who is the object of a devotion and love which kings might envy and emperors sigh for in vain!'[21]

Disappointed that the Bahá'ís refused to become involved in Iranian politics, Browne transferred his interest to the Azalís. Browne recognized he had a unique opportunity to study and record at first hand the birth of a faith which 'whatever its actual destiny may be, is of that stuff whereof world-religions are made',[22] although some of his colleagues belittled his interest in the subject. One judged Browne's translation of *A Traveller's Narrative* 'quite unworthy of the learning and labour which the author has brought to bear upon it . . .' and concluded: 'There are no signs that Mírzá 'Alí Muḥammad will leave any permanent mark on religious or political history . . . Time may vindicate the author: but for the present we can only record our belief that the prominence given to the "Báb" in this book is an absurd violation of historical perspective; and the translation of the *Traveller's Narrative* a waste of the powers and opportunities of a Persian scholar.'[23]

E. G. Browne in Oriental dress

Buddha A title meaning 'Enlightened One', given to Siddhartha Gautama, the founder of the religion of Buddhism. Bahá'ís accept Buddha as a Manifestation of God and believe that prophecies attributed to Buddha about the coming of the Buddha Maitreya, the Buddha of universal fellowship, refer to Bahá'u'lláh.

burial, Bahá'í The body is the temple of the spirit, therefore it must be respected and treated with honour. Its burial in the earth after death and its gradual decomposition is natural. Thus, according to Bahá'í law, cremation of the dead is forbidden and the body must not be transported more than one hour's journey from the place of death. The body 'should be wrapped in a shroud of silk or cotton, and on its finger should be placed a ring bearing the inscription, "I came forth from God, and return unto Him, detached from all save Him, holding fast to His Name, the Merciful, the Compassionate"; and that the coffin should be of crystal, stone or hard fine wood. A specific *Prayer for the Dead* is ordained, to be said before interment . . . The formal prayer and the ring are meant to be used for those who have attained the age of maturity [age fifteen].'[24] The parts of the law regarding cremation, the transportation of the body and the *Prayer for the Dead* are the only ones binding on all Bahá'ís, Bahá'ís in the West being exempt at present from the others.

See also death, life after; *and* death, nature of.

Buzurg [Pers] Great. A title of respect accorded a man of rank.

Buzurg, Áqá *See* Badí'.

Left Mírzá Buzurg

Buzurg-i-Vazír, Mírzá Mírzá 'Abbás of Núr, known as Mírzá Buzurg the Vizier, the father of Bahá'u'lláh. Renowned for, in the words of Mullá Ḥusayn, 'his character, his charm, and artistic and intellectual attainments',[25] he served as a vizier to a son of Fatḥ-'Alí Sháh. Under Muḥammad Sháh he was governor of Burújird and Luristán, but lost his official posts and much of his wealth through the antagonism of Ḥájí Mírzá Áqásí. Bahá'u'lláh was Mírzá Buzurg's third child by his second wife, Khadíjih Khánum. Mírzá Buzurg died in 1839.

Calligraphy of Mírzá Buzurg

C

calamity Sometimes called 'the calamity' although not necessarily one single event. World-shaking catastrophic events and upheaval destined to afflict mankind before the establishment of world peace as part of the simultaneous two-fold processes of the collapse and disintegration of the old world order and the rise and development of the New World Order. Shoghi Effendi explained that 'Adversity, prolonged, world-wide, afflictive, allied to chaos and universal destruction, must needs convulse the nations, stir the conscience of the world, disillusion the masses, precipitate a radical change in the very conception of society'[1] before world unity can be achieved.

calendar, Bahá'í Also called the Badí' calendar. The Bahá'í calendar was established by the Báb in the *Kitáb-i-Asmá'* and approved by Bahá'u'lláh, who stated that it should begin in 1844 (AH 1260). It is based on the solar year of 365 days, five hours and some fifty minutes. Each year is divided into nineteen months of nineteen days each with four Intercalary Days (five in leap year), called Ayyám-i-Há, which Bahá'u'lláh specified should precede the nineteenth month. New Year's Day (Naw-Rúz) falls on the Spring Equinox. This usually occurs on 21 March but if the equinox takes place after sunset on 21 March, Naw-Rúz is to be celebrated on 22 March, for the Bahá'í day begins and ends at sunset.

See also days of the month; Kull-i-Shay'; months, Bahá'í *and* years.

Caliph (Khalífih) A successor of Muḥammad as the head of Islam.

Shoghi Effendi calls the Caliph 'the self-styled vicar of the Prophet of Islam' who 'exercised a spiritual sovereignty, and was invested with a sacred character'[2] and who 'usurped the authority of the lawful successors of the Apostle of God (the Imáms)'.[3]

Caliph

The Caliphate is an institution of Sunní Islam.
See also Imám.

calligraphy Generally, beautiful and elegant penmanship; specifically, the drawing-like renderings of Arabic and Persian words, phrases or text. Many of the writings of Bahá'u'lláh and the Báb were executed in fine calligraphy. The best-known Bahá'í calligrapher was Mishkín-Qalam, whose calligraphy of the Greatest Name is widely used among Bahá'ís as a symbol of their Faith.
See also Greatest Name *and* Mishkín-Qalam.

An example of fine calligraphy

calumny Uttering false charges with malicious intent, in order to damage another person's reputation. Along with backbiting, calumny is specifically prohibited in the *Kitáb-i-Aqdas*. Bahá'u'lláh wrote: 'Material fire consumeth the body, whereas the fire of the tongue devoureth both heart and soul. The force of the former lasteth but for a time, whilst the effects of the latter endure a century.'[4]

Carmel, Mount The mountain spoken of by Isaiah as the 'mountain of the Lord'. Site of the Bahá'í World Centre including several Bahá'í Holy Places, the most important of which are the Shrine of the Báb and the Monument Gardens. Mount Carmel is also the location of the Bahá'í world administrative institutions: the Seat of the Universal House of Justice, the International Archives building, and the other present and future institutions of the World Bahá'í Administrative

Order, including the International Teaching Centre, the Centre for the Study of the Sacred Texts and the International Bahá'í Library as well as the Mashriqu'l-Adhkár of Haifa which will one day stand on Mount Carmel on a site already designated.

See also Arc, Ark, Haifa *and* Tablet of Carmel.

Mount Carmel, before its development in the twentieth century

Carmel, Tablet of *See* Tablet of Carmel.

Cause of God Today, the Bahá'í Faith.

Bahá'í Cemetery, Haifa

cemetery, Bahá'í Plots of land set aside by some Bahá'í communities for the burial of Bahá'ís. This is done particularly in places where all other cemeteries are used exclusively by other religious groups, or where Bahá'ís are not allowed to be buried in a particular cemetery. No special dedication or consecrating ceremony is necessary for land to become a Bahá'í cemetery.

The Bahá'í cemetery in Haifa is situated at the tip of the promontory of Mount Carmel as its northern face plunges to the plain. It is a six-acre plot purchased at the behest of 'Abdu'l-Bahá. Its first recorded burial was in August 1911. Several early Bahá'ís are buried there including Ḥájí Mírzá Ḥaydar-'Alí and many Hands of the Cause.

Central Figures According to Shoghi Effendi, the Báb, Bahá'u'lláh and 'Abdu'l-Bahá are regarded as the 'Central Figures' of the Bahá'í Faith.

Centre, Bahá'í *See* Ḥaẓíratu'l-Quds.

'Abdu'l-Bahá, the Centre of the Covenant

Centre of the Covenant 'Abdu'l-Bahá.
See also City of the Covenant, Covenant of Bahá'u'lláh, *and Kitáb-i-Ahdí.*

century of light The twentieth century, so designated by 'Abdu'l-Bahá in a Tablet known as The Seven Candles of Unity: '. . . the unity of all mankind can in this day be achieved. Verily this is none other but one of the wonders of this wondrous age, this glorious century. Of this past ages have been deprived, for this century – the century of light – has been endowed with unique and unprecedented glory, power and illumination.'[5]

Certitude, Book of *See Kitáb-i-Íqán*

chant The unaccompanied musical rendering of the holy scriptures in any language. Generally, however, Bahá'ís use this term to refer to forms of devotional song, adapted from traditional Islamic practices, using the original Persian and Arabic texts of the sacred writings, the prayers of Shoghi Effendi, and other devotional poems and songs.

Chase, Thornton Designated by 'Abdu'l-Bahá as 'the first American believer' and surnamed 'Thábit' (Steadfast), Thornton Chase became a Bahá'í in 1894 in Chicago. He travelled extensively for his employers, and wherever he went he taught and served the Faith, not only by speech and dissertation but also by the radiance of his person. 'Abdu'l-Bahá said of him, 'He served the Cause faithfully and his services will ever be remembered throughout future ages and cycles . . . For the present his worth is not known, but in the future it will be inestimably dear. His sun will ever be shining, his star will ever bestow the light.'[6] Thornton Chase died in Los Angeles in 1912 just before 'Abdu'l-Bahá arrived in California.

Thornton Chase, the first American believer

chastity A high standard of moral behaviour which should distinguish the lives of Bahá'ís of both sexes and which Shoghi Effendi has explained 'must contribute its proper share to the strengthening and vitalization of the Bahá'í community, upon which must in turn depend the success of any Bahá'í plan or enterprise . . . A chaste and holy life must be made the controlling principle in the behaviour and conduct of all Bahá'ís, both in their social relations with the members of their own community, and in their contact with the world at large.

'Such a chaste and holy life, with its implications of modesty, purity, temperance, decency, and clean-mindedness, involves no less than the exercise of moderation in all that pertains to dress, language, amusements, and all artistic and literary avocations. It demands daily vigilance in the control of one's carnal desires and corrupt inclinations. It calls for the abandonment of a frivolous conduct, with its excessive attachment to trivial and often misdirected pleasures. It requires total abstinence from all alcoholic drinks, from opium, and from similar habit-forming drugs. It condemns the prostitution of art and of literature, the practices of nudism and of companionate marriage, infidelity in marital relationships, and all manner of promiscuity, of easy familiarity, and of sexual vices. It can tolerate no compromise with the theories, the standards, the habits, and the excesses of a decadent age. Nay rather it seeks to demonstrate, through the dynamic force of its example, the pernicious character of such theories, the falsity of such standards, the hollowness of such claims, the perversity of such habits, and the sacrilegious character of such excesses.'[7]

Shoghi Effendi points out, however, that the law of chastity does not imply that Bahá'ís are puritanical: 'the maintenance of such a high standard of moral conduct is not to be associated or confused with any form of asceticism, or of excessive and bigoted puritanism. The standard inculcated by Bahá'u'lláh, seeks, under no circumstances, to deny any one the legitimate right and privilege to derive the fullest advantage and benefit from the manifold joys, beauties, and pleasures with which the world has been so plentifully enriched by an All-Loving Creator.'[8]

The prison at C̲h̲ihríq

Chihríq A fortress in Ádharbáyján, northeastern Iran, where the Báb was imprisoned for almost all of the last two years of His life. Because He was more strictly confined there than He had been in Máh-Kú, the Báb named Chihríq 'Jabal-i-Shadíd' (the Grievous Mountain). Many of His writings were revealed in Chihríq, including the Arabic *Bayán* and His Tablet to Ḥájí Mírzá Áqásí. One of the purposes of the Conference of Badasht was to find a way to free the Báb from His imprisonment in Chihríq.
See also Máh-Kú.

Chosen Branch, the 'Abdu'l-Bahá.

Christ *See* Jesus.

City of the Covenant On 19 June 1912 'Abdu'l-Bahá named New York the City of the Covenant. At a gathering there, He spoke of Bahá'u'lláh's Tablet of the Branch and declared His own station to be the 'Centre of the Covenant'.

Hand of the Cause Amelia Collins

civilization, divine The civilization which will be brought about by the establishment of the World Order of Bahá'u'lláh, 'the foundations of which the unerring hand of Bahá'u'lláh has laid, and the essential elements of which the Will and Testament of 'Abdu'l-Bahá has disclosed.'[9]

'The emergence of a world community, the consciousness of world citizenship, the founding of a world civilization and culture . . . should, by their very nature, be regarded, as far as this planetary life is concerned, as the furthermost limits in the organization of human society . . .'[10]

clergy The Bahá'í Faith has no clergy. 'We have no priests,' Shoghi Effendi stated in a letter written on his behalf, 'therefore the service once rendered by priests to their religions is the service every single Bahá'í is expected to render individually to his religion. He must be the one who enlightens new souls, confirms them, heals the wounded and weary upon the road of life, and gives them to quaff from the chalice of everlasting life . . . the knowledge of the Manifestation of God in His Day.'[11] In His writings, Bahá'u'lláh forbids the monastic practices of asceticism and living in seclusion, bids priests to marry and prohibits the confession of sins.

Collins, Amelia American Hand of the Cause who accepted the Faith in 1919. She served for many years on the National Spiritual Assembly of the United States and Canada and in 1951 was appointed to the first

Collins, Amelia

International Bahá'í Council as its Vice-President. In December 1951 she was made a Hand of the Cause. She passed away on 1 January 1962.

Collins Gate Large wrought-iron gate erected by Shoghi Effendi at the northern approach to the Shrine of Bahá'u'lláh. It is named after Hand of the Cause Amelia Collins.

The Collins Gate at Bahjí, soon after its erection

Commonwealth, World *See* World Commonwealth.

community, Bahá'í The term often used by Bahá'ís to describe those Bahá'ís who live in a particular administrative unit, locally or nationally. It may also refer to the followers of the Bahá'í Faith worldwide.

Bahá'í community of Manchester in October 1921. Shoghi Effendi is seated to the left of the centre

Conclave of the Hands of the Cause Meetings in the Holy Land of all the Hands of the Cause. The first of these was held in November 1957 after the passing of Shoghi Effendi when nine Hands of the Cause were chosen to serve as Custodians of the Bahá'í Faith residing in the Holy Land.

See also Hands of the Cause of God.

Concourse on High *See* Supreme Concourse.

Constantinople in the nineteenth century

consolidation Term used by Bahá'ís to describe the process of Bahá'í community development whereby the Bahá'ís increasingly understand the teachings of the Faith, abide by its precepts, and take on the responsibilities of teaching and administration.

Constantinople (Istanbul) The city in Turkey, and former capital of the Ottoman Empire, to which Bahá'u'lláh went from Baghdád at the request of the Turkish government in 1863. He arrived in Constantinople on 16 August and remained there for about four months, after which time He was exiled to Adrianople.

consultation A form of discussion between individuals and within groups. It is the method by which Bahá'ís make decisions within their administrative bodies. Bahá'ís are also encouraged to use consultation in making personal or family decisions. It is 'a process for producing change in order to accomplish some definite purpose. This involves a

Consultation requires frankness and courtesy

sharing and interaction of thoughts and feelings in a spirit of love and harmony.'[12]

Consultation is one of the 'two luminaries' of the 'heaven of divine wisdom', the 'lamp of guidance'. Bahá'u'lláh enjoined, 'Take ye counsel together in all matters, inasmuch as consultation is the lamp of guidance which leadeth the way, and is the bestower of understanding.'[13]

Consultation requires the 'subjugation of all egotism and unruly passions, the cultivation of frankness and freedom of thought as well as courtesy, openness of mind, and wholehearted acquiescence in a majority decision'.[14]

Continental Board of Counsellors An institution created in 1968 by the Universal House of Justice as a means of developing 'the institution of the Hands of the Cause with a view to extension into the future of its appointed functions of protection and propagation,' as the House had already indicated that it saw 'no way in which additional Hands of the Cause of God' could be appointed.[15]

The duties of the Counsellors include 'directing the Auxiliary Boards in their respective areas, consulting and collaborating with national spiritual assemblies, and keeping the Hands of the Cause and the Universal House of Justice informed concerning the conditions of the Cause in their areas.'[16] Counsellors are appointed for terms of five years and function as Counsellors only when in the continent to which

Continental Board of Counsellors for the Americas, 1988

they have been appointed, unless they are appointed to the International Teaching Centre. Counsellors are not eligible for any elective office, except the Universal House of Justice. If elected to the Universal House of Justice, the Counsellor ceases to be a member of the Board of Counsellors.

convention A gathering of delegates for the purpose of electing an administrative body or for electing delegates who will in turn elect that body. Unit, district, state or other sub-national conventions are held to elect delegates who will in turn vote for the national spiritual assembly.

All the adult Bahá'ís in a given geographic locality will comprise the delegates for a particular sub-national convention, which takes place annually. They elect one of their number to serve as a delegate to the National Convention. The number of delegates to the National Convention is determined by the Universal House of Justice and advised to the national assembly which draws up the electoral units.

The National Convention is generally held annually during the Riḍván period (21 April–2 May). The delegates to the National Convention vote for the members of the national assembly. They are free to vote for any adult Bahá'í in the country and are not limited to voting for other delegates. Apart from this election, the function of the Convention is to consult with the incoming national assembly.

Shoghi Effendi wrote: 'It is the vital duty of the delegates to unburden their hearts, state their grievances, disclose their views, and explain their motives. It is the duty of the National Assembly to give earnest, prompt and prayerful consideration to the views of the delegates, weigh carefully their arguments and ponder their considered judgements, before they resort to voting and undertake to arrive at a decision according to the dictates of their conscience. They should explain their motives and not dictate: seek information and invite discussion.'[17]

The International Convention takes place in Haifa during the Riḍván period, at present once every five years. Its purpose is to elect the members of the Universal House of Justice. The delegates to this convention are the members of the national spiritual assemblies currently serving. They are free to vote for any adult male Bahá'í in the world and are not limited to voting for other national assembly members. In addition to the election, delegates also consult on a variety of topics of importance to the Faith.

Covenant, Day of the *See* Day of the Covenant.

Covenant, Greater and Lesser In a letter written on his behalf, Shoghi Effendi explained that there were 'two forms of Covenant both of which are explicitly mentioned in the literature of the Cause. First is the Covenant that every Prophet makes with humanity or, more definitely, with His people that they will accept and follow the coming Manifestation who will be the reappearance of His reality. The second form of Covenant is such as the one Bahá'u'lláh made with His people that they should accept the Master. This is merely to establish and strengthen the succession of the series of Lights that appear after every Manifestation.

Bahá'í Convention for the United States and Canada, 28 April 1923

Under the same category falls the Covenant the Master made with the Bahá'ís that they should accept His administration after Him.'[18]

The first of these is known as the Greater Covenant, the second as the Lesser Covenant.

Covenant of Bahá'u'lláh The divinely-ordained 'instrument' provided by Bahá'u'lláh 'to direct and canalize these forces let loose by this Heaven-sent process [the Revelation of Bahá'u'lláh], and to ensure their harmonious and continuous operation after His ascension.'[19] In His Will and Testament, the *Kitáb-i-'Ahdí* (The Book of My Covenant, Bahá'u'lláh clearly appointed 'Abdu'l-Bahá as His successor, identifying Him as 'Him Whom God hath purposed',[20] to whom all should turn after Bahá'u'lláh's passing. 'Abdu'l-Bahá is the Centre of the Covenant.

The intention of the Covenant is the protection of the unity of the Bahá'í Faith: 'The purpose of the Blessed Beauty in entering into this Covenant and Testament was to gather all existent beings around one point so that the thoughtless souls, who in every cycle and generation have been the cause of dissension, may not undermine the Cause.'[21]

'Abdu'l-Bahá has called the appointment of the Centre of the Covenant 'the most great characteristic of the revelation of Bahá'u'lláh.'[22] 'By this appointment and provision He has safeguarded and protected the religion of God against differences and schisms, making it impossible for anyone to create a new sect or faction of belief. To ensure unity and agreement He has entered into a Covenant with all the people of the world, including the interpreter and explainer of His teachings, so that no one may interpret or explain the religion of God

according to his own view or opinion and thus create a sect founded upon his individual understanding of the divine Words.'[23]

The Covenant of Bahá'u'lláh is unique in religious history: 'So firm and mighty is this Covenant that from the beginning of time until the present day no religious Dispensation hath produced its like.'[24]

Further, the Covenant provides the basis for the primary social teaching of the Bahá'í Revelation: 'It is indubitably clear that the pivot of the oneness of mankind is nothing else but the power of the Covenant.'[25]

See also 'Abdu'l-Bahá; Centre of the Covenant; Covenant, Greater and Lesser; *and Kitáb-i-'Ahdí.*

Covenant-breaker One who publicly denies the line of succession (i.e. Bahá'u'lláh, 'Abdu'l-Bahá, Shoghi Effendi, the Universal House of Justice) or who rebels against the Centre of the Covenant and actively works to undermine the Covenant. In the time of 'Abdu'l-Bahá the arch-breaker of the Covenant was His half-brother Mírzá Muḥammad-'Alí.

The decision to expel someone from the community as a Covenant-breaker is taken, at present, by the Hands of the Cause with the approval of the Universal House of Justice. It is a very rare occurrence.

It is forbidden for Bahá'ís to associate with Covenant-breakers. 'Abdu'l-Bahá explains the reason for this: '. . . just as the bodily diseases like consumption . . . are contagious, likewise the spiritual diseases are also infectious. If a consumptive should associate with a thousand safe and healthy persons, the safety and health of these thousand persons would not affect the consumptive and would not cure him of his consumption. But when this consumptive associates with those thousand souls, in a short time the disease of consumption will infect a number of those healthy persons.'[26] However, Bahá'ís are to pray for Covenant-breakers, as 'these souls are not lost forever'.[27]

cradle of the administration America. Shoghi Effendi wrote: 'the role played by the American Bahá'í community, since the passing of 'Abdu'l-Bahá until the termination of the first Bahá'í century, has been such as to lend a tremendous impetus to the development of the Faith throughout the world . . . Indeed so preponderating has been the influence of its members in both the initiation and the consolidation of Bahá'í administrative institutions that their country may well deserve to be recognized as the cradle of the Administrative Order which Bahá'u'lláh Himself has envisaged . . .'[28]

cradle of the Faith Iran (Persia).

creation *See* evolution.

Crimson Book *See Kitáb-i-'Ahdí.*

Crimson Spot (Buq'atu'l -Ḥamrá') A hill called Samaríyyih near Bahjí where red flowers grew in abundance in the time of Bahá'u'lláh. Today it is occupied by the army.

'In the springtime when the hill was verdant and covered with red flowers such as poppies and anemones, Bahá'u'lláh would have His tent pitched there. Many years later, when 'Abdu'l-Bahá was again incarcerated within the city walls of 'Akká, He would wistfully ask those who had gone to visit the Shrine of His Father: "Were red, red flowers blooming on Buq'atu'l-Ḥamrá'?"'[29]

Cycle, Prophetic The great period of time, inaugurated by Adam, during which many Manifestations appeared who prophesied the advent of Bahá'u'lláh. The Prophetic Cycle has been succeeded by the Era of Fulfilment.[30]

See also Adamic Cycle.

D

***Dalá'il-i-Sab'ih* (*The Seven Proofs*)** A book revealed by the Báb during His imprisonment in Máh-Kú. According to Shoghi Effendi, it is 'the most important of the polemical works of the Báb . . . Remarkably lucid, admirable in its precision, original in conception, unanswerable in its argument, this work, apart from the many and divers proofs of His mission which it adduces, is noteworthy for the blame it assigns to the "*seven powerful sovereigns ruling the world*" in His day, as well as for the manner in which it stresses the responsibilities, and censures the conduct, of the Christian divines of a former age who, had they recognized the truth of Muḥammad's mission, He contends, would have been followed by the mass of their co-religionists.'[1]

Seven Bahá'í dervishes who came on foot to 'Akká to visit Bahá'u'lláh

darvísh (dervish) [Pers] Literally, beggar [Arabic, faqír: poor one]. More specifically, a travelling religious mendicant of one of several Sufi orders or other Muslim mystic traditions.

Darvísh Muḥammad-i-Írání The name taken by Bahá'u'lláh when he sought seclusion in the mountains of Sulaymáníyyih in 1856.
See also Sulaymáníyyih.

Dawn-Breakers The heroes and martyrs of the earliest days of the Bábí-Bahá'í Dispensation, so-called because of their association with the beginning of a new age: 'The call of the Báb was a call to awakening, a claim that a New Day had dawned.'[2] Their story is told in *The Dawn-Breakers: Nabíl's Narrative of the Early Days of the Bahá'í Revelation* by Muḥammad-i-Zarandí (Nabíl-i-A'ẓam), translated from the Persian by Shoghi Effendi.

The Dawn-Breakers is the main account of the events of the period beginning with the missions of Shaykh Aḥmad and Siyyid Káẓim, and including the Revelation of the Báb and His Martyrdom, the Conference of Badasht and the deeds of many heroes and martyrs including Mullá Ḥusayn, Quddús, Ṭáhirih, Vaḥíd and Ḥujjat. The volume describes the role of Bahá'u'lláh during the Bábí Dispensation and ends with His banishment to Baghdád.

Shoghi Effendi, in a letter written on his behalf, said about *The Dawn-Breakers* that 'The life of those who figure in it is so stirring that every one who reads those accounts is bound to be affected and impelled to follow their footsteps of sacrifice in the path of the Faith. The Guardian believes, therefore, that it should be studied by the friends, especially the youth who need some inspiration to carry them through these troubled days.'[3]

Day of the Covenant Festival observed on 26 November to commemorate Bahá'u'lláh's appointment of 'Abdu'l-Bahá as the Centre of His Covenant. 'Abdu'l-Bahá had instructed that His own birthday should not be celebrated because it falls on the Declaration of the Báb and that day should be devoted to the Báb's anniversary. At the believers' request 'Abdu'l-Bahá gave them the Day of the Covenant to observe in His honour. It is also known as the Greatest Festival (Jashn-i-A'ẓam). Suspension of work is not obligatory on this Holy Day.

Day of God Generally, the dispensation of each Manifestation. Specifically, the period, or universal cycle, ushered in by Bahá'u'lláh, 'whose advent has been hailed in the Heavenly Books as the advent of the Day of God Himself'.[4] Bahá'u'lláh Himself states: 'Great indeed is this Day! The allusions made to it in all the sacred Scriptures as the Day of God attest its greatness. The soul of every Prophet of God, of every Divine Messenger, hath thirsted for this wondrous Day. All the divers kindreds of the earth have, likewise, yearned to attain it.'[5] 'This is the King of Days, the Day that hath seen the coming of the Best-beloved, Him Who through all eternity hath been acclaimed the Desire of the World.'[6] 'It is evident that every age in which a Manifestation of God hath lived is divinely ordained and may, in a sense, be characterized as God's appointed Day. This Day, however, is unique and is to be distinguished from those that have preceded it. The designation "Seal of the Prophets" fully reveals and demonstrates its high station.'[7]

days of the week The days of the Bahá'í week are:

1 Jalál	Glory	(Saturday)
2 Jamál	Beauty	(Sunday)
3 Kamál	Perfection	(Monday)
4 Fiḍál	Grace	(Tuesday)
5 'Idál	Justice	(Wednesday)
6 Istijlál	Majesty	(Thursday)
7 Istiqlál	Independence	(Friday)

The Bahá'í day of rest is Istiqlál (Friday)[8] and the Bahá'í day begins and ends at sunset.

See also calendar, Bahá'í.

Dayspring of Revelation The Manifestation of God, specifically Bahá'u'lláh.

Daystar The sun. Literary allusion to the Manifestation of God, specifically Bahá'u'lláh.

death, life after In the Bahá'í teachings death is regarded as the passage of the soul to another plane of existence, which is spiritual rather than physical.

The concept of death as annihilation is regarded as a mistaken idea, for even the physical elements of which the body is composed do not cease to exist, but rather undergo a transformation. While the physical body of man decomposes after death, the soul or spirit is indestructible and goes on to another existence where the soul continues on its journey towards God. The nature of this level of existence cannot be comprehended, except in the most elementary way by analogy: 'The world beyond', Bahá'u'lláh states, 'is as different from this world as this world is different from that of the child while still in the womb of its mother.'[9] In the physical existence of life on earth the soul progresses through its own efforts; in the spiritual world beyond it is dependent for its development on the mercy of God and intercession through the prayers of other souls.

'Abdu'l-Bahá was asked, 'How should one look forward to death?' He answered: 'How does one look forward to the goal of any journey? With hope and with expectation. It is even so with the end of this earthly journey.'[10] Bahá'u'lláh wrote, 'O Son of the Supreme! I have made death a messenger of joy to thee. Wherefore dost thou grieve? I made the light to shed on thee its splendour. Why dost thou veil thyself therefrom?'[11]

See also burial, Bahá'í; death, nature of; heaven and hell; resurrection; *and* soul.

death, nature of The separation of the soul from the body. In *The Hidden Words* Bahá'u'lláh reveals, 'I have made death a messenger of joy to thee.'[12] In the *Ḥurúfát-i-'Állín* (The Exalted Letters), here paraphrased by Adib Taherzadeh, Bahá'u'lláh 'directs His attention to physical death and dwells on the afflictions which befall the human temple. At this point the vehicle of so precious an entity as the soul becomes useless, is discarded and buried under the dust . . . The perfect union which for a lifetime brought the soul and the body together is now ended, as one is elevated to great heights and the other abased and condemned to perish. In this Tablet Bahá'u'lláh refers to death as an affliction for the body and confirms that since the spiritual worlds of God are hidden from the eyes of men, it is difficult for those who are bereaved by the death of their loved ones not to feel the anguish of separation in their hearts. He therefore counsels them to fix their attention on the spiritual realms of God and the immortality of the soul.'[13]

See also death, life after.

declaration The statement of belief made by one who wishes to become a Bahá'í, including acceptance of the stations of Bahá'u'lláh as the Manifestation of God for this day, of the Báb as His Forerunner and of 'Abdu'l-Bahá as the Centre of Bahá'u'lláh's Covenant and Perfect Exemplar of His Faith, as well as acceptance of all that they have revealed.

The Universal House of Justice has stated: 'The declarants need not know all the proofs, history, laws, and principles of the Faith, but in the process of declaring themselves they must, in addition to catching the spark of faith, become basically informed about the Central Figures of the Faith, as well as the existence of laws they must follow and an administration they must obey.'[14]

See also enrolment; *and* maturity, age of.

Declaration of Bahá'u'lláh *See* Riḍván, Feast or Festival of.

Declaration of the Báb A Bahá'í Holy Day commemorating the Declaration of the Báb to Mullá Ḥusayn that the Báb was the Promised One. This event occurred at two hours and eleven minutes after sunset on the evening of 22 May 1844 in the House of the Báb in Shíráz. It is considered to mark the opening of the Bahá'í Dispensation and the beginning of the Bahá'í Era.

'This night', said the Báb to Mullá Ḥusayn, 'this very hour will, in the days to come, be celebrated as one of the greatest and most significant of all festivals.'[15] The Declaration of the Báb is observed about two hours after sunset on 22 May and work is prohibited on this Holy Day (23 May).

deeds Actions.

In *The Hidden Words* Bahá'u'lláh states, 'Verily I say unto thee: Of all men the most negligent is he that disputeth idly and seeketh to advance himself over his brother. Say, O brethren! Let deeds, not words, be your adorning.'[16]

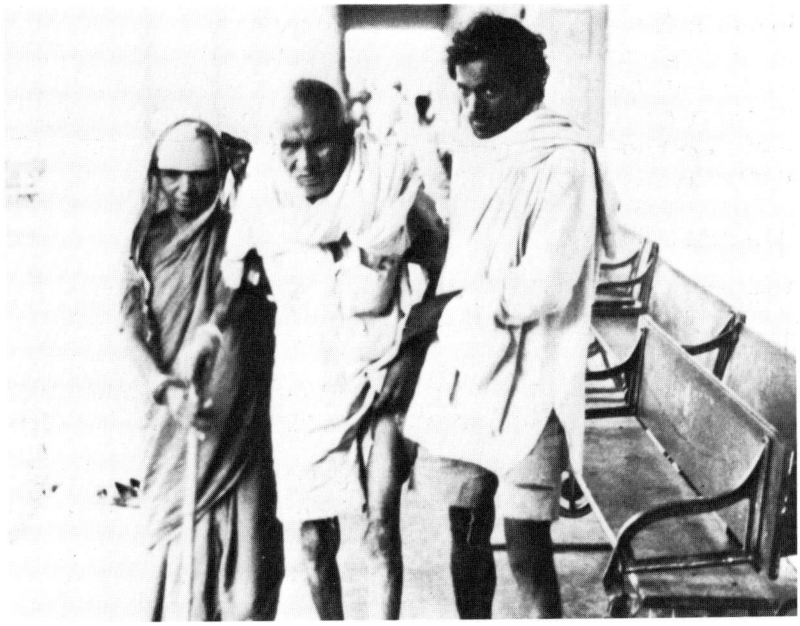

Mere words are not enough; deeds must be our 'adorning'. An elderly patient is guided to an Eye Camp conducted under Bahá'í auspices in India, where doctors treated 1900 patients in one week in 1983

deepening The study of the Bahá'í Faith in all its aspects.

Shoghi Effendi has stated, in a letter written on his behalf: 'To deepen in the Cause means to read the writings of Bahá'u'lláh and the Master so thoroughly as to be able to give it to others in its pure form.'[17] In addition to the thorough study of the history, literature and teachings of the Bahá'í Faith, to deepen in the Faith also means to 'assimilate its laws and principles, ponder its admonitions, tenets and purposes, commit to memory certain of its exhortations and prayers, master the essentials of its administration, and keep abreast of its current affairs and latest developments.'[18]

In 1967 the Universal House of Justice, in its Riḍván message, wrote a lengthy description of the nature of deepening and the imperative need for the Bahá'ís to deepen in the Cause: 'A detailed and exact knowledge of the present structure of Bahá'í administration, or of the bylaws of national and local spiritual assemblies, or of the many and varied applications of Bahá'í law under the diverse conditions prevailing around the world, while valuable in itself, cannot be regarded as the sort of knowledge primarily intended by deepening. Rather it is suggested a clearer apprehension of the purpose of God for man, and particularly His immediate purpose as revealed and directed by Bahá'u'lláh, a purpose as far removed from current concepts of human well-being and happiness as is possible . . . this is the theme we must pursue in our efforts to deepen in the Cause. What is Bahá'u'lláh's purpose for the human race? For what ends did He submit to the appalling cruelties and indignities heaped upon Him? What does he mean by "a new race of men"? What are the profound changes He will bring about? The answers are to be found in the Sacred Writings of our Faith and in their interpretation by 'Abdu'l-Bahá and our beloved Guardian. Let the friends immerse themselves in this ocean, let them organize regular study classes for its constant consideration, and, as reinforcement to their effort, let them remember conscientiously the requirements of daily prayer and reading of the Word of God enjoined upon all Bahá'ís by Bahá'u'lláh.'[19]

Deepening forms the basis for individual steadfastness and faith, for teaching through both word and deed and for the establishment and functioning of the institutions of the administrative order.

deputization The provision of financial support for a pioneer or teacher by another person. 'Centre your energies', Bahá'u'lláh wrote, 'in the propagation of the Faith of God. Whoso is worthy of so high a calling, let him arise and promote it. Whoso is unable, it is his duty to appoint him who will, in his stead, proclaim this Revelation . . .'[20]

See also funds.

detachment To submit one's will to the will of God and to seek His good pleasure above one's own. Attachment to this world can be described as anything which prevents the soul from drawing nearer to God. Detachment does not mean renunciation of the world, mendicancy or asceticism. Bahá'u'lláh has stated, 'Should a man wish to adorn himself with the ornaments of the earth, to wear its apparels, or partake of the benefits it can bestow, no harm can behall him, if he alloweth nothing whatever to intervene between him and God, for God hath ordained every good thing, whether created in the heavens or in the earth, for such of His servants as truly believe in Him.'[21]

Possession of earthly goods is not the only form of attachment. Pride in one's accomplishments, knowledge, position or own self can also be a barrier between oneself and God. Ridding oneself of these is also detachment.

development, social and economic The process of maturation of social institutions together with the increase in participation of individuals and groups in, and access to, those institutions; and the improvement in the economic welfare, wealth, standard of living and material comfort of individuals, groups and whole populations.

For Bahá'ís, material development cannot be successfully pursued unless spiritual development is also sought. 'Abdu'l-Bahá elaborated this concept of development in several of His talks in America, collected under the title of *The Promulgation of Universal Peace*: 'No matter how far the material world advances, it cannot establish the happiness of mankind. Only when material and spiritual civilization are linked and coordinated will happiness be assured.' '. . . until material achievements, physical accomplishments and human virtues are reinforced by spiritual perfections, luminous qualities and characteristics of mercy, no fruit or result shall issue therefrom, nor will the happiness of the world of humanity, which is the ultimate aim, be attained.'

Many of the social teachings of the Bahá'í Faith are of central importance to development issues: universal education, the equality of men and women, the need for government officials to maintain a rectitude of conduct, the use of consultation as a means of making decisions and solving problems, the abolition of the extremes of wealth and poverty, the establishment of economic justice, the oneness of mankind and the need for unity.

Bahá'ís have been involved in the process of social and economic development from the early days of the religion. In 1875 'Abdul'-Bahá Himself, in *The Secret of Divine Civilization*, made proposals for the social and economic reform of Iran. The Bahá'ís in Iran established schools and took the lead in the provision of education to girls. The status of Bahá'í women was also higher than in the general population. The Bahá'ís of 'Ishqabád, who were largely free of the persecution which befell the Iranian Bahá'ís, went even further in their efforts and built schools, a medical clinic and a library. Illiteracy was eliminated in their community.

Between the passing of 'Abdu'l-Bahá in 1921 and the 1980s the Bahá'ís concentrated on developing a network of local spiritual assemblies around the world. These provided, among many other functions, a system of communication at grassroots level, a framework in which to develop the skill of consultation as a method of decision-making, and a way for individuals to participate in decision-making. During this period the Bahá'í Faith spread into Africa, the Pacific and Latin America, as well as increasing the communities in Asia, Europe and North America. In many places Bahá'ís responded to local needs by creating small, specific development projects, often establishing schools or literacy centres.

In October 1983, in a letter addressed to the Bahá'ís of the world, the Universal House of Justice stated that the Bahá'í community had grown to the stage where the 'processes of this development' were to be incorporated into its regular pursuits'.

'The steps to be taken', the House of Justice continued, 'must necessarily begin in the Bahá'í community itself, with the friends endeavouring, through their application of spiritual principles, their rectitude of conduct and the practice of the art of consultation, to uplift themselves and thus become self-sufficient and self-reliant.

'Moreover, these exertions will conduce to the preservation of human honour, so desired by Bahá'u'lláh. In the process and as a consequence, the friends will undoubtedly extend the benefits of their efforts to society as a whole, until all mankind achieves the progress intended by the Lord of the Age.'

In this same letter the Universal House of Justice established the Office of Social and Economic Development to 'assist [it] to promote and coordinate the activities of the friends throughout the world in this new field'. However, the Universal House of Justice pointed out that 'progress in the development field will depend largely on natural stirrings at the grassroots, and it should receive its driving force from those sources rather than from an imposition of plans and programmes from the top'.

Since 1983 the number of community-based development projects has grown enormously. In September 1984 there were 487 such projects; by October 1987 this number had risen to 1482, 805 of which are schools, tutorial schools and literacy schemes.

Agricultural projects have been particularly successful in India, although all of the rural developments projects have an agricultural

Robert Turner

Dr J. G. Augur

Helen S. Goodall

Joseph Hannen

component. Some of the rural development projects are based on schools which provide training in a wide range of skills, such as carpentry and metal-working.

Projects providing medical and dental care, health education and counselling have been established in several communities, and free medical and dental clinics have been arranged on a permanent or temporary basis in India, Pakistan and Bangladesh.

Another type of development project helps to restore the pride of indigenous peoples in their own cultures. Bahá'í radio stations in the Americas and in West Africa have played a major role in re-introducing people to their own music and traditions. Annual festivals of traditional music, folklore and dancing, as well as music festivals for children, ensure that the rich cultural diversity of the world's people will be preserved.

Arthur P. Dodge

Dhi'b [Ar] *See* Muḥammad-Báqir, Shaykh.

dhikr [Ar] Remembrance, mention; praise or glorification. Dhikru-'lláh (Remembrance of God) is a title the Báb took in the early days of His ministry.

Disciples of 'Abdu'l-Bahá Nineteen eminent Western Bahá'ís, men and women, designated by this title by Shoghi Effendi. They were also entitled 'Heralds of the Covenant'. They are:

Dr John E. Esslemont, author of *Bahá'u'lláh and the New Era*
Thornton Chase, the first American Bahá'í
Howard MacNutt
Sarah Farmer, founder of Green Acre
Hippolyte Dreyfus-Barney
Lillian Kappes
Robert Turner, first Black Bahá'í in America
Dr Arthur Brauns
W. H. Randall
Lua Getsinger
Joseph Hannan
Chester I. Thatcher
Charles Greenleaf
Mrs J. D. Brittingham
Mrs Thornburgh
Helen S. Goodall
Arthur P. Dodge
William H. Hoar
Dr J. G. Augur

Charles Greenleaf

dispensation The period of time during which the authority of a Manifestation of God's social or temporal teachings endure. (The eternal, spiritual truths taught by each Manifestation are not abrogated but affirmed by subsequent Manifestations.) A prophet's dispensation begins with the declaration of His prophetic mission and ends with the declaration of the next Manifestation of God, whose Teachings supersede those of the former prophet. The dispensation of the Báb, which began on 23 May 1844, is closely linked to that of Bahá'u'lláh and is considered part of the Bahá'í Era. The dispensation of the Báb ended at Riḍván 1863 when Bahá'u'lláh declared His Mission. Bahá'u'lláh has stated in the *Kitáb-i-Aqdas* that the Bahá'í Dispensation shall last no less than a thousand years.

diversity, unity in *See* unity in diversity.

Divine Plan *See Tablets of the Divine Plan*

divorce According to Bahá'í law, divorce is strongly condemned but is permitted under certain circumstances. It is allowed only in the case of extreme antipathy and aversion on the part of either spouse and after a period of one full year of separation, called the year of waiting (or year of patience).

See also year of waiting.

dowry The payment of a dowry by the groom to the bride is specified in the *Kitáb-i-Aqdas* as a requirement for Bahá'í marriage, but this law is not yet in general effect. The dowry is fixed at a minimum of nineteen mith̲qáls and no more than ninety-five mith̲qáls of pure gold for city dwellers and of silver for village dwellers, one mith̲qál being equal to a little over 3.5 grammes.

See also marriage, Bahá'í; *and* mith̲qál.

dreams In *The Seven Valleys* Bahá'u'lláh states, 'One of the created phenomena is the dream. Behold how many secrets are deposited therein, how many wisdoms treasured up, how many worlds concealed. Observe, how thou art asleep in a dwelling, and its doors are barred; on a sudden thou findest thyself in a far-off city, which thou enterest without moving thy feet or wearying thy body; without using thine eyes, thou seest; without taxing thine ears, thou hearest; without a tongue, thou speakest. And perchance when ten years are gone, thou wilt witness in the outer world the very things thou hast dreamed tonight . . . Consider the difference between these two worlds . . .'[22]

In the *Súriy-i-Vafá*, Bahá'u'lláh again refers to dreams: 'Consider thy state when asleep. Verily, I say, this phenomenon is the most mysterious of the signs of God amongst men . . . Behold how the things which thou hast seen in thy dream is, after a considerable lapse of time, fully realized. Had the world in which thou didst find thyself in thy dream been identical with the world in which thou livest, it would have been necessary for the event occurring in that dream to have transpired in this world at the very moment of its occurrence . . . This not being the case, however, it must necessarily follow that the world in which thou livest is different and apart from that which thou hast experienced in thy dream. This latter world hath neither beginning nor end. It would be true if thou wert to contend that this same world is . . . within thy proper self and is wrapped up within thee. It would equally be true to maintain that thy spirit, having transcended the limitations of sleep and having stripped itself of all earthly attachment, hath, by the act of God, been made to traverse a realm which lieth hidden in the innermost reality of this world.'[23]

In a letter written on behalf of Shoghi Effendi it is stated: 'That truth is often imparted through dreams no one who is familiar with history, especially religious history, can doubt. At the same time dreams and visions are always coloured and influenced more or less by the mind of the dreamer and we must beware of attaching too much importance to them . . . In many cases dreams have been the means of bringing people to the truth or of confirming them in the Faith . . . We should test impressions we get through dreams, visions or inspirations, by comparing them with the revealed Word and seeing whether they are in harmony therewith.'[24]

drugs and alcohol The use of all intoxicants, including drugs and alcohol, is forbidden in the *Kitáb-i-Aqdas*. An exception is made in the case of drugs which are prescribed by a physician for medical treatment.

Alcohol is prohibited, 'Abdu'l-Bahá states, because 'it is the cause of chronic diseases, weakeneth the nerves, and consumeth the mind'.[25] 'Abdu'l-Bahá described ḥashísh (cannabis) as 'the worst of all intoxicants, and its prohibition is explicitly revealed. Its use causeth the disintegration of thought and the complete torpor of the soul.'[26]

Of the effects of smoking opium 'Abdu'l-Bahá has stated: 'Reason showeth that smoking opium is a kind of insanity, and experience attesteth that the user is completely cut off from the human kingdom. May God protect all against the perpetration of an act so hideous as this, an act which layeth in ruins the very foundation of what it is to be human, and which causeth the user to be dispossessed for ever and ever. For opium fasteneth on the soul, so that the user's conscience dieth, his mind is blotted away, his perceptions are eroded. It turneth the living into the dead.'[27]

drugs and alcohol

Strong measures may be used to prevent the use of opium: '. . . violence and force, constraint and oppression, are one and all condemned. It is, however, mandatory that the use of opium be prevented by any means whatsoever, that perchance the human race may be delivered from this most powerful of plagues.'[28]

du'a [Ar, Pers] Prayer.

E

economic problems, spiritual solution to One of the principles or tenets of Bahá'í social teaching, it includes the abolition of extremes of wealth and poverty, to be achieved through taxation as well as the spiritual transformation of attitudes so that the rich engage in philanthropy from inner conviction. 'The essence of the matter', said 'Abdu'l-Bahá, 'is that divine justice will become manifest in human conditions and affairs, and all mankind will find comfort and enjoyment in life. It is not meant that all will be equal, for inequality in degree and capacity is a property of nature. Necessarily there will be rich people and also those who will be in want of their livelihood, but in the aggregate community there will be equalization and readjustment of values and interests. In the future there will be no very rich nor extremely poor.'[1] One of the institutions established to bring this principle into effect is the Ḥuqúqu'lláh.

Refugees from drought and famine. Bahá'u'lláh says that there must be a spiritual solution to economic problems

The Bahá'í Faith provides the spiritual stimulus and framework necessary for the complete restructuring of human society, of which economics is a part. It does not provide a complete economic system or programme of reform: 'There are practically no technical teachings on economics in the Cause, such as banking, the price system, and others. The Cause is not an economic system . . . The contribution of the Faith to this subject is essentially indirect, as it consists of the application of spiritual principles to our present-day economic system. Bahá'u'lláh has given us a few basic principles which should guide future Bahá'í economists in establishing such institutions which will adjust the economic relationships of the world . . .'[2]

However, there are several practical solutions to specific economic problems to be found in the Bahá'í Writings, such as the creation of a general storehouse of agricultural goods for a community, profit-sharing, the voluntary sharing of one's property with others, the redistribution of wealth so that there are no extremes of wealth and poverty, justice in opportunity,[3] graduated taxation, recognition of the importance of agriculture and the abolition of war.

See also wealth and poverty, elimination of extremes of.

Edirne *See* Adrianople.

education, nature of That process which enables a person to understand God, the Manifestation, and his own self, as well as to acquire particular skills and knowledge useful to himself and to the world.

Bahá'u'lláh writes: 'The Prophets and Messengers of God have been

Bahá'u'lláh has stated that it is compulsory for everyone to learn to read and write

sent down for the sole purpose of guiding mankind to the straight Path of Truth. The purpose underlying their revelation hath been to educate all men, that they may, at the hour of death, ascend, in the utmost purity and sanctity and with absolute detachment, to the Throne of the Most High.'[4] 'We have decreed, O people, that the highest and last end of all learning be the recognition of Him Who is the Object of all knowledge . . .'[5] 'Regard man as a mine rich in gems of inestimable value. Education can, alone, cause it to reveal its treasures, and enable mankind to benefit therefrom.'[6] 'It is not desirable that a man be left without knowledge or skills, for he is then but a barren tree.'[7] 'The learned of the day must direct the people to acquire those branches of knowledge which are of use, that both the learned themselves and the generality of mankind may derive benefits therefrom.'[8]

As women are the educators of the next generation, the education of girls takes precedence over that of boys

education, universal One of the principles or tenets of Bahá'í social teaching. 'Abdu'l-Bahá explained: 'Bahá'u'lláh has announced that inasmuch as ignorance and lack of education are barriers of separation among mankind, all must receive training and instruction. Through this provision the lack of mutual understanding will be remedied and the unity of mankind furthered and advanced. Universal education is a universal law. It is, therefore, incumbent upon every father to teach and instruct his children according to his possibilities. If he is unable to educate them, the body politic, the representative of the people, must provide the means for their education.'[9] And: 'education is essential, and all standards of training and teaching throughout the world of mankind should be brought into conformity and agreement; a universal curriculum should be established, and the basis of ethics be the same.'[10] 'Daughters and sons must follow the same curriculum of study, thereby promoting unity of the sexes.'[11]

'Furthermore, the education of woman is more necessary and important than that of man, for woman is the trainer of the child from its infancy . . . If the educator be incompetent, the educated will be correspondingly lacking . . . The mothers are the first educators of mankind; if they be imperfect, alas for the condition and future of the race.'[12]

Effendi [Turk] A term of respect meaning 'sir' or 'mister' affixed to a person's name.

elections The selection of membership of local and national spiritual assemblies and the Universal House of Justice. All Bahá'í elections are conducted by secret ballot without nominations, canvassing or any form of electioneering.

Election of the Local Spiritual Assembly of Chi Ma Wan, a closed refugee camp in Hong Kong, Riḍván 1985

elections

The election process requires the elector to write down the names of those individuals (presently nine for local and national spiritual assemblies and the Universal House of Justice, generally one for election of delegates to the national convention) whom he feels are the most suitable for service. There is no discussion of personalities before an election. Those people with the highest number of votes assume office. Local and national assemblies elect their officers from among their own number. The election of officers is conducted as other Bahá'í elections, except that a person must receive at least five votes to be elected to a particular office.

All adult Bahá'ís in good standing in a specific locality are eligible to vote for, and to be elected to, the local spiritual assembly. All adult Bahá'ís in good standing in a particular electoral unit are eligible to vote for, or to be elected as, a delegate to the national convention. Delegates to the national convention vote for the members of the national spiritual assembly, the members of which are drawn from all adult Bahá'ís in the country, and not merely from the body of the delegates. National spiritual assembly members elect the members of the Universal House of Justice from among the adult Bahá'í males of the world community.

See also convention, local spiritual assembly, national spiritual assembly *and* Universal House of Justice.

endowed with constancy *See* Prophets, Greater.

enrolment The administrative process by which a person who has declared his or her belief in Bahá'u'lláh officially becomes a member of the Bahá'í community, enjoying the rights and privileges of membership including voting in Bahá'í elections, attending Nineteen Day Feasts and serving in elective and appointed administrative positions. Each national spiritual assembly determines the manner for registering new believers. In most countries this involves signing a card stating one's desire to become enrolled in the Bahá'í community.

See also declaration.

epistle A letter. Often refers to major Writings of Bahá'u'lláh addressed to particular individuals, as *Epistle to the Son of the Wolf*.

Epistle to the Son of the Wolf The last volume revealed by Bahá'u'lláh, in 1891 in Bahjí. It was addressed to Shaykh Muḥammad-Taqí, the son of an enemy of the Bahá'í Faith whom Bahá'u'lláh had named 'The Wolf'. In this Epistle Bahá'u'lláh calls upon Shaykh Muḥammad-Taqí to repent his evil deeds, quotes selected passages from His own writings and describes the deeds of the Covenant-breakers in Constantinople.

See also Muḥammad-Báqir, Shaykh; *and* Son of the Wolf.

epoch Period or division of the three ages through which the Bahá'í Faith must pass. The Heroic, or Apostolic Age, 'fell into three distinct epochs, of nine, of thirty-nine and of twenty-nine years' duration, associated respectively with the Bábí Dispensation and the ministries of Bahá'u'lláh and of 'Abdu'l-Bahá'.[13] The first epoch of the Formative Age (1921–44/46) witnessed the 'birth and the primary stages in the erection of the framework of the Administrative Order of the Faith.'[14] The second epoch (1946–63) witnessed the 'formulation of a succession of teaching plans designed to facilitate the development of the Faith beyond the confines of the Western Hemisphere and the continent of Europe'.[15] The second epoch also witnessed the 'appointment of the Hands of the Cause, the introduction of Auxiliary Boards and the establishment of the International Bahá'í Council. The culminating event of the epoch was the election of the Universal House of Justice in 1963.'[16] The third epoch (1963–86) witnessed 'the emergence of the Faith from obscurity and the initiation of activities designed to foster the social and economic development of communities'.[17] The institution of the Continental Boards of Counsellors was brought into existence leading to the establishment of the International Teaching Centre. Assistants to the Auxiliary Boards were also introduced. The Seat of the Universal House of Justice was designed and built in this epoch. The fourth epoch (1986–) saw the beginning of the process whereby 'the specific goals for each national community will be formulated, within the framework of the overall objectives of the [Six Year Teaching] Plan, by means of consultation between the particular National Spiritual Assembly and the Continental Board of Counsellors.'[18]

In addition, the term 'epoch' was also used by Shoghi Effendi to refer to the phases in the unfoldment of 'Abdu'l-Bahá's Divine Plan. The first epoch of this Plan began in 1937 with the inception of the First Seven Year Plan by the North American Bahá'í community and concluded with the completion of the Ten Year Crusade in 1963. The second epoch began in 1964 with the inauguration of the Nine Year Plan of the Universal House of Justice.

See also ages of the Bahá'í Faith *and Tablets of the Divine Plan.*

equality of men and women One of the principles or tenets of Bahá'í social teaching. Bahá'u'lláh has stated: 'Praised be God, the Pen of the Most High hath lifted distinctions from between His servants and handmaidens and . . . hath conferred upon all a station and rank on the same plane.'[19]

'Abdu'l-Bahá spoke much about this principle when touring the West in 1911–13. While in America He spoke at a Woman's Suffrage Meeting in New York, stating: 'In past ages it was held that woman and man were not equal – that is to say, woman was considered inferior to man, even from the standpoint of her anatomy and creation. She was considered especially inferior in intelligence, and the idea prevailed universally that it was not allowable for her to step into the arena of important affairs. In some countries man went so far as to believe and teach that woman belonged to a sphere lower than human. But in this century, which is the century of light and the revelation of mysteries, God is proving to the satisfaction of humanity that all this is ignorance and error; nay, rather, it is well established that mankind and womankind as parts of composite humanity are coequal and that no difference in estimate is allowable, for all are human. The conditions in past centuries were due to woman's lack of opportunity. She was denied the right and privilege of education and left in her undeveloped state. Naturally, she could not and did not advance. In reality, God has created all mankind, and in the estimation of God there is no distinction as to male and female. The one whose heart is pure is acceptable in His sight, be that one man or woman. God does not inquire, "Art thou woman or art thou man?" He judges human actions. If these are acceptable in the threshold of the Glorious One, man and woman will be equally recognized and rewarded.

'Furthermore, the education of woman is more necessary and important than that of man, for woman is the trainer of the child from its infancy. If she be defective and imperfect herself, the child will necessarily be deficient; therefore, imperfection of woman implies a condition of imperfection in all mankind, for it is the mother who rears, nurtures and guides the growth of the child. This is not the function of the father. If the educator be incompetent, the educated will be correspondingly lacking. This is evident and incontrovertible. Could the student be brilliant and accomplished if the teacher is illiterate and ignorant? The mothers are the first educators of mankind; if they be imperfect, alas for the condition and future of the race . . .

'The world of humanity consists of two parts: male and female. Each is the complement of the other. Therefore, if one is defective, the other will necessarily be incomplete, and perfection cannot be attained. There is a right hand and a left hand in the human body, functionally equal in service and administration. If either proves defective, the defect will naturally extend to the other by involving the completeness of the whole; for accomplishment is not normal unless both are perfect. If we say one hand is deficient, we prove the inability and incapacity of the other; for single-handed there is no full accomplishment. Just as physical accomplishment is complete with two hands, so man and woman, the two parts of the social body, must be perfect. It is not natural that either should remain undeveloped; and until both are perfected, the happiness of the human world will not be realized.'[20]

See also women, status of.

The equality of men and women is one of the prerequisites of world peace

Hand of the Cause
John E. Esslemont

Esperanto *See* Bahá'í Esperanto League.

Esslemont, Dr John Ebenezer Hand of the Cause of God, born in Aberdeenshire, Scotland, in 1874. He was introduced to the Bahá'í Faith in 1914. His major book, *Bahá'u'lláh and the New Era*, the first nine chapters of which he wrote during the First World War, was submitted to 'Abdu'l-Bahá for approval. Esslemont visited 'Abdu'l-Bahá in 1919–20 and returned to the Holy Land in 1925 to undertake work for Shoghi Effendi. He died there in November 1925 and was posthumously named a Hand of the Cause. *Bahá'u'lláh and the New Era* has been translated into many languages and has become one of the most widely used of the introductory books to the Bahá'í Faith.

evil 'Evil' is explained in the Bahá'í Writings as being the absence of good, in the same way that darkness is the absence of light. Evil is not seen as an independent force in its own right.

'Abdu'l-Bahá explained: '. . . the intellectual realities, such as all the qualities and admirable perfections of man, are purely good, and exist. Evil is simply their non-existence. So ignorance is the want of knowledge, error is the want of guidance, forgetfulness is the want of memory, stupidity is the want of good sense. All these things have no real existence.'[21]

Although the creation of God is entirely good, man's free will allows him the capacity to use his natural gifts for positive good or to pervert them to evil uses, by following his selfish, baser desires. In a letter written on his behalf, Shoghi Effendi further explained: 'We know absence of light is darkness, but no one would assert darkness was not a fact. It exists even though it is only the absence of something else. So evil exists too, and we cannot close our eyes to it, even though it is a negative existence. We must seek to supplant it by good, and if we see an evil person is not influenceable by us, then we should shun his company for it is unhealthy.'[22] However, Bahá'ís do not believe that people are inherently evil.

See also Satan, satanic.

evolution The change and development of the physical or spiritual self. 'Abdu'l-Bahá states: 'Know that nothing which exists remains in a state of repose, that is to say, all things are in motion. Everything is either growing or declining, all things are either coming from non-existence into being, or going from existence into non-existence.'[23]

As to spiritual evolution, 'Abdu'l-Bahá says, '. . . as the spirit continues to exist after death, it necessarily progresses or declines; and in the other world, to cease to progress is the same as to decline; but it never leaves its own condition, in which it continues to develop.'[24]

evolution

Regarding physical evolution, Bahá'ís do not believe that man was once another species, although in physical form man may have resembled other species of animals. 'Abdu'l-Bahá states: '. . . as man in the womb of the mother passes from form to form, from shape to shape, changes and develops, and is still the human species from the beginning of the embryonic period – in the same way man, from the beginning of his existence in the matrix of the world, is also a distinct species, that is, man, and has gradually evolved from one form to another. Therefore this change of appearance, this evolution of members, this development and growth, even though we admit the reality of growth and progress (i.e. if we admit, for example, that man had formerly been a quadruped, or had had a tail), does not prevent the species from being original. Man from the beginning was in this perfect form and composition, and possessed capacity and aptitude for acquiring material and spiritual perfections, and was the manifestation of these words, "We will make man in our image and likeness." He has only become more pleasing, more beautiful, and more graceful.'[25]

Exemplar, Perfect *See* 'Abdu'l-Bahá.

expansion The growth and development of the Bahá'í Faith resulting from the introduction of new people to it.

See also teaching.

F

faith Belief in God. Faith has two aspects: belief and action. Bahá'u-'lláh writes: 'True belief in God and recognition of Him cannot be complete save by acceptance of that which He hath revealed and by observance of whatsoever hath been decreed by Him and set down in the Book by the Pen of Glory.'[1]

There is no implication of faith being blind; faith must be balanced by knowledge: 'Regarding the "two wings" of the soul: These signify wings of ascent. One is the wing of knowledge, the other of faith, as this is the means of the ascent of the human soul to the lofty station of divine perfections.'[2] 'If religion is opposed to reason and science, faith is impossible; and when faith and confidence in the divine religion are not manifest in the heart, there can be no spiritual attainment.'[3]

Every created thing has 'faith' in that it must respond to the laws of God. Man's soul also has this sort of faith. However, it is better for a man to choose to know and worship God: 'Know thou that faith is of two kinds. The first is objective faith that is expressed by the outer man, obedience of the limbs and senses. The other faith is subjective, and unconscious obedience to the will of God . . . This condition of unconscious obedience constitutes subjective faith. But the discerning faith that consists of true knowledge of God and the comprehension of divine words, of such faith there is very little in any age.'[4]

Faith is personal and must be personally cultivated: '. . . the faith of no man can be conditioned by any one except himself.'[5] 'The essence of faith is fewness of words and abundance of deeds . . .'[6]

faqíh [Ar] (Pl. fuqahá) A Muslim jurist.

farmán (also, firmán) [Pers] In Persia or Turkey, a royal decree or edict.

farrásh [Pers] Literally, carpet-spreader; attendant, footman.

farrásh-bashí [Pers] Head farrásh. The farrásh-bashí to the Sháh was able, at times, to exert power and influence.

farsakh [Pers] A measure of distance used in Iran, equivalent to between three and four miles. It is based on the distance a laden mule can walk in an hour.

fasting The abstinence from food and drink between sunrise and sunset in the month of 'Alá' (2–20 March). 'It is essentially a period of meditation and prayer, of spiritual recuperation, during which the believer must strive to make the necessary readjustments in his inner life, and to refresh and reinvigorate the spiritual forces latent in his soul. Its significance and purpose are, therefore, fundamentally spiritual in character. Fasting is symbolic, and a reminder of abstinence from selfish and carnal desires.'[7]

Fath-'Alí Sháh

Fatḥ-'Alí Sháh Qájár Sháh of Iran who reigned from 1798 to 1834. He bestowed the name 'Mírzá Buzurg' on the father of Bahá'u'lláh principally on account of his calligraphic prowess.

Fáṭimih, Book of *See Hidden Words of Bahá'u'lláh, The*

Fáṭimih Khánum *See* Munírih Khánum.

fatvá [Ar] A judgement or sentence made by a Muslim muftí.

Feast, Nineteen Day The principal gathering of Bahá'ís of a particular locality. The Nineteen Day Feast is, ideally, held on the first day of every Bahá'í month, and brings together the members of the Bahá'í community for worship, consultation and fellowship.

The programme for each Feast is divided into three parts to correspond to these purposes. The devotional portion of the feast consists of reading primarily from the Writings of Bahá'u'lláh, the Báb and 'Abdu'l-Bahá or, occasionally, from the sacred scriptures of other religions.[8] The purpose of the consultative portion of the Feast 'is to enable individual believers to offer any suggestion to the local assembly which in its turn will pass it to the [national spiritual assembly]'. The social portion of the Feast consists in the serving of refreshments. Attendance at the Feast is not obligatory but very important. In general, only Bahá'ís are permitted to attend the Nineteen Day Feast.

Fiḍál [Ar] Grace. The fourth day of the Bahá'í week, corresponding to Tuesday.

Firdaws Garden (Paradise Garden) A garden lying to the west of the Riḍván Garden in the Holy Land. It covers an extensive agricultural area. Bahá'u'lláh once pitched His tent near a pool in the garden. In 1881 the garden was purchased in the name of Bahá'u'lláh.

fireside A meeting held in one's home for the purpose of teaching the Bahá'í Faith.

According to Shoghi Effendi, 'The principle of the fireside meeting, which was established in order to permit and encourage the individual to teach in his own home, has been proven the most effective instrument for spreading the Faith.'[9] '. . . The most effective method of teaching is the Fireside group, where new people can be shown Bahá'í hospitality, and ask all the questions which bother them. They can feel there the true Bahá'í spirit . . .'[10] Bahá'ís are encouraged to hold a fireside once every nineteen days.

See also teaching.

Five Year Plan *See* plans, teaching.

Formative Age Also called the Iron or Transitional Age, corresponding to the period since the passing of 'Abdu'l-Bahá in 1921. As described by Shoghi Effendi, the phase or age of the Bahá'í era, 'ushered in by ['Abdu'l-Bahá's] Will and Testament, which defines its character and establishes its foundation.'[11] This age is to 'witness the crystallization and shaping of the creative energies' released by the Revelation of Bahá'u'lláh.[12]

The Formative Age is divided into epochs which mark stages in the development of the Bahá'í community and its institutions. The first epoch (1921–44/46) saw the formation of local and international institutions in all five continents, the first Seven Year Plan and several national plans. The second epoch (1946–63) witnessed the development, through a series of teaching plans, of the Bahá'í Faith in East and West and the development of the World Centre. The third epoch (1963–86) included three world teaching plans under the direction of the Universal House of Justice and saw the emergence of the Faith from obscurity and the beginning of the social and economic development of Bahá'í communities. The fourth epoch, which began in 1986 with the Six Year Plan, marks a new stage in the development of the Bahá'í Administrative Order. The Formative Age will see its ultimate flowering in the Golden Age.

See also ages of the Bahá'í Faith *and* epoch.

free will The freedom given to man by God to choose whether or not to acknowledge Him and obey His commands: 'the choice of good and evil belongs to the man himself.'[13]

'Some things are subject to the free will of man, such as justice, equity, tyranny, and injustice, as well as all the good and evil actions; it is evident and clear that these actions are, for the most part, left to the will of man. But there are certain things to which man is forced and compelled: such as sleep, death, sickness, decline of power, injuries, and misfortunes; these are not subject to the will of man, and he is not responsible for them, for he is compelled to endure them. But in the choice of good and bad actions he is free, and he commits them according to his own will.'[14]

Frequented Fane (Baytu'l-Ma'múr) In Islam, the Ka'bih or its archetype in heaven. Bahá'u'lláh refers to it in one of the prayers for the Fast: '. . . this Revelation whereby darkness hath been turned into light, through which the Frequented Fane hath been built . . .'[15]

Friend of God Abraham.

Friends Name by which Bahá'ís often address each other collectively.

funds The moneys contributed by the Bahá'ís to the different institutions of the Faith. 'And as the progress and execution of spiritual activities is dependent and conditioned upon material means, it is of absolute necessity that immediately after the establishment of local as well as National Spiritual Assemblies, a Bahá'í Fund be established, to be placed under the exclusive control of the Spiritual Assembly. All donations and contributions should be offered to the Treasurer of the Assembly, for the express purpose of promoting the interests of the

Cause throughout that locality or country. It is the sacred obligation of every conscientious and faithful servant of Bahá'u'lláh who desires to see His Cause advance, to contribute freely and generously for the increase of that Fund . . .'[16]

The amount given to the Funds is not important: 'Contributing to the Fund is a service every believer can render, be he poor or wealthy; for this is a spiritual responsibility in which the amount given is not important. It is the degree of the sacrifice of the giver, and the love with which he makes his gift, and unity of all the friends in this service which brings spiritual confirmations . . .'[17]

Contributions to the Bahá'í funds are not accepted from non-Bahá'ís. 'One of the distinguishing features of the Cause of God is its principle of non-acceptance of financial contributions for its own purposes from non-Bahá'ís: support of the Bahá'í Fund is a bounty reserved by Bahá'u'lláh to his declared followers.'[18]

There are several Bahá'í Funds. Each local spiritual assembly will establish its own Fund which is used to support local teaching, proclamation and consolidation activities; similarly, each national spiritual assembly will administer a National Fund which supports activities on a national level. The Continental Fund supports the work of the Hands of the Cause, the Continental Boards of Counsellors and the Auxiliary Board Members, while the International Fund, administered by the Universal House of Justice, supports Bahá'í work on an international level. There are also funds for various projects, such as the building of a House of Worship and the building of the Arc on Mount Carmel, for deputizing travel teachers or pioneers to undertake these activities in one's stead, and for assisting those believers who have suffered from persecution in Iran.

G

gambling Playing games for money, betting on an uncertain outcome. Gambling is forbidden in the *Kitáb-i-Aqdas*.

generation of the half-light People living today, that is, before the establishment of the World Commonwealth: 'the "generation of the half-light", living at a time which may be designated as the period of the incubation of the World Commonwealth envisaged by Bahá'u'lláh . . . We stand on the threshold of an age whose convulsions proclaim alike the death-pangs of the old order and the birth-pangs of the new.'[1]

Lua Getsinger

Getsinger, Lua (née Louisa A. Moore) American Bahá'í to whom 'Abdu'l-Bahá gave the name Livá (Banner) – Banner of the Cause. Shoghi Effendi designated her as 'the mother teacher of the West'. Lua Getsinger travelled extensively in order to teach the Bahá'í Faith. In 1898 she was among the first Western pilgrims to visit 'Abdu'l-Bahá in 'Akká. She died in Cairo in 1916.

Geyserville Bahá'í School Property in northern California given to the Bahá'í Faith by John Bosch and used for the first time as a summer school in 1927. The school was superseded by the Bosch School.

g͟huṣn [Ar] Branch. A son or male descendant of Bahá'u'lláh.

G͟huṣn-i-A'ẓam *See* Greatest Branch.

G͟huṣn-i-Mumtáz The Chosen Branch, that is, Shoghi Effendi.

Glory of God Bahá'u'lláh.

goals Objectives. Usually refers to objectives of the various teaching plans, such as the Six Year Plan (1986–92). Goals may include establishing a certain number of local spiritual assemblies, creating social and economic development projects, developing particular aspects of Bahá'í community life, and the like. Bahá'ís are also encouraged to set personal goals, such as overcoming bad habits, trying to acquire certain virtues, memorizing prayers and so on.

God The deity. Bahá'ís believe there is only one God, unknowable in His essence, who is the creator and absolute ruler of the universe. 'All existence is dependent upon Him, and from Him all beings derive their sustenance. He is independent of all things. He is alone and without equal. No being can know or approach Him.'[2] It is not possible to describe God.

'To every discerning and illuminated heart it is evident that God, the unknowable Essence, the Divine Being, is immensely exalted beyond every human attribute, such as corporeal existence, ascent and descent, egress and regress. Far be it from His glory that human tongue should adequately recount His praise, or that human heart comprehend His fathomless mystery. He is, and hath ever been, veiled in the ancient eternity of His Essence, and will remain in His Reality everlastingly hidden from the sight of men.'[3]

However, man's purpose is to 'know' and to 'worship' God. This paradox lies in the centre of the Bahá'í conception of God. One can come to know God only through His attributes and signs, particularly through His word and command as revealed through His manifestations. In the world of creation, God's attributes are revealed through created things. Each created thing has been made the bearer of some sign of divine reality, so that the whole of creation mirrors forth the beauty of God. Human beings have been made the bearers of all the divine names and attributes, so that they may be said to be made in the 'image of God'. However, the chief locus of the attributes of God in this world is the Manifestation of God, who exemplifies most perfectly God's attributes and provides a channel for the revelation of His command.[4]

See also attributes of God *and* Manifestation.

God, Day of *see* Day of God.

God Passes By Volume by Shoghi Effendi, first published in 1944, outlining events in the history of the first hundred years of the Bahá'í Faith including the Mission of the Báb, the Revelation of Bahá'u'lláh, the Ministry of 'Abdu'l-Bahá and the development of the Bahá'í Administrative Order.

Golden Age A future age of the Bahá'í Era, the arrival of which will be signalized by the establishment of the World Order of Bahá'u'lláh. The Golden Age of the Bahá'í Era will, Shoghi Effendi writes, 'witness the unification of all the peoples and nations of the world, the establishment of the Most Great Peace, the inauguration of the Kingdom of the Father upon earth, the coming of age of the entire human race and the birth of a world civilization, inspired and directed by the creative energies released by Bahá'u'lláh's World Order . . .'[5]

See also ages of the Bahá'í Era.

gossip *See* backbiting *and* calumny.

government, obedience to One of the laws of Bahá'u'lláh is that Bahá'ís must obey the laws of the government of the land in which they live. They are forbidden to take part in subversive movements.

In His Will and Testament 'Abdu'l-Bahá has stated: 'According to the direct and sacred command of God . . . we must obey and be the well-wishers of the governments of the land, regard disloyalty unto a just king as disloyalty to God Himself and wishing evil to the government a transgression of the Cause of God.'[6]

'Abdu'l-Bahá has further written, '. . . each and every one is required to show obedience, submission and loyalty to his own government . . . the Bahá'ís are the well-wishers of the government, obedient to its laws and bearing love towards all peoples.'[7] And, 'Let them willingly subject themselves to every just king, and to every generous ruler be good citizens. Let them obey the government and not meddle in political affairs . . .'[8]

Shoghi Effendi, in a letter written on his behalf, has explained that, 'What the Master's statement really means is obedience to a duly constituted government, whatever that government may be in form. We are not the ones, as individual Bahá'ís, to judge our government as just or unjust – for each believer would be sure to hold a different viewpoint, and within our own Bahá'í fold a hotbed of dissension would spring up and destroy our unity.'[9]

However, Shoghi Effendi stated in a letter to the Bahá'ís of Germany and Austria in 1934 written on his behalf: '. . . whereas the friends should obey the government under which they live, even at the risk of sacrificing all their administrative affairs and interests, they should under no circumstances suffer their inner religious beliefs and convictions to be violated and transgressed by any authority whatever. A distinction of fundamental importance must, therefore, be made between *spiritual* and *administrative* matters. Whereas the former are sacred and inviolable and hence cannot be subject to compromise, the latter are secondary and can consequently be given up and even sacrificed for the sake of obedience to the laws and regulations of the government . . . In matters of belief, however, no compromise whatever should be allowed, even though the outcome of it be death or expulsion.'[10]

See also politics.

Greater Branch *See* Muḥammad-'Alí, Mírzá.

Greater Plan of God Also known as the Major Plan of God. God's purpose for mankind in this age, which is 'one and indivisible, whose Source is God, whose author is Bahá'u'lláh, the theatre of whose operations is the entire planet, and whose ultimate objectives are the unity of the human race and the peace of all mankind.'[11] '. . . two great processes are at work in the world: [the first is] the great Plan of God, tumultuous in its progress, working through mankind as a whole, tearing down barriers to world unity and forging humankind into a unified body in the fires of suffering and experience. This process will produce, in God's due time, the Lesser Peace . . .'[12] The various teaching plans of Shoghi Effendi and the Universal House of Justice are parts of the Greater Plan and may be called the Minor or Lesser Plan.

See also Minor Plan of God.

Greatest Branch A variant translation of Ghuṣn-i-A'ẓam. The Most

Greatest Branch

Great Branch, 'Abdu'l-Bahá.

Greatest Holy Leaf *See* Bahíyyih Khánum.

The Greatest Name, in the calligraphy of Mishkín-Qalam

Greatest Name, the In Islam there is a tradition that among the various names of God, one is the greatest. However, the identity of this Greatest Name is hidden. Bahá'ís believe that the Greatest Name of God is Bahá, which means glory, splendour or light. Bahá, or any of its derivatives such as Abhá, as well as certain phrases such as Alláh'u'-Abhá, Yá Bahá'u'lláh, or Yá Baha'u'l-Abhá, are all referred to as the Greatest Name. Yá Bahá'u'l-Abhá is an invocation which can be translated either as 'O Glory of Glories' or 'O Glory of the All-Glorious'. This invocation calligraphically designed by Mishkín-Qalam is used by Bahá'ís in their homes as a dignified wall-hanging. The ringstone symbol is another representation of the Greatest Name.

See also ringstone symbol.

Green Acre Bahá'í School

Green Acre Bahá'í School Property in Eliot, Maine, USA, given to the Bahá'í Faith by Sarah Farmer for use as a summer school. The first Bahá'í summer school was established there in 1929.

Gregory, Louis Hand of the Cause born in Charleston, South Carolina, USA, in 1874, the son of a freed slave. He attended Fisk University and later studied law at Howard University. He practised law until 1906 when he took a position in the United States Treasury Department. Louis Gregory first heard about the Bahá'í Faith in 1908. He visited 'Abdu'l-Bahá in Egypt and later in Haifa and 'Akká. He travelled extensively throughout the United States teaching the Bahá'í Faith and was for thirty-five years the mainspring behind the work for Race Amity. He was a member of the National Spiritual Assembly of the United States for many years. Louis Gregory passed away in 1951 and was designated by Shoghi Effendi as the first Hand of the Cause of his race.

groups, Bahá'í Communities of Bahá'ís whose adult members number less than nine. Bahá'í groups have no administrative status but are encouraged to hold their own Nineteen Day Feasts and to teach. When a Bahá'í group increases to nine or more members, generally a local spiritual assembly will be formed at the next Riḍván. Occasionally there are Bahá'í groups of more than nine where it is impossible by law, or inadvisable, to form a local spiritual assembly.

Guardian The Guardianship as an institution was anticipated in the *Kitáb-i-Aqdas* and formally stated in 'Abdu'l-Bahá's Will and Testament, in which He named Shoghi Effendi as 'the guardian of the Cause of God' and 'the expounder of the words of God',[13] whose word was to be infallible and binding on all. His successor was to be appointed by him from his descendants. The Guardian was to act as sole interpreter of the Bahá'í Scriptures, while power to legislate on questions not mentioned in the Sacred Texts was given exclusively to the Universal House of Justice as whose permanent head he was to serve. When Shoghi Effendi died in 1957, however, the Universal House of Justice had not yet been elected.

The successor to the Guardian was to be his first-born son or another male member of the family of Bahá'u'lláh. However, Shoghi Effendi died without children and was unable to appoint a successor from among the members of Bahá'u'lláh's family as they had all broken the Covenant. In 1963 the Universal House of Justice sent the following cable to the Bahá'ís of the world: 'After prayerful and careful study of the Holy Texts bearing upon the question of the appointment of the successor to Shoghi Effendi as Guardian of the Cause of God, and after prolonged consultation . . . the Universal House of Justice finds that there is no way to appoint or legislate to make it possible to appoint a second Guardian to succeed Shoghi Effendi.'[14]

Thus in one sense the institution of the Guardianship came to an end, because there could be no new Guardians; but in another sense the institution continues on, as the voluminous writings of Shoghi Effendi set a lasting standard of guidance for the future.

See also Guardianship *and* Shoghi Effendi.

Guardianship Institution created by 'Abdu'l-Bahá in His Will and Testament to carry on into the future the function of authoritative interpretation of the Sacred Writings and the care and protection of the Bahá'í Faith provided by 'Abdu'l-Bahá. The Guardian is the 'sacred head and the distinguished member for life' of the Universal House of Justice. The Guardian and the Universal House of Justice are 'under the care and protection of the Abhá Beauty, under the shelter and unerring guidance of His Holiness, the Exalted One . . .'[15]

'Abdu'l-Bahá appointed his grandson Shoghi Effendi as the first Guardian. He provided that 'after him will succeed the first-born of his lineal descendants' or, if his child should not manifest the necessary characteristics, that the Guardian would 'choose another branch to succeed him'.[16] Shoghi Effendi had no children nor did he appoint a successor from among the family of Bahá'u'lláh and therefore no further Guardians can be appointed. The institution of the Guardianship, however, continues.

The Universal House of Justice wrote in 1977: '. . . the word "guardianship"; is used with various meanings in different contexts. In certain contexts it indicates the office and function of the Guardian himself, in others it refers to the line of Guardians, in still others it bears a more extended meaning embracing the Guardian and his attendant institutions . . . In the specific sense of referring to the office and function of the Guardian himself, the House of Justice finds that the prerogatives and duties vested in him are of three kinds. First . . . there are a number of functions and objects which the Guardianship shares with the Universal House of Justice and which the House of Justice must continue to pursue. Secondly, there are functions of the Guardianship which, in the absence of a Guardian devolve upon the Universal House of Justice, for example the Headship of the Faith, the responsibility for directing the work of the Institution of the Hands of the Cause and of ensuring the continuing discharge of the functions of protection and propagation vested in that Institution, and the right to administer the Ḥuqúqu'lláh. Thirdly, there are those prerogatives and duties which lie exclusively within the sphere of the Guardian himself and, therefore, in the absence of a Guardian, are inoperative except insofar as the monumental work already performed by Shoghi Effendi continues to be of enduring benefit to the Faith. Such a function is that of authoritative interpretation of the Teachings.'[17]

See also Shoghi Effendi.

H

Há [Ar] The letter 'h'. The numerical value of há is five and is identical with that of 'Báb'.

Há, Days of The Intercalary Days.

ḥadí<u>th</u> [Ar] Tradition. In Islam, oral traditions about things which Muḥammad said or did which were handed down for several generations before being written. In <u>Sh</u>í'ih Islam, ḥadí<u>th</u> about the Imáms were also transmitted.

Ḥaḍrat [Pers] Holiness. In Persian it is impolite not to use the word Ḥaḍrat before the name of the Manifestation or other figures with a high spiritual station such as 'Abdu'l-Bahá, but this is generally not translated in the English translations of the Bahá'í scriptures.

Ḥaḍrat-i-A'lá His Holiness the Most Exalted One. A title of the Báb.

Nineteenth-century Haifa

Haifa Town in the north of Israel on a large bay, four times visited by Bahá'u'lláh. The area of Haifa was assigned by Jacob and Joshua to the Tribe of Zebulon. In the late 1860s and 1870s a German sect from Württemberg, the Temple Society, settled in Haifa. The town continued to expand in the twentieth century with the opening of a railroad between Haifa and Damascus and the Ḥijáz in 1905 coupled with the decision of the British to make Haifa their principal Middle Eastern naval and oil port. Today Haifa is a major commercial city and port.

Bahá'u'lláh first landed in Haifa on 31 August 1868 after His journey of eleven days from Gallipoli by steamer. He and His companions were transferred from the steamer to a sailing vessel which carried them to 'Akká. Bahá'u'lláh visited Haifa three more times: in August 1883, in April 1890, and in the summer of 1891 for about three months. It was during this last visit that He revealed the Tablet of Carmel and pointed out to 'Abdu'l-Bahá 'the site which was to serve as the permanent resting-place of the Báb, and on which a befitting mausoleum was later to be erected'.[1]

'Abdu'l-Bahá made this prophecy about Haifa: 'In the future the distance between 'Akká and Haifa will be built up, and the two cities will join and clasp hands, becoming the two terminal sections of one mighty metropolis . . . The mountain and the plain will be dotted with the most modern buildings and palaces. Industries will be established and various institutions of philanthropic nature will be founded. The flowers of civilization and culture from all nations will be brought here to blend their fragrances together and blaze the way for the brotherhood of man. Wonderful gardens, orchards, groves and parks will be laid out on all sides. At night the great city will be lighted by electricity. The entire harbour from 'Akká to Haifa will be one path of illumination. Powerful searchlights will be placed on both sides of Mount Carmel to guide the steamers. Mount Carmel itself, from top to bottom, will be submerged in a sea of lights. A person standing on the summit of Mount Carmel, and the passengers of the steamers coming to it, will look upon the most sublime and majestic spectacle of the whole world.'[2]

'Abdu'l-Bahá built the Shrine of the Báb on the site pointed out to Him by Bahá'u'lláh, and the remains of the Báb were interred there on Naw-Rúz 1909. Shoghi Effendi later embellished the shrine with the golden-domed superstructure. Shoghi Effendi also began the construction of the arc, around which the administrative offices of the Faith are being built. Haifa thus serves both as a spiritual centre and point of pilgrimage and as the international administrative centre of the Bahá'í Faith.

See also Arc; Carmel, Mount; *and* Tablet of Carmel.

Ḥáj, Ḥájj [Ar] Pilgrimage to Mecca instituted in the Qur'án.

Ḥájí [Pers] One who has made the pilgrimage to Mecca. The term is placed before the person's name, preceding other titles such as Mírzá, Siyyid or S͟hayk͟h.

Hands of the Cause of God Individuals appointed first by Bahá'u'lláh, and later by Shoghi Effendi, who were charged with the specific duties of protecting and propagating the Faith. Bahá'u'lláh appointed four individuals to this position: Mírzá 'Alí-Muḥammad (Ibn-i-Aṣdaq), Ḥájí Mullá 'Alí-Akbar-i-S͟hahmírzádí (Ḥájí Ák͟húnd), Mírzá Muḥammad-Taqí (Ibn-i-Abhar) and Mírzá Ḥasan-i-Adíb (Adíb). 'Abdu'l-Bahá did not appoint any living Hands of the Cause, but in *Memorials of the*

Hands of the Cause of God at their Plenary Meeting, April 1963

Hands of the Cause of God

Faithful named four people as having been Hands of the Cause: Áqá Muḥammad-i-Qá'iní (Nabíl-i-Akbar), Mírzá 'Alí-Muḥammad-i-Varqá, Shaykh Muḥammad Riḍáy-i-Yazdí and Mullá Ṣádiq-i-Muqaddas (Ismu'lláhu'l-Aṣdaq).

In His Will and Testament, 'Abdu'l-Bahá developed the institution of the Hands of the Cause: 'The Hands of the Cause of God must be nominated and appointed by the guardian of the Cause of God. All must be under his shadow and obey his command . . . The obligations of the Hands of the Cause are to diffuse the Divine Fragrances, to edify the souls of men, to promote learning, to improve the character of all men and to be, at all times and under all conditions, sanctified and detached from earthly things. They must manifest the fear of God by their conduct, their manners, their deeds and their words. This body of the Hands of the Cause of God is under the direction of the guardian of the Cause of God.'[3]

One of the responsibilities of the Hands of the Cause is to protect the Faith from those wishing to harm it and to expel those who attack it: '. . . the Hands of the Cause of God must be ever watchful and so soon as they find anyone beginning to oppose and protest against the guardian of the Cause of God cast him out from the congregation of the people of Bahá and in no wise accept any excuse from him.'[4]

Further, the Hands of the Cause must assent to the choice of a successor to the guardian. They 'must elect from their own number nine persons that shall at all times be occupied in the important services in the work of the guardian of the Cause of God. The election of these nine must be carried either unanimously or by majority from the company of the Hands of the Cause and these, whether unanimously or by a majority vote, must give their assent to the choice of the one whom the guardian of the Cause of God hath chosen as his successor.'[5]

Several people were posthumously appointed Hands of the Cause by Shoghi Effendi, among them Martha Root, John E. Esslemont and Louis Gregory. In December 1951 he appointed the first contingent of living Hands of the Cause, twelve in number. A second contingent of seven Hands was appointed in February 1952. Five Hands were appointed singly between March 1952 and March 1957, and a final contingent of eight Hands was appointed in October 1957.

In the letter appointing this final contingent, Shoghi Effendi referred to the Hands of the Cause as the 'Chief Stewards of Bahá'u'lláh's embryonic World Commonwealth'.[6] It was this phrase which enabled the Hands of the Cause legally to take charge of the Bahá'í properties in the Holy Land on the unexpected death of Shoghi Effendi in November 1957.

In the period between the passing of Shoghi Effendi in 1957 and the election of the Universal House of Justice in 1963, the Hands of the

Cause directed the affairs of the Faith, enabled the Bahá'ís to complete the Ten Year Crusade and called for the election of the House of Justice, for which they decreed themselves ineligible. This period is known as the Interregnum of the Hands of the Cause.

In November 1964 the Universal House of Justice made the following announcement: 'There is no way to appoint, or to legislate to make it possible to appoint, Hands of the Cause of God.'[7] The functions of the institution of the Hands of the Cause were extended into the future by the creation in 1968 of the Continental Boards of Counsellors.

The Universal House of Justice stated in 1964 that 'the exalted rank and specific functions of the Hands of the Cause of God make it inappropriate for them to be elected or appointed to administrative institutions, or to be elected as delegates to national conventions.' All of the Hands are, however, members of the International Teaching Centre based in the Holy Land.

See also Continental Board of Counsellors; Guardianship; Interregnum; Will and Testament of 'Abdu'l-Bahá; *and individual Hands of the Cause by name.*

ḥaqíqat [Pers] Truth, the object of the mystic searcher.

Ḥaram [Ar] The sacred sanctuary at Mecca where no blood may be spilled.

Ḥaram-i-Aqdas Most holy sanctuary (or precincts). The northwestern quadrant of the gardens at Bahjí immediately around and enclosing the Shrine of Bahá'u'lláh. It was designed and constructed by Shoghi Effendi with five gates and nine paths.

The Ḥarám-i-Aqdas, the area immediately surrounding the Shrine of Bahá'u'lláh

Ḥasan-i-Adíb, Mírzá (Adíb) Hand of the Cause and Apostle of Bahá'u'lláh born in Ṭalaqán in 1848, the son of an eminent cleric. He was given the title Adíbu'l-'Ulamá (litterateur of the 'ulamá) for his services to Islamic literature and was a poet of considerable talent. He became a Bahá'í about 1889 after prolonged discussions with Nabíl-i-Akbar and soon afterwards was designated by Bahá'u'lláh a Hand of the Cause. After the passing of Bahá'u'lláh he was much involved with dealing with the activities of the Covenant-breakers. Between 1897 and 1898 he participated in the meetings of the Hands of the Cause which evolved over several years into the Central Spiritual Assembly of Ṭihrán, the precursor of the Iranian National Spiritual Assembly. He was chairman of this body, and he also played an important part in the founding of the Tarbíyat Schools in Ṭihrán. He was briefly imprisoned in Iṣfahán in 1903 during the upheaval there. He travelled to 'Akká where 'Abdu'l-Bahá instructed him to travel through India and Burma with the American Bahá'í Sidney Sprague. He died in Ṭihrán in 1919.[8]

Ḥájí Mírzá Ḥaydar-'Alí

Ḥaydar-'Alí, Ḥájí Mírzá Born into a Shaykhí family of Iṣfáhán, Ḥaydar-'Alí was for a time a disciple of Karím Khán, the Shaykhí opponent of the Báb. But after studying the Báb's Writings and seeing the behaviour of the martyrs, Ḥaydar-'Alí became a Bábí. When Bahá'u'lláh declared Himself to be the Promised One, Ḥaydar-'Alí accepted Him and met Bahá'u'lláh in Adrianople. He was sent to Egypt where the Persian consul had him arrested. At the end of ten years' imprisonment in the Sudan, he was sent by Bahá'u'lláh to Persia and Iraq where he spent some twenty-five years travelling throughout the land, encouraging and inspiring the Persian Bahá'ís. After the passing of Bahá'u'lláh, Ḥaydar-'Alí devoted himself to 'Abdu'l-Bahá and was a staunch defender of the Covenant. He spent his last years in Haifa where he became known as 'the Angel of Mount Carmel' and wrote his memoirs, *The Delight of Hearts*. He died in 1920 and is buried in the Bahá'í cemetery at the foot of Mount Carmel.

Ḥaẓíratu'l-Quds [Ar] The Sacred Fold. The 'official and distinctive title' of the headquarters of Bahá'í administrative activity, whether on a local or national level. The national Ḥaẓíratu'l-Quds is the seat of the national spiritual assembly and 'the pivot of all Bahá'í administrative activity'.[9]

'Complementary in its function to those of the Mashriqu'l-Adhkár . . . this institution, whether local or national, will, as its component parts, such as the Secretariat, the Treasury, the Archives, the Library, the Publishing Office, the Assembly Hall, the Council Chamber, the Pilgrims' Hostel, are brought together and made jointly to operate in one spot, be increasingly regarded as the focus of all Bahá'í

Bahá'ís of Pikosa Village, Papua New Guinea, gather in front of their new Bahá'í Centre (left) in 1984

A Bahá'í centre is dedicated in the tribal area of Dang in Gujarat State, India, in 1983

National Ḥaẓíratu'l-Quds of the Mariana Islands at Malojloj, Inarajan, southeastern Guam

administrative activity, and symbolize, in a befitting manner, the ideal of service animating the Bahá'í community in its relation alike to the Faith and to mankind in general.'[10]

He Who Discoursed with God Moses.

healing In the *Kitáb-i-Aqdas* Bahá'u'lláh counsels his followers to 'consult competent physicians when ill'.

'Abdu'l-Bahá, in a discussion about healing in 1904–6, said: 'The science of medicine is still in a condition of infancy; it has not reached maturity; but when it has reached this point, cures will be performed by things which are not repulsive to the smell and taste of man . . . it is possible to cure by foods, aliments, and fruits; but as today the science of medicine is imperfect, this fact is not yet fully grasped. When the science of medicine reaches perfection, treatment will be given by foods, aliments, fragrant fruits, and vegetables, and by various waters, hot and cold in temperature.'[11]

Healing is possible through physical medicine, pyschological treatment and spiritual means, through prayer. Of healing through prayer, 'Abdu'l-Bahá wrote: 'The prayers which were revealed to ask for healing apply both to physical and spiritual healing. Recite them, then, to heal both the soul and the body. If healing is right for the patient, it will certainly be granted; but for some ailing persons, healing would only be the cause of other ills, and therefore wisdom doth not permit an affirmative answer to the prayer.'[12]

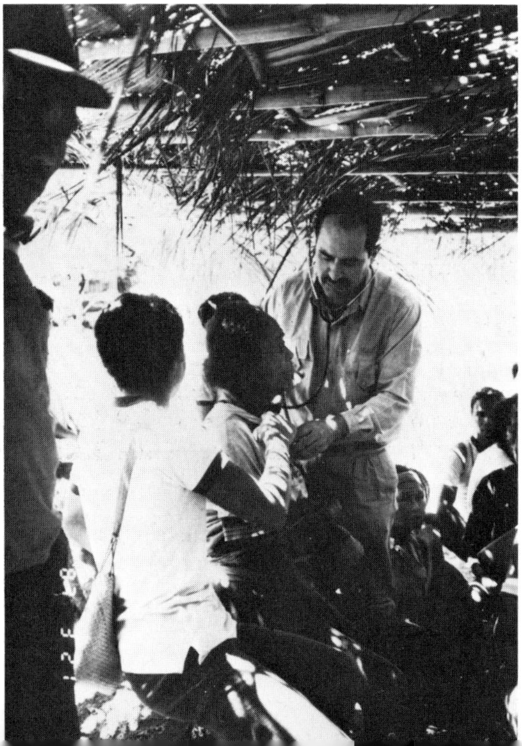

A Bahá'í, when ill, must seek the advice of a qualified physician

Bahá'ís are encouraged to apply the appropriate treatment, physical or spiritual, for their illnesses: 'Disease is of two kinds: material and spiritual. Take for instance a cut hand; if you pray for the cut to be healed and do not stop its bleeding, you will not do much good; a material remedy is needed.'[13] However, 'Physical healing cannot be complete and lasting unless it is reinforced by spiritual healing. And this last one can be best obtained through obedience to the laws and commandments of God as revealed to us through His Manifestations.'[14] 'Healing through purely spiritual forces is undoubtedly as inadequate as that which materialist physicians and thinkers vainly seek to obtain by resorting entirely to mechanical devices and methods. The best result can be obtained by combining the two processes, spiritual and physical.'[15]

heart The symbolic centre of an individual's spirituality. In the Hidden Words Bahá'u'lláh says, 'Thy heart is My home; sanctify it for My descent.'[16] 'O Son of Spirit! My first counsel is this: Possess a pure, kindly and radiant heart, that thine may be a sovereignty ancient, imperishable and everlasting.'[17] 'O Friend! In the garden of thy heart plant naught but the rose of love . . .'[18]

heaven and hell The highest and lowest conditions a human soul can experience.

In the Bahá'í Writings these terms are used in a spiritual rather than a literal, material sense. These conditions of 'heaven' and 'hell' are not limited to life after death: 'the paradise and hell of existence are found in all the worlds of God, whether in this world or in the spiritual heavenly worlds.'[19]

'Heaven' is the state of perfection and nearness to God, achieved by a soul who has striven to acquire virtues during its life on earth, while 'hell' is the condition of imperfection, remoteness and the awareness of the deprivation one has brought by one's actions. Bahá'u'lláh wrote, 'They say: "Where is Paradise, and where is Hell?" Say: "The one is reunion with Me; the other thine own self . . ."'[20] Bahá'u'lláh explains in the *Kitáb-i-Íqán* that the use of the word 'heaven' in earlier prophecies such as the 'cleaving asunder of the heaven' is metaphorical not literal.

See also death, life after; *and* death, nature of.

Herald, the The Báb.

Heroic Age Also called the Apostolic or Primitive Age, corresponding roughly with the first eighty years of the first Bahá'í century (1844–1944). It commences with the Declaration of the Báb, includes the

mission of Bahá'u'lláh and terminates with the passing of 'Abdu'l-Bahá or, more particularly, with the passing of Bahíyyih Khánum in 1932.
See also ages of the Bahá'í Era.

Hidden Imám *See* Twelfth Imám.

Hidden Words of Bahá'u'lláh, The A collection of passages revealed by Bahá'u'lláh in Baghdád in 1858. *The Hidden Words*, which Shoghi Effendi termed a 'marvellous collection of gem-like utterances'[21] were revealed as Bahá'u'lláh 'paced, wrapped in His meditations, the banks of the Tigris'.[22] The book consists of seventy-one passages in Arabic and eighty-two in Persian, and was originally called the 'Hidden Book of Fáṭimih'. In Shí'ih Islam, the 'Hidden Book of Fáṭimih' is believed to have been dictated to the Imám 'Alí by the Angel Gabriel to console Muḥammad's daughter Fáṭimih after the Prophet's death. The 'Hidden Book of Fáṭimih' is thought to be in the possession of the awaited Qá'im.

A calligraphic rendering of *The Hidden Words*

Hand of the Cause
Horace Holley

Hijra [Ar] (Also Hijrat) The Hejira, the flight of Muḥammad from Mecca to Medina in 622. The first year of the Muslim calendar is taken to be the year of the Hijra.

Him Whom God Shall Make Manifest In His writings the Báb frequently refers in this way to a figure who will come in the future. Bahá'ís believe that this is a reference to Bahá'u'lláh.

Holley, Horace Hotchkiss Hand of the Cause born in 1887 in Torrington, Connecticut, USA. In 1909 he read *Abbas Effendi, His Life and Teachings* by Myron H. Phelps and accepted the Bahá'í Faith. He met 'Abdu'l-Bahá in France in 1911. Holley wrote many books of poetry and in 1913 wrote the first of his books on the Bahá'í Faith, *Baha'ism – The Modern Social Religion*. In 1923 he was elected a member of the American National Spiritual Assembly. He served on that body until 1959, for 34 years as its secretary. Shoghi Effendi greatly valued Holley's qualities and abilities. He often expressed the wish that Holley would some day come to assist him in the Holy Land but the time was never right for this.

It was Holley who titled the general letters of Shoghi Effendi to the Bahá'ís of America and the West, picking out such phrases as 'The Promised Day is Come', 'The Goal of a New World Order' and 'The Dispensation of Bahá'u'lláh'. He also put subtitles throughout the texts to facilitate their study, a practice of which Shoghi Effendi approved.

In 1951 Shoghi Effendi appointed Holley a Hand of the Cause. In 1959 he went to the Holy Land as one of the nine Hands of the Cause serving there. He died in July 1960 and is buried in the Bahá'í cemetery at the foot of Mount Carmel.

holy days, Bahá'í Days commemorating significant Bahá'í anniversaries. These are:

Festival of Naw-Rúz (Bahá'í New Year)	21 March
Festival of Riḍván (Declaration of Bahá'u'lláh)	21 April – 2 May
Declaration of the Báb	23 May
Ascension of Bahá'u'lláh	29 May
Martyrdom of the Báb	9 July
Birth of the Báb	20 October
Birth of Bahá'u'lláh	12 November
Day of the Covenant	26 November
Ascension of 'Abdu'l-Bahá	28 November

holy days, Bahá'í

Work is to be suspended, and children should not attend school, on Holy Days (during the Festival of Riḍván, on the first, ninth and twelfth days) with the exception of the last two anniversaries. There are no prescribed ceremonies for the commemoration of Holy Days, but many Bahá'í communities combine a devotional programme with fellowship or appropriate social activities.

Holy Family Generally, the family of Bahá'u'lláh. However, this term has meant different things at different periods of Bahá'í history. In the time of Bahá'u'lláh the whole of Baha'u'lláh's family was considered to be the Holy Family. Today, however, Bahá'ís generally include only Bahá'u'lláh, Navváb and their children ('Abdu'l-Bahá, Bahíyyih Kh͟ánum and Mírzá Mihdí) and not 'Abdu'l-Bahá's half-brothers and half-sister. In the time of 'Abdu'l-Bahá the 'Holy Family' referred to 'Abdu'l-Bahá, Munírih Kh͟ánum, and their daughters and grandchildren.

Left 'Abdu'l-Bahá in His youth. *Centre* The Greatest Holy Leaf as a young woman. *Right* The Purest Branch

Holy Land The area associated with present-day Israel. Bahá'u'lláh calls it 'the nest of all the Prophets of God', 'the Vale of God's unsearchable Decree, the snow-white Spot, the Land of unfading splendour'.[23] Shoghi Effendi says it is 'the Land promised by God to Abraham, sanctified by the Revelation of Moses, honoured by the lives and labours of the Hebrew patriarchs, judges, kings and prophets, revered as the cradle of Christianity, and as the place where Zoroaster, according to 'Abdu'l-Bahá's testimony, had "held converse with some of the Prophets of Israel", and associated by Islam with the Apostle's night-journey, through the seven heavens, to the throne of the Almighty.'[24]

Holy Mariner, Tablet of the A Tablet revealed by Bahá'u'lláh on the fifth day after Naw-Rúz 1863, not long before leaving Ba<u>gh</u>dád for Constantinople. In it Bahá'u'lláh prophesied 'the severe afflictions' that were to befall Him.[25] Its 'gloomy prognostications . . . aroused the grave apprehensions of His Companions . . .': 'Oceans of sorrow surged in the hearts of the listeners when the Tablet of the Holy Mariner was read aloud to them.'[26]

Holy Mother *See* Munírih <u>Kh</u>ánum.

Holy Places Places linked with important events in Bahá'í history. The residences of the Báb, Bahá'u'lláh and 'Abdu'l-Bahá and their shrines, as well as those of other holy souls and martyrs, are considered Holy Places to Bahá'ís. The most sacred spot on earth for Bahá'ís is the Shrine of Bahá'u'lláh in Bahjí.

'Abdu'l-Bahá explained in a Tablet that 'Holy places are undoubtedly centres of the outpouring of Divine grace, because on entering the illumined sites associated with martyrs and holy souls, and by observing reverence, both physical and spiritual, one's heart is moved with great tenderness. But there is no obligation for everyone to visit such places, other than the three, namely: the Most Holy Shrine, the Blessed House in Ba<u>gh</u>dád, and the venerated House of the Báb in <u>Sh</u>íráz . . . These three Holy Places are consecrated to pilgrimage. But as to the other resting places of martyrs and holy souls, it is pleasing and acceptable in the sight of God if a person desires to draw nigh unto Him by visiting them; this, however, is not a binding obligation.'[27]

See also pilgrimage.

Holy Spirit The entity which acts as an intermediary between God and His Manifestations. 'This link is similar to the rays of the sun by which energy is transmitted to the planets.'[28] It is impossible for man to understand the nature of the Holy Spirit. In all Dispensations 'the Holy

Spirit manifested itself to the Founders of the great world religions and enabled them to reveal the teachings of God to humanity.'[29] In order for the Manifestation to convey to His followers that He was animated by the power of God, He has used symbolic language concerning the appearance of the Holy Spirit to Him. Thus Moses heard the voice of God through the Burning Bush, the Dove descended upon Jesus, Muḥammad saw the Angel Gabriel, and Bahá'u'lláh refers to the Maid of Heaven proclaiming to Him His mission.

The House of 'Abbúd

House of 'Abbúd The house in 'Akká, once belonging to Ilyás 'Abbúd and adjacent to the House of 'Údí Khammár (the two connected houses are known today as the House of 'Abbúd). It was occupied by Bahá'u'lláh and His family in late 1873 and He lived there until June 1877 when He left the city of 'Akká for Mazra'ih. The family of 'Abdu'l-Bahá continued to live in the House of 'Abbúd, and Bahá'u-'lláh returned to visit it a number of times. It was here that 'Abdu'l-Bahá wrote *The Secret of Divine Civilization* and *A Traveller's Narrative*. Bahá'u'lláh's wife Navváb died in the House of 'Abbúd in 1886.

See also 'Abbúd, Ilyás.

House of ‘Abdu’l-Bahá at 7 Haparsim Street, Haifa

House of ‘Abdu’l-Bahá A house designed and built by ‘Abdu’l-Bahá in the German colony at the foot of Mount Carmel in Haifa on a lane later to be called Persian (Haparsim) Street. It was completed in 1908, although from 1907 ‘Abdu’l-Bahá began the transfer of the Holy Family to it. In the next few years all the Holy Family moved from ‘Akká, including the Greatest Holy Leaf and Shoghi Effendi, and in August 1910 ‘Abdu’l-Bahá Himself moved to the house and it became His official residence. On His return from His travels in the West, this house became the place of reception of pilgrims. The Master ascended to the Abhá Kingdom in the room on the right as one enters the house. An apartment was built on the roof in the early 1920s for Shoghi Effendi, and this was expanded in 1937 after his marriage to Rúḥíyyih Khánum. More recently, the reception room directly opposite the entrance door has been used by her to receive pilgrims and guests.

The House of ‘Abdu’lláh Páshá and its outbuildings are outlined in white

House of 'Abdu'lláh Páshá A group of buildings in 'Akká, built by 'Alí Páshá around 1810, and later serving as the Governorate of 'Abdu'lláh Páshá. It was the home of 'Abdu'l-Bahá from 1896 to 1910, and the birthplace of Shoghi Effendi. The remains of the Báb were concealed there for ten years before being moved to the Shrine on Mount Carmel. It was in the House of 'Abdu'lláh Páshá that the first group of Western pilgrims met 'Abdu'l-Bahá in 1898, and where Laura Clifford Barney recorded His table talks, which were later published as *Some Answered Questions*. 'Abdu'l-Bahá wrote the first part of His Will and Testament while residing in the House of 'Abdu'lláh Páshá. In 1975 the property was purchased by the Bahá'ís and restored as a place of pilgrimage.

See also 'Abdu'lláh Páshá.

House of the Báb The House of the Báb in Shíráz designated by Bahá'u'lláh in the *Kitáb-i-Aqdas* as a centre for pilgrimage. It was in this House that the Báb declared His mission to Mullá Ḥusayn on the eve of 23 May 1844. Mullá Ḥusayn recounts that it was 'of modest appearance'.

The House was restored by order of 'Abdu'l-Bahá and became increasingly a focus of Bahá'í life and activity for those who were deprived by circumstances of visiting either the Most Great House in Baghdád or the Most Holy Tomb in 'Akká.[30] In 1942–3 it was damaged by fire in an attack by enemies of the Faith, and in 1955 was destroyed by persecutors, but later restored.

In 1979 the focal point of the persecution mounted against the Bahá'ís by the Iranian revolutionaries was the attack and desecration of the House of the Báb. The demolition of the House took place between 8 and 10 September 1979 and in 1981 the site was made into a road and public square.

The House of the Báb

House of Bahá’u’lláh in Baghdád (Bayt-i-A‘ẓam) The ‘extremely modest’ house in which Bahá’u’lláh resided during nearly all of His ten-year exile in Iraq from 1853 to 1863. It is situated in the Karkh quarter of the city, near the western bank of the river. Named by Him the ‘Most Great House’ and the ‘House of God’, it is designated in the *Kitáb-i-Aqdas* as a place of pilgrimage and is considered a holy shrine by Bahá’ís. During the 1920s the House was seized by Shí‘ih enemies of the Faith and although the Council of the League of Nations upheld the Bahá’ís’ claim to it, this ruling was never carried out and the House has not yet been returned to the Bahá’ís. Bahá’u’lláh, in His Tablets, prophesied the abasement and future exaltation of the House.

House of Justice The administrative and governing institution of a Bahá’í community. Local and national (or secondary) Houses of Justice are presently called spiritual assemblies, but Shoghi Effendi has stated that these will eventually evolve into and be named ‘Houses of Justice’.[31] At the international level, however, the name of the supreme authority in the Bahá’í world is the Universal House of Justice.

The House of Justice was first ordained in the *Kitáb-i-Aqdas* of Bahá’u’lláh. Bahá’u’lláh calls for the formation of a House of Justice wherever ‘shall gather counsellors to the number of Bahá (9)’.[32] ‘Abdu’l-Bahá laid down that they should be elected bodies: the local Houses of Justice to be elected by all the Bahá’ís in an area; the national body through indirect election by delegates; and the Universal House of Justice by the national bodies.

Among the functions of the House of Justice are the following: to promulgate the Cause of God; to educate the souls of men; to preserve the law; to make the land prosperous; to administer social affairs; to educate the children; and to take care of the old, the weak and the ill who have fallen into poverty.

See also local spiritual assembly, national spiritual assembly *and* Universal House of Justice.

House of ‘Údí Khammár House adjacent to the House of ‘Abbúd in ‘Akká, occupied by Bahá’u’lláh and His family from September 1871 to late 1873. It was here, in 1873, that Bahá’u’lláh revealed the *Kitáb-i-Aqdas*, His Book of Laws, and it was also in this house that ‘Abdu’l-Bahá married Munírih Khánum. However, during the period of Bahá’u’lláh’s residence in this house antagonism broke out anew against the exiles after seven Bahá’ís murdered three Azalís, including Siyyid Muḥammad-i-Iṣfahání. As a result of this, Bahá’u’lláh was imprisoned and interrogated. In late 1873 the adjacent House of ‘Abbúd was acquired and the two houses joined into one residence. The two combined houses are known today as the House of ‘Abbúd.

See also House of ‘Abbúd *and* Khammár, ‘Údí.

House of ‘Údí <u>Kh</u>ammár

The House of ‘Údí <u>Kh</u>ammár

Howdah

House of Worship *See* Mashriqu'l-Adhkár.

howdah A seat or covered pavilion accommodating two persons, carried by a mule, camel or other animal.

Bahá'u'lláh travelled in a howdah for much of the caravan journey of His exile from Baghdád to Constantinople. On the last day of the ten-day land journey, as they approached the Black Sea, Mírzá Áqá Ján asked Bahá'u'lláh to reveal a Tablet on the occasion. From inside His howdah, Bahá'u'lláh revealed the Tablet known as the Tablet of the Howdah. In it He warned of tests ahead, which would come from Mírzá Yaḥyá.

Húd A prophet of God who appeared before Abraham to the people of 'Ád. He is said to have been a fourth-generation descendant of Noah. He 'proclaimed to his people that God had chosen him as a prophet, and preached to them the one true God and the destruction of their idols. But they rejected him, and only a few became his followers.'[33] A calamity took place in which all perished except Húd and his followers. According to tradition, Húd is buried in Hadhramaut in the south of the Arabian peninsula.

There is a chapter of the Qur'án known as the Súrih of Húd. Bahá'u'lláh refers to Húd in the *Kitáb-i-Íqán* and the Lawḥ-i-Burhán.

Ḥujjat The Proof; Mullá Muḥammad-'Ali of Zanján. He was called Ḥujjatu'l-Islám, 'an appellation given to highly-placed and well-recognized divines'.[34] The Báb gave him the designation Ḥujjat-i-Zanjání.

Ḥujjat sent Mullá Iskandar to investigate the claims of the Báb. On Mullá Iskandar's return, he acquainted himself with the Writings of the Báb and from the pulpit directed his disciples to embrace the Báb's cause. He was detained in Ṭihrán and kept under surveillance. Upon his return to Zanján he was the target of concealed hostility on the part of the authorities. Zanján split into two opposing camps and Ḥujjat and his companions were forced to seek safety in a nearby fort. About three hundred of Ḥujjat's supporters held the fort against repeated attack and siege for almost nine months. Ḥujjat was wounded after a final month-long siege and his wife and baby son were killed. Ḥujjat himself died a few days later. In a fierce attack the Bábís were finally overcome, the survivors being tortured, killed and their bodies mutilated. The body of Ḥujjat was exposed for three days to dishonour in the public square, after which it was carried away by unknown hands.[35]

Human Rights Day A United Nations-sponsored special event day observed on 10 December by many Bahá'í communities around the world, as well as by United Nations Associations, to mark the anniversary of the United Nations Universal Declaration of Human Rights in 1948.

Ḥuqúqu'lláh [Ar] The Right of God. A monetary payment, instituted in the *Kitáb-i-Aqdas*, made by the believers to God, the proceeds of which 'revert to the Authority in the Cause to whom all must turn'[36] (in the time of Bahá'u'lláh, the Manifestation Himself; in the time of 'Abdu'l-Bahá, the Centre of the Covenant; in the time of Shoghi Effendi, the Guardian; and, presently, the Universal House of Justice): 'Should a person acquire one hundred mithqáls of gold, nineteen mithqáls thereof belong unto God, the Creator of earth and heaven.'[37] The payment of Ḥuqúqu'lláh 'serves as a means of purifying the earthly possessions' of those who pay it.[38]

The payment of Ḥuqúqu'llah is worked out thus: 'If a person has possessions equal in value to at least 19 mithqáls in gold, it is a spiritual obligation for him to pay 19% of the total amount, once only, as Ḥuqúqu'lláh. Certain categories of possessions, such as one's residence, are exempt from this. Thereafter, whenever his income, after all expenses have been paid, increases the value of his possessions by the amount of at least 19 mithqáls of gold, he is to pay 19% of this increase, and so on for each further increase.'[39]

Bahá'u'lláh describes the payment of Ḥuqúqu'lláh as a spiritual obligation and bounty; 'It is incumbent upon everyone to discharge the obligation of Ḥuqúq. The advantages gained from this deed revert to the persons themselves.'[40] However, the payment must be made in the right spirit for it to be acceptable: '. . . the acceptance of the offerings dependeth on the spirit of joy, fellowship and contentment that the righteous souls who fulfil this injunction will manifest. If such is the attitude acceptance is permissible, and not otherwise.'[41]

Ḥuqúqu'lláh is not payable on certain possessions: 'We have exempted the residence and the household furnishings, that is, such furnishings as are needful.'[42] The Universal House of Justice has clarified this further: 'It is clear from the Writings that a person is exempt from paying Ḥuqúqu'lláh on his residence and such household and professional equipment as are needful. It is left to the discretion of the individual to decide which items are necessary and which are not.'[43]

Bahá'u'lláh appointed Trustees who acted on His behalf in matters related to the Ḥuqúqu'lláh. Today the Universal House of Justice appoints the Trustees.

'Bahá'u'lláh was very anxious that no one should ever feel forced to pay the Ḥuqúq' and 'insisted that no one should be solicited to pay'.[44] For many years He did not accept any payments at all.

The Ḥuqúqu'lláh is not for the personal use of the Centre of the

Cause but is rather to be spent on the promotion of the Faith and for charitable purposes.[45] At present it is spent for the same purposes as the International Fund.[46]

However, 'the Ḥuqúq should not be confused with the normal contributions of a believer to the International Funds. Although both are donated to the Centre of the Cause – today to the House of Justice – there is a great difference between the two. The Ḥuqúq in reality does not belong to the individual, as it is the right of God, whereas ordinary donations are given by the believer from his own resources . . .'[47]

The law of Ḥuqúqu'llah is not yet binding on any but the Iranian believers, although all Bahá'ís are free to observe it.

See also funds.

Ḥúrí *See* Maiden of Heaven

Ḥurúf-i-Ḥayy *See* Letters of the Living.

Ḥusayn, Imám The third Imám, in Shí'ih Islam, son of 'Alí and Fáṭimih, grandson of the Prophet Muḥammad. He was martyred at Karbilá in 680 AD.

Ḥusayn-'Alíy-i-Núrí, Mírzá The given name of Bahá'u'lláh and the name by which He was known outside the community of Bábís in Iran.

Ḥusayn-i-Bushrú'í, Mullá The one to whom the Báb declared His mission and the first to believe in the Báb as the Promised One.

Mullá Ḥusayn was born in Bushrúyih, Khurásán. At the age of eighteen he became a disciple of Siyyid Káẓim. After Siyyid Káẓim's death Mullá Ḥusayn went to Shíráz to search for the Promised One. There, on 22 May 1844, he encountered the Báb and, during a dramatic interview with Him, declared his belief. Designated the Bábu'l-Báb (Gate of the Gate), Mullá Ḥusayn was the first of eighteen Letters of the Living or disciples of the Báb. He was a leader of the Bábís during savage persecution in Iran and fell as a martyr at the Fort of Shaykh Ṭabarsí on 2 February 1849 at the age of thirty-five. Nabíl writes of him: 'The traits of mind and of character which, from his very youth, he displayed, the profundity of his learning, the tenacity of his faith, his intrepid courage, his singleness of purpose, his high sense of justice and unswerving devotion, marked him as an outstanding figure among those who, by their lives, have borne witness to the glory and power of the new Revelation.'[48]

See also Declaration of the Báb.

Ḥusayníyyih In Shí'ih Islam, a place used to mourn the death of the

Ḥusayníyyih

Imám Ḥusayn. The House of Bahá'u'lláh in Baghdád was changed into a Ḥusayníyyih by Shí'ihs in 1928 when it was awarded to them after a court decision.

I

ibn [Ar] Son.

Ibn-i-Abhar (Mullá Muḥammad Taqí) Hand of the Cause appointed by Bahá'u'lláh, born in Abhar, Iran. His father became a Bábí, and because of persecution the family moved to Qazvín. In about 1868 the family became Bahá'ís. After the death of his father in 1874, Ibn-i-Abhar moved to Zanján where he reinvigorated the Bábí community and caused most of them to become Bahá'ís. He was imprisoned in Zanján for fourteen months, after which he travelled throughout Iran. In 1886 he visited the Holy Land and was appointed a Hand of the Cause. He travelled extensively in Iran, Caucasia, Turkmenistan and India. From 1890 to 1894 he was imprisoned in Ṭihrán and for a time wore the same chains as Bahá'u'lláh had worn as a prisoner in the Síyáh-Chál. After his release he went to the Holy Land and then to 'Ishqábád. He participated in the 1897 gathering of Hands in Ṭihrán which led to the formation of the Central Spiritual Assembly there. He finally settled in Ṭihrán where he assisted with the establishment of the Tarbíyat Bahá'í School. His wife, Munírih Khánum, the daughter of Ḥájí Ákhúnd, helped to found the Girls' School. In 1907 he travelled in India with Harlan Ober, Hooper Harris and Mírzá Maḥmúd Zarqání. Ibn-i-Abhar passed away in 1917.

Mullá Muḥammad-Taqí (Ibn-i-Abhar) in chains

Ibn-i-Aṣdaq (Mírzá 'Alí-Muḥammad) Hand of the Cause appointed by Bahá'u'lláh. He was the son of Mullá Ṣádiq-i-Muqaddas-i-Khurásání, a veteran of the Bábí Faith. As a boy Ibn-i-Aṣdaq was, with his father, confined in the dungeon of Ṭihrán. While still a youth he met Bahá'u'lláh in Baghdád, and again met Him in the Most Great Prison. Ibn-i-Aṣdaq longed for martyrdom, and Bahá'u'lláh designated him Shahíd Ibn-i-Shahíd (Martyr, son of the Martyr) in 1882. He then travelled extensively, teaching the Faith. The first mention of the concept of Hand of the Cause is within a Tablet revealed by Bahá'u'lláh in his honour in April 1887. His marriage to a great-granddaughter of Fatḥ-'Alí Sháh brought him into contact with highly placed people, to whom he gave the message of Bahá'u'lláh's coming. He continued to travel widely, in India, Turkistan and Burma, as well as in Iran. After the passing of Bahá'u'lláh he worked to counter the activities of the Covenant-breakers. He, with the other Hands of the Cause, was appointed by 'Abdu'l-Bahá to the Spiritual Assembly of Ṭihrán, which eventually became the National Spiritual Assembly of Iran. Together with Aḥmad Yazdání, Ibn-i-Aṣdaq delivered in person the Tablet addressed by 'Abdu'l-Bahá to the Central Organization for a Durable Peace at the Hague. Ibn-i-Aṣdaq died in 1928 in Ṭihrán.

Ibn-i-Dhi'b (Son of the Wolf) *See* Shaykh Muḥammad-Taqíy-i-Najafí.

'Idál [Ar] Justice. The fifth day of the Bahá'í week, corresponding to Wednesday.

'Ilm [Ar] Knowledge. The twelfth month of the Bahá'í year (from sunset 15 October to sunset 3 November).

imám In Islam, the divine who leads the prayers in the mosque; a religious leader.

Imám In Shí'ih Islam, one of the twelve legitimate, hereditary successors of Muḥammad, beginning with 'Alí and ending with the Hidden Imám.
See also Caliph.

imám-jum'ih The leader of the Friday prayers in the mosque.

Imám-Zádih Ḥasan, Shrine of Shrine in Ṭihrán where the Báb's body was kept at the instruction of Bahá'u'lláh.

Imám-Zádih Ma'ṣúm, Shrine of Shrine where for a time the Báb's body was concealed. In 1867–8 Bahá'u'lláh directed that the remains be immediately transferred elsewhere. Not long after this the shrine was rebuilt.

Imám-Zádih Zayd, Shrine of Shrine where the Báb's body was kept for a time. The casket containing the remains of the Báb was buried beneath the floor of the inner sanctuary.

immortality *See* death, life after.

independent investigation of truth One of the principles or tenets of Bahá'í social teaching. 'Abdu'l-Bahá explained, '. . . know ye that God has created in man the power of reason, whereby man is enabled to investigate reality. God has not intended man to imitate blindly his fathers and ancestors. He has endowed him with mind, or the faculty of reasoning, by the exercise of which he is to investigate and discover the truth, and that which he finds real and true he must accept. He must not be an imitator or blind follower of any soul. He must not rely implicitly upon the opinion of any man without investigation; nay, each soul must seek intelligently and independently, arriving at a real conclusion and bound only by that reality. The greatest cause of bereavement and disheartening in the world of humanity is ignorance based upon blind imitation.'[1]

Further, 'man must endeavour in all things to investigate the fundamental reality. If he does not independently investigate, he has failed to utilize the talent God has bestowed upon him.'[2]

'Abdu'l-Bahá explained that the concept of the independent investigation of truth refers to the investigation of the underlying unity of the fundamental, original teachings of all the religions of the past: 'Man must cut himself free from all prejudice and from the result of his own imagination, so that he may be able to search for truth unhindered. Truth is one in all religions . . . All the peoples have a fundamental belief in common. Being one, truth cannot be divided, and the differences that appear to exist among nations only result from their attachment to prejudice. If only men would search out truth, they would find themselves united.'[3]

infallibility Free from error.

The doctrine of the 'Most Great Infallibility' of the Manifestation of God was enunciated by Bahá'u'lláh in the *Kitáb-i-Aqdas* and expanded upon in the Tablet of Ishráqát. He makes a distinction between 'conferred' and 'the Most Great Infallibility' and asserts that the Most Great Infallibility is the inherent and exclusive right of the Prophet. The former derives its authority from the latter. Bahá'u'lláh Himself possessed the Most Great Infallibility while He conferred infallibility upon ‘Abdu’l-Bahá, Shoghi Effendi and the Universal House of Justice. In His Will and Testament ‘Abdu’l-Bahá states that ‘God hath ordained’ the Universal House of Justice ‘as the source of all good and freed from all error’.[4]

A letter written on behalf of Shoghi Effendi further elucidates this doctrine of infallibility: ‘The infallibility of the Guardian is confined to matters which are related strictly to the Cause and interpretation of the teachings; he is not an infallible authority on other subjects, such as economics, science, etc.’[5]

insh<u>á</u>’lláh [Ar] If God wills.

institutes, teaching Instructional sessions designed to assist Bahá’ís to deepen their knowledge of the Faith to prepare them for teaching work. In some countries teaching institutes are conducted in Bahá’í centres or in rented facilities, while in other countries permanent institutes offer regular courses. Subjects taught at institutes include Bahá’í history, laws and teachings, and the Administrative Order. Special emphasis is given to living the Bahá’í life, the importance of teaching, prayer, fasting, Nineteen Day Feasts, Bahá’í elections and contribution to the Funds.

intellect The capacity for knowledge, for rational thought; the power to know.

‘Abdu’l-Bahá states that ‘the light of the intellect is the highest light that exists, for it is born of the Light Divine . . . The light of the intellect enables us to understand and realize all that exists.’[6] However, though all people possess intelligence and capacities, ‘the intelligence, the capacity, and the worthiness of men differ’.[7]

Intercalary Days *See* Ayyám-i-Há.

intercession Prayer or entreaty to God on behalf of another.

‘Abdu’l-Bahá has revealed, ‘In this Most Great Dispensation Thou dost accept the intercession of children in behalf of their parents. This is one of the infinite bestowals of this Dispensation.’[8] ‘The wealth of the other world is nearness to God. Consequently it is certain that those who are near the Divine Court are allowed to intercede, and this intercession is approved by God. But intercession in the other world is not like intercession in this world; it is another thing, another reality, which cannot be expressed in words.’[9] ‘The progress of man’s spirit in the divine world . . . is through the bounty and grace of the Lord alone, or through the intercession and the sincere prayers of other human souls, or through the charities and important good works which are performed in its name.’[10]

International Bahá'í Bureau An office set up in Geneva in 1925 following a visit to Haifa of Mrs Stannard. It was designed to promote in Europe the affairs of the Faith as well as to stimulate its international functions throughout the world. The work of the Bureau was encouraged and directed by Shoghi Effendi, who wrote of it: 'Geneva is auxiliary to the Centre in Haifa. It does not assume the place of Haifa, but is auxiliary. It exercises no international authority; it does not try to impose, but helps and acts as intermediary between Haifa and other Bahá'í centres.'[11] The Bureau was recognized by the League of Nations and its bulletin, *Messager Bahá'í*, was published in English, French and German. The work of the International Bahá'í Bureau was largely taken over by the Bahá'í International Community.

International Bahá'í Council An institution created by Shoghi Effendi in 1951 as the forerunner of the Universal House of Justice. It was invested with three functions: to forge links with the authorities in the newly-emerged State of Israel, to assist Shoghi Effendi in the erection of the superstructure of the Shrine of the Báb, and to conduct negotiations related to matters of personal status with the civil authorities. To these were added further functions as the Council developed. The members of the first Council were appointed by Shoghi Effendi: its President was Charles Mason Remey and its Vice-President Amelia Collins. The Council was enlarged to eight members in 1952 and to nine in 1955. Following the passing of Shoghi Effendi the Council continued to perform its duties at the World Centre under the direction of the Hands of the Cause residing in the Holy Land. At Riḍván 1961 the Council was elected for the first time. Its nine members were elected by the members of all the national and regional spiritual assemblies in the Bahá'í world by postal ballot. The Hands of the Cause ruled that they themselves were not eligible for election to this body. The following people were elected: Jessie Revell, 'Alí Nakhjavání, Luṭfu'lláh Ḥakím, Ethel Revell, Charles Wolcott, Sylvia Ioas, Mildred Mottahedeh, Ian Semple and H. Borrah Kavelin. These members served until the election of the Universal House of Justice in 1963.

International Fund *See* funds.

International Teaching Centre An institution established in 1973 by the Universal House of Justice to bring to fruition the work of the Hands of the Cause and to provide for its extension into the future. Its duties are 'to coordinate, stimulate and direct the activities of the Continental Boards of Counsellors and to act as liaison between them and the Universal House of Justice'; to be fully informed of the state of the

Cause in all parts of the world, to make reports and recommendations to the House of Justice based on this information and to give advice to the Counsellors; to be alert to the possibility of extending the teaching work into receptive or needy areas and to make recommendations for action; and 'to determine and anticipate needs for literature, pioneers and travelling teachers and to work out teaching plans, both regional and global, for the approval of the Universal House of Justice.'[12]

All the Hands of the Cause are members of the Teaching Centre plus those Counsellors so appointed by the Universal House of Justice. The permanent seat of the International Teaching Centre will be on the arc on Mount Carmel.

International Teaching Centre 1988

interpretation Providing an explanation of the Sacred Writings.

The function of authoritative interpretation of the Bahá'í Scriptures is limited to 'Abdu'l-Bahá and the Guardian of the Bahá'í Faith. Bahá'u'lláh designated 'Abdu'l-Bahá as the only authorized Interpreter of His Teachings: 'When the Mystic Dove will have winged its flight from its Sanctuary of Praise and sought its far-off goal, its hidden habitation, refer ye whatsoever ye understand not in the Book to Him Who hath branched from this mighty stock.'[13] In the *Kitáb-i-'Ahdí* Bahá'u'lláh states: '"When the ocean of My presence hath ebbed and the Book of My Revelation is ended, turn your faces toward Him Whom God hath purposed, Who hath branched from this Ancient

Root." The object of this sacred Verse is none other except the most Mighty Branch ['Abdu'l-Bahá].'[14]

In His Will and Testament 'Abdu'l-Bahá appointed His grandson to be the Interpreter: 'After the passing of this wronged one, it is incumbent upon the Aghṣán, the Afnán of the Sacred Lote-Tree, the Hands of the Cause of God and the loved ones of the Abhá Beauty to turn unto Shoghi Effendi . . . as he is the sign of God, the chosen branch, the guardian of the Cause of God . . . He is the expounder of the words of God . . .'[15]

As no further Guardians could be appointed after the passing of Shoghi Effendi, the function of authoritative interpretation ceased: 'there are those prerogatives and duties which lie exclusively within the sphere of the Guardian himself and, therefore, in the absence of a Guardian, are inoperative except insofar as the monumental work already performed by Shoghi Effendi continues to be of enduring benefit to the Faith. Such a function is that of authoritative interpretation of the Teachings.'[16]

The exclusive nature of authoritative interpretation does not preclude individuals from having their own understandings of the Writings: 'A clear distinction is made in our Faith between authoritative interpretation and the interpretation or understanding that each individual arrives at for himself from his study of its teachings. While the former is confined to the Guardian, the latter, according to the guidance given to us by the Guardian himself, should by no means be suppressed. In fact such individual interpretation is considered the fruit of man's rational power and conducive to a better understanding of the teachings, provided that no disputes or arguments arise among the friends and the individual himself understands and makes it clear that his views are merely his own.'[17]

Interpreter The Centre of the Covenant. 'Abdu'l-Bahá Himself stated: 'In accordance with the explicit text of the *Kitáb-i-Aqdas* Bahá'u'lláh hath made the Centre of the Covenant the Interpreter of His Word . . .'[18] and further, 'I am the Interpreter of the Word of God . . .'[19] In His Will and Testament 'Abdu'l-Bahá appointed Shoghi Effendi as the 'expounder of the words of God' after Him. Apart from 'Abdu'l-Bahá and Shoghi Effendi, no one can authoritatively interpret the Writings.

A view of Iṣfáhán

Interregnum The period between the passing of Shoghi Effendi in 1957 and the election of the Universal House of Justice in 1963 when the affairs of the Bahá'í Faith were under the care of the Hands of the Cause.

Iran Country in southwest Asia bordering the Caspian Sea and the

Iran

USSR on the north, the Persian Gulf and the Gulf of Oman on the south, Iraq on the west and Afghanistan and Pakistan on the east. Also known as Persia, its capital is Ṭihrán. Iran is the homeland of both the Báb and Bahá'u'lláh.

Iraq Country in southwest Asia in Mesopotamia bordering Turkey on the north, Saudi Arabia and Kuwait on the south, Syria and Jordan on the west and Iran on the east. Its capital is Baghdád, where Bahá'u'lláh was in exile for ten years. It was in Iraq, in the Garden of Riḍván near Baghdád, that Bahá'u'lláh made the public proclamation of His mission in 1863. The House of Bahá'u'lláh in Baghdád is the site of formal pilgrimage for Bahá'ís.

Iron Age *See* Formative Age.

Iṣfáhán City in west central Iran, formerly the capital. The Báb stayed four months in the private residence of the Governor of Iṣfáhán, Manúchihr Khán.

Isfandíyár The black servant of Bahá'u'lláh and 'Abdu'l-Bahá who paid the debts of the Holy Family when Bahá'u'lláh was imprisoned in Ṭihrán. In the Holy Land, 'Abdu'l-Bahá had another servant named Isfandíyár who for many years drove 'Abdu'l-Bahá's carriage.

'Ishqábád (Ashkabad) A city in Russian Turkistan, once the location of a large Bahá'í community and the site of the first Mashriqu'l-Adhkár of the Bahá'í world. Begun in 1902 and carried out at the instruction of 'Abdu'l-Bahá, 'this enterprise must rank', Shoghi Effendi writes, 'not only as the first major undertaking launched through the concerted efforts of His followers in the Heroic Age of His Faith, but as one of the most brilliant and enduring achievements in the history of the first Bahá'í century.'[20] Its dependent institutions included two Bahá'í schools, a traveller's hostel, a medical dispensary and Ḥaẓíratu'l-Quds. In 1928 it was seized by the Soviet government, in 1938 converted into a museum, then after being damaged by earthquake, it was demolished by government order in 1963.

Ishráqát [Ar] Splendours. A Tablet of Bahá'u'lláh addressed to Jalíl-i-Khu'í, a coppersmith, revealed in answer to his questions, particularly those on the subject of supreme infallibility.

Islam The religion founded by Muḥammad in Arabia in the seventh century AD. The core teachings of Islam which are accepted by all Muslims are the oneness of God, the prophethood of Muḥammad and belief in a Day of Judgement. Shí'ihs add to these belief in the rightful succession of the Imáms and justice. The secondary principles of Islam are prayer, fasting, pilgrimage, almsgiving, enjoining to good acts and admonishing of wrongdoing, and holy war. The Bahá'í Faith has its historical roots in Islam in the same way that Christianity has its roots in

The Mashriqu'l-Adhkár in 'Ishqábád. The building has since been destroyed by earthquake

Judaism yet is a completely independent religion, not a sect of the former faith.

Ism-i-A'ẓam [Ar] *See* Greatest Name.

Ismu'lláhi'l-Ákhir [Ar] The Last Name of God. This was the title given by the Báb to Quddús.

Istanbul Constantinople.

Istijlál [Ar] Majesty. The sixth day of the Bahá'í week, corresponding to Thursday.

Istiqlál [Ar] Independence. The seventh day of the Bahá'í week, corresponding to Friday.

Ithná-'Asharíyyih Twelver Shí'ihs, who believe in the succession of the twelve Imáms after Muḥammad and who expect the return of the Twelfth Imám.

'Izzat [Ar] Might. The tenth month of the Bahá'í year (from sunset 7 September to sunset 26 September).

J

Jalál [Ar] Glory. The first day of the Bahá'í week, corresponding to Saturday; also, the second month of the Bahá'í year (from sunset 8 April to sunset 27 April).

Jamál [Ar] Beauty. The second day of the Bahá'í week, corresponding to Sunday; also, the third month of the Bahá'í year (from sunset 27 April to sunset 16 May).

Jamál-i-Mubárak The Blessed Beauty. Bahá'u'lláh. A title sometimes applied to Him by Bahá'ís.

Jamál-i-Qidam [Ar] The Ancient Beauty. A title of Bahá'u'lláh.

Javáhiru'l-Asrár Tablet of Bahá'u'lláh revealed in Baghdád dealing with verses from the Bible.

Jesus Founder of the religion of Christianity and accepted by Bahá'ís as a Manifestation of God.

Bahá'ís believe that Jesus' promise to return 'in the glory of the Father' was fulfilled by the coming of Bahá'u'lláh. As in the Qur'án, in the Bahá'í Writings Jesus is often referred to as 'the Spirit of God' and 'the Son'.

Jináb [Ar] Honour or Excellency. A term of respect prefixed to a person's name. After the Conference of Badas͟ht Bahá'u'lláh was known among the Bábís as 'Jináb-i-Bahá'.

jubbih [Pers] Outer coat, overcoat.

Judgement, Day of In Islam and Christianity, an awaited day when the dead would be raised, good and evil separated, and the return of Jesus and the coming of the Mihdí (or Mahdi) would occur. It is also known as the 'Day of Resurrection', the 'Last Day' and 'the Hour'. Bahá'ís interpret this event spiritually rather than physically and believe that it refers to the appearance of the Manifestation of God on earth.

Junaynih Garden An extensive garden northwest of Mazra'ih owned by several Bahá'ís which Bahá'u'lláh often visited. In 1901 it was registered under the names of 'Abdu'l-Bahá and a brother. E. G. Browne mentions seeing Bahá'u'lláh at this garden during his visit in 1890.

justice Equity, fairness, righteousness.

Justice is the virtue which characterizes the Dispensation of Bahá'u'lláh. 'The best beloved of all things in My sight is Justice.'[1] 'Justice is a powerful force. It is, above all else, the conqueror of the citadels of the hearts and souls of men, and the revealer of the secrets of the world of being, and standard-bearer of love and bounty.'[2]

At the global level, justice is the guarantor for the establishment in the future of a world community based on the principle of the oneness of mankind. 'No light can compare with the light of justice. The establishment of order in the world and the tranquillity of the nations depend upon it.'[3] To uphold the standard of justice, Bahá'u'lláh has decreed that, 'The structure of world stability and order hath been reared upon, and will continue to be sustained by, the twin pillars of reward and punishment.'[4] Further, He states, 'That which traineth the world is Justice, for it is upheld by two pillars, reward and punishment. These two pillars are the sources of life to the world.'[5]

At the individual level, Bahá'u'lláh states, 'If thine eyes be turned towards justice, choose thou for thy neighbour what thou choosest for thyself.'[6] He further states: 'Be fair to yourselves and to others, that the

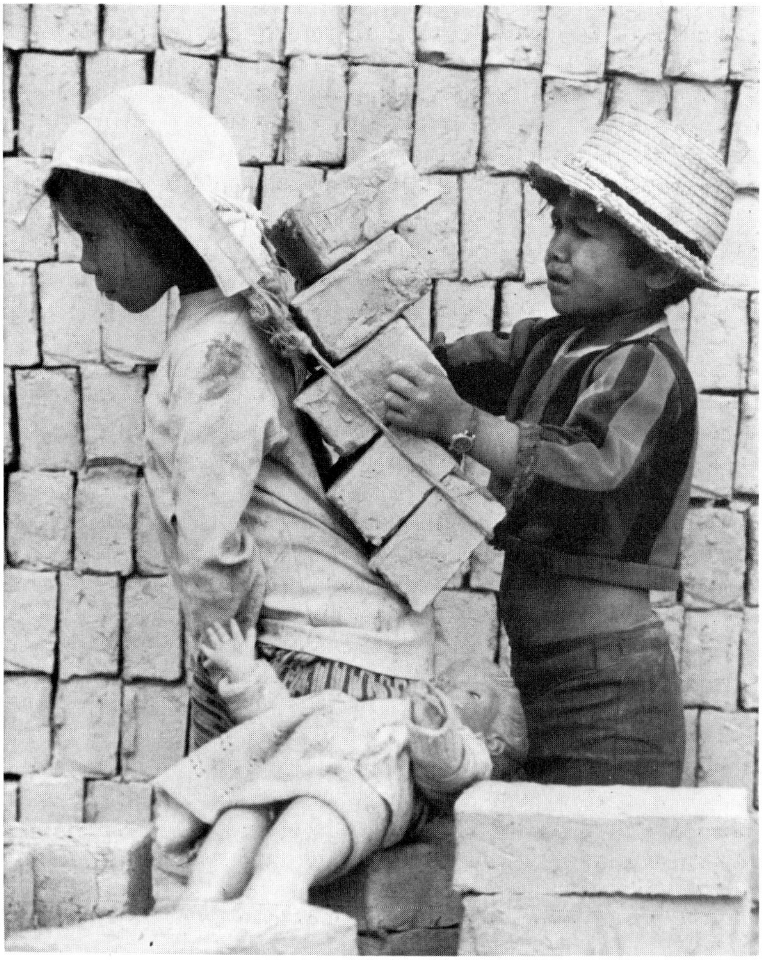

The injustice of child labour

evidences of justice may be revealed, through your deeds, among Our faithful servants.'[7] 'Whoso cleaveth to justice, can, under no circumstances, transgress the limits of moderation. He discerneth the truth in all things, through the guidance of Him Who is the All-Seeing.'[8]

The Bahá'í Houses of Justice, the present-day spiritual assemblies, are to act with justice: 'The administrators of the Faith of God must be like unto shepherds. Their aim should be to dispel all the doubts, misunderstandings and harmful differences which may arise in the community of the believers. And this they can adequately achieve provided they are motivated by a true sense of love for their fellow-brethren, coupled with the firm determination to act with justice in all the cases which are submitted to them for their consideration.'[9]

K

Kaaba (also, ka'bih) [Ar] Literally, cube. The cube-like building in the court of the Great Mosque at Mecca containing the sacred black stone. It is the Qiblih (point of adoration) of Islam and the goal of pilgrimage for Muslims. In the Bahá'í Writings the term is used metaphorically and refers to Bahá'u'lláh.

Kad-khudá In Iran, the head man of a village or the chief of a section of a town.

kalántar In Iran, a mayor or magistrate.

Kalimát [Ar] Words. The seventh month of the Bahá'í year (from sunset 12 July to sunset 31 July).

Kalimát-i-Firdawsíyyih (Words of Paradise). A Tablet revealed by Bahá'u'lláh in honour of Ḥájí Mírzá Ḥaydar-'Alí. It contains eleven passages called 'Leaves of the Most Exalted Paradise' which include exhortations to the rulers, the peoples of the world and the believers to show justice, wisdom, unity and moderation, and to abandon ascetic practices. In it Bahá'u'lláh instructs the House of Justice to 'take counsel together regarding those things which have not outwardly been revealed in the Book, and to enforce that which is agreeable to them', assuring that 'God will verily inspire them with whatsoever He willeth'.[1]

In this Tablet, Bahá'u'lláh warns against weapons of destruction, adding: 'Strange and astonishing things exist in the earth but they are hidden from the minds and the understanding of men. These things are capable of changing the whole atmosphere of the earth and their contamination would prove lethal.'[2]

Kamál [Ar] Perfection. The third day of the Bahá'í week, corresponding to Monday; also, the eighth month of the Bahá'í year (from sunset 31 July to sunset 19 August).

Karbilá Shrine city of the Imám Ḥusayn in Iraq and the site of his martyrdom.

kashkúl [Pers] Globe-shaped alms-basket carried by dervishes.

Kawthar [Ar] Abundance. According to Islamic tradition, the lake or river in Paradise which Muḥammad saw on his mystic night journey.

Káẓim-i-Rashtí, Siyyid The disciple and chosen successor of Shaykh

Aḥmad. Born in Rasht, Iran, in 1793, as a boy he showed great intellect and spirituality. At the age of twenty-two he went to Yazd, became a disciple of Shaykh Aḥmad and was designated to succeed him and continue the work of preparing his disciples to recognize the Promised Qá'im. After Shaykh Aḥmad's death, the tide of opposition to Shaykhí doctrines rose and Siyyid Káẓim was attacked and denounced by the 'ulamá.

Siyyid Káẓim knew the identity of the Promised One and alluded to it clearly when Siyyid 'Alí-Muḥammad (the Báb) attended his lecture one day in Karbilá. Seeing Him, Siyyid Káẓim fell silent. When asked to continue his discourse he said: 'What more shall I say? . . . Lo, the Truth is more manifest than the ray of light that has fallen upon that lap!'[3] But none understood his meaning.

Towards the end of his life, feeling that the advent of the Qá'im was at hand, he charged his disciples to scatter and search for the Promised One. One of those who arose in response was Mullá Ḥusayn, the first to find the Báb. Siyyid Káẓim died on 31 December 1843.

Khadíjih-Bagum The wife of the Báb. Khadíjih-Bagum and Siyyid 'Alí-Muḥammad, the Báb, were neighbours and playmates as children in Shíráz. Before their betrothal Khadíjih-Bagum dreamed that Fáṭimih, daughter of Muḥammad, asked for her hand in marriage to her son, the Imám Ḥusayn. The Báb and Khadíjih-Bagum were married in the House of the Báb in Shíráz in August 1842. They had one child, a son Aḥmad, who died in infancy.

The Báb revealed to Khadíjih-Bagum His station as the Qá'im even before making His Declaration to Mullá Ḥusayn. Nabíl writes: 'The wife of the Báb, unlike His mother, perceived at the earliest dawn of His Revelation the glory and uniqueness of His Mission and felt from the very beginning the intensity of its force. No one except Ṭáhirih, among the women of her generation, surpassed her in the spontaneous character of her devotion nor excelled the fervour of her faith. To her the Báb confided the secret of His future sufferings, and unfolded to her eyes the significance of the events that were to transpire in His Day.'[4] The Báb revealed for her the prayer known as the 'Remover of Difficulties' and directed her to recite it before going to sleep, promising He Himself would appear to her to banish her anxiety.

When Khadíjih-Bagum learned Bahá'u'lláh had declared Himself to be the Promised One of the *Bayán*, Whose advent the Báb had foretold, she gave Him her allegiance instantly. She died in 1882.

Khadíjih Khánum The mother of Bahá'u'lláh. Khadíjih Khánum was a widow and had one son and two daughters by her first marriage when she became the second wife of Mírzá Buzurg. They had two daughters –

Sárih Khánum and Nisá' Khánum – and three sons – Bahá'u'lláh, Mírzá Músá and Mírzá Mihdí (who died within his father's lifetime).
See also Buzurg-i-Vazír, Mírzá.

Khammár, 'Údí A successful Christian merchant of 'Akká. His house in 'Akká backed onto that of Ilyás 'Abbúd, and he also owned a mansion in the countryside which had been built by 'Abdu'lláh Páshá.

'Údí Khammár vacated his town house to live in his country mansion and the Holy Family was able to move into the house in 'Akká. This house faces onto Genoa (then ''Abbúd') Square in the former Genoese quarter of 'Akká. The house was so insufficient to the needs of the Holy Family that at one time thirteen people lived in one room. It was in the House of 'Údí Khammár that Bahá'u'lláh revealed the *Kitáb-i-Aqdas*.

'Údí Khammár restored the mansion in the countryside at great expense and inscribed in Arabic this verse over the door: 'Greetings and salutation rest upon this Mansion which increaseth in splendour through the passage of time. Manifold wonders and marvels are found therein, and pens are baffled in attempting to describe them.'[5] The area round about this mansion was known as al-Bahja, Place of Delight. 'Údí Khammár and his family moved to the mansion by mid-1871; but in 1879 an epidemic disease, probably bubonic plague, struck 'Akká and the Khammár family, fleeing from it, left the mansion. It was rented to 'Abdu'l-Bahá for the use of Baha'u'lláh and was known as Bahjí.

'Údí Khammár died in 1879 and was buried in a room of the eastern housing complex, at the southeast corner of the mansion wall.
See also 'Abbúd, Ilyás; *and* House of 'Údí Khammár.

'Údí Khammár

The Khán-i-'Avámíd

khán Originally, from the Mongolian term for a ruler; a title meaning prince, chieftain or man of rank. Also, [Ar] a caravanserai, or inn for travellers.

khánum The feminine form of 'khán'. A lady. Also, a title conveying respect; when placed after the name, it denotes 'lady' or 'madam'.

Kheiralla (also Khayru'lláh), Ibráhím George The first Bahá'í teacher in America. Born in 1849, he was a Syrian Orthodox Christian who was converted to the Bahá'í Faith in Cairo. In 1892–3 he went to the United States to promote one of his business ventures, but when it failed he remained to open a faith healing practice in Chicago and teach the Bahá'í Faith. He converted a large number of people in Chicago, Illinois, and Kenosha, Wisconsin, through his 'Truth Seeker' classes. However, his presentation of 'Bahá'í' teachings included a number of erroneous doctrines and beliefs of his own. When 'Abdu'l-Bahá refused to sanction them, or to give him authority over the Bahá'í community in the West, Kheiralla broke with 'Abdu'l-Bahá, becoming a Covenant-breaker. He died in 1929.

khuṭbih [Ar] In Islam, the Friday sermon delivered by the imám at noon.

King of Glory Bahá'u'lláh.

King of Martyrs and Beloved of Martyrs (Sulṭánu'sh-Shuhadá' *and* Maḥbúbu'sh-Shuhadá') Mírzá Muḥammad-Ḥasan and Mírzá Muḥammad-Ḥusayn, two brothers of Iṣfáhán who were condemned to death by Shaykh Muḥammad-Báqir after they were denounced as 'Bábís' by the Imám-Jum'ih of Iṣfáhán, Mír Muḥammad-Ḥusayn, who owed them a sum of money.

Right King of Martyrs Mírzá Muḥammad Ḥasan

Far right Beloved of Martyrs Mírzá Muḥammad Ḥusayn

King of Martyrs

The King and Beloved of Martyrs were successful merchants and were held in high esteem in Iṣfáhán. Their prosperity enabled them to alleviate some of the hardships of Bahá'u'lláh and the Holy Family during their exiles and confinements,[6] and they were also generous to the poor. The Imám-Jum'ih put his financial affairs in the hands of these two brothers who were 'the most trustworthy persons he could find'.[7] Eventually, however, he discovered that he owed the two brothers a considerable sum of money for the work they had done for him, and he decided that rather than pay this he would take their lives. He realized that this would not be difficult, as the two brothers were Bahá'ís, and all that had to be done was for a mujtahid to write their death warrant. Shaykh Báqir, the leading mujtahid of the city, plotted with the Imám-Jum'ih to do just this. They approached the Prince, who was the Governor of Iṣfáhán, and asked him to implement their plans.

The two brothers were arrested and taken to government headquarters where they were interviewed by the Prince. The Sháh then asked that they be transferred to Ṭihrán, but the Prince did not comply. On the sixth day of their imprisonment, 17 March 1879, the King and Beloved of Martyrs were executed in Iṣfáhán.

Bahá'u'lláh lamented their loss for many years and revealed many Tablets in their honour.

See also Raqshá *and* Muḥammad-Baqir, Shaykh.

Kingdom, the Often used to refer to the next life, e.g. 'The outer expression used for the Kingdom is heaven; but this is a comparison and similitude, not a reality or fact, for the Kingdom is not a material place, it is sanctified from time and place.'[8] It is also used to refer to the World Order of Bahá'u'lláh where the people of the world will live under the laws of God and the world is transformed into a paradise.

kingdoms of God The levels of creation: mineral, vegetable, animal, human. Each manifests some of the qualities of God, except man, who potentially manifests them all: '. . . whatever is in the heavens and whatever is on the earth is a direct evidence of the revelation within it of the attributes and names of God . . . To a supreme degree is this true of man . . . For in him are potentially revealed all the attributes and names of God to a degree that no other created being hath excelled or surpassed.'[9] Lower kingdoms do not bear all of the characteristics of higher ones, nor can lower kingdoms comprehend higher ones: 'An inferior degree can never comprehend a higher degree or kingdom. The mineral, no matter how far it may advance, can never attain knowledge of the vegetable. No matter how the plant or vegetable may progress, it cannot perceive the reality of the animal kingdom – in other words, it cannot grasp a world of life that is endowed with the power of the senses. The animal may develop a wonderful degree of intelligence, but it can never attain the powers of ideation and conscious reflection which belong to man . . . This being so, how can the human reality, which is limited, comprehend the eternal, unmanifest Creator?'[10]

Kings, Tablets to the Letters written by Bahá'u'lláh to the various kings and rulers of the time proclaiming His advent and instructing them in how to achieve the Most Great Peace. Bahá'u'lláh began His proclamation to the kings and rulers with His first Tablet to Sulṭán 'Abdu'l-'Azíz of Turkey, revealed while Bahá'u'lláh was in Constantinople. He revealed three other Tablets towards the end of His stay in Adrianople. One major Tablet, the *Súriy-i-Mulúk*, is addressed to all the kings and rulers collectively. Others revealed in this period are addressed to Náṣiri'd-Dín Sháh and Napoleon III. Bahá'u'lláh continued His Tablets to the kings and rulers with the revelation of the *Kitáb-i-Aqdas* in the first few years of His imprisonment in 'Akká. Kings and rulers addressed at this time included Kaiser Wilhelm I, Napoleon III (a second Tablet), Francis Joseph of Austria and Hungary, Pope Pius IX, Czar Alexander II and Queen Victoria.

Kings and Rulers addressed by Bahá'u'lláh

Kaiser Wilhelm I

Naṣíri'd-Dín Sháh

Czar Alexander II

Napoleon III

Pope Pius IX

kingship, station of One of the signs of God. Bahá'u'lláh has stated that 'the majesty of kingship is one of the signs of God. We do not wish that the countries of the world should remain deprived thereof . . .'[11] However, Bahá'u'lláh also states that 'One of the signs of the maturity of the world is that no one will accept to bear the weight of kingship. Kingship will remain with none willing to bear alone its weight. That day will be the day whereon wisdom will be manifested among mankind. Only in order to proclaim the Cause of God and spread abroad His Faith will anyone be willing to bear this grievous weight.'[12] Shoghi Effendi writes that in the Writings of Bahá'u'lláh 'the principle of kingship is eulogized, the rank and conduct of just and fair-minded kings is extolled, the rise of monarchs, ruling with justice and even professing His Faith, is envisaged, and the solemn duty to arise and insure the triumph of Bahá'í sovereigns is inculcated.'[13]

kitáb [Ar] Book.

***Kitáb-i-'Ahdí* (Book of My Covenant)** Bahá'u'lláh's Will and Testament, written entirely in His own hand and unsealed on the ninth day after His passing. Referred to by Him as the 'Most Great Tablet' and 'the Crimson Book', it designates 'Abdu'l-Bahá as Bahá'u'lláh's successor and the one to whom all should turn for guidance after Bahá'u'lláh's death. As a written covenant clearly stating the succession of authority by a Manifestation of God, this document is unique in religious scripture. The Will and Testament of Bahá'u'lláh, Shoghi Effendi has written, together with the *Kitáb-i-Aqdas* and those Tablets describing the station of 'Abdu'l-Bahá, 'constitute the chief buttresses designed by the Lord of the Covenant Himself to shield and support, after His ascension, the appointed Centre of His Faith and the Delineator of its future institutions'.[14]

***Kitáb-i-Aqdas* (Most Holy Book)** Bahá'u'lláh's book of laws, revealed in 'Akká in 1873 while He resided in the House of 'Údí Khammár. The *Kitáb-i-Aqdas*, revealed in Arabic, sets forth the laws and ordinances of Bahá'u'lláh's Dispensation but is much more than 'a mere code of laws'. Shoghi Effendi has described it as 'the Mother Book of His Dispensation', the 'Charter of His New World Order',[15] and as the 'Charter of the future world civilization'.[16] In it Bahá'u'lláh sets forth the succession of 'Abdu'l-Bahá and His authority as Interpreter, anticipates the Guardianship and ordains the institution of the House of Justice and its functions and revenues. He reveals laws, ordinances and exhortations concerning subjects including prayer, fasting, marriage, divorce, burial, wills and inheritance, pilgrimage, the Ḥuqúqu'lláh, the Mashriqu'l-Adhkár, the Bahá'í calendar, Feasts and holy days, the age of maturity, the obligation to work and its elevation to worship, obedience to government, and education. He sets forth prohibitions including the institution of priesthood and its practices including confession of sins; forbids slavery; condemns mendicancy, idleness, cruelty to animals, backbiting and calumny, gambling, the use of drugs and intoxicants; and outlines the punishment for certain crimes.

In addition the *Kitáb-i-Aqdas* contains many exhortations by Bahá'u'lláh to His followers as to the high standard of conduct they should follow in their individual lives and in carrying out their responsibilities towards family, society and their faith, as well as statements directed to the rulers and peoples of the world.

Bahá'u'lláh sets forth the infallibility of the Manifestation of God and fixes the duration of His Dispensation at no less than a thousand years.

After the Revelation of the *Kitáb-i-Aqdas* Bahá'u'lláh continued to reveal supplementary ordinances and explanations of the laws in the *Aqdas* such as those contained in the *Questions and Answers*.

Not all of the provisions of the *Kitáb-i-Aqdas* are in practice at the present time and certain laws (such as the Ḥuqúqu'lláh) apply only to Iranians. Bahá'u'lláh Himself urged the Bahá'ís to implement the laws gradually with tact and wisdom.

Shoghi Effendi explained, in a letter written on his behalf, that to avoid disturbance and dissension, the laws of the *Kitáb-i-Aqdas* 'are, whenever practicable and not in direct conflict with the Civil Laws of the land, absolutely binding on every believer or Bahá'í institution whether in the East or in the West. Certain laws, such as fasting, obligatory prayers, the consent of parents before marriage, avoidance of alcoholic drinks, monogamy, should be regarded by all believers as universally and vitally applicable at the present time. Others have been formulated in anticipation of a state of society destined to emerge from the chaotic conditions that prevail today.'[17]

The entire text of the *Kitáb-i-Aqdas* is not yet available in translation, as it is to be published with detailed explanatory material, drawing on the related Tablets elucidating its laws. However, its contents are summarized in *A Synopsis and Codification of the Kitáb-i-Aqdas, the Most Holy Book of Bahá'u'lláh*.

Kitáb-i-Asmá' **(The Book of Names)** A work written by the Báb counselling His followers to remain unified, to be sincere in their allegiance to 'Him Whom God Shall Make Manifest', and warning them not to let anything, even the *Bayán*, keep them from recognizing the Promised One when He should appear. The *Kitáb-i-Asmá'* is the source of the Bahá'í (Badí') calendar.

***Kitáb-i-Íqán* (Book of Certitude)** Volume revealed by Bahá'u'lláh in Bag̲h̲dád two years before His declaration. It was written in answer to questions posed to Him by an uncle of the Báb, Ḥájí Mírzá Siyyid Muḥammad, who was not convinced as yet that his nephew fulfilled all the prophecies concerning the Promised Qá'im. In the *Kitáb-i-Íqán*, which was written in two days and two nights, Bahá'u'lláh proclaims the oneness of God, the station of His manifestations as 'mirrors' through whom alone man can obtain knowledge of God, and the essential unity of their teachings. He describes how the prophets of the past faced opposition and denial through the blindness and greed of religious leaders and presents the essential qualities of the 'true seeker' after religious truth. Bahá'u'lláh further explains the spiritual meaning of prophecies about the return of Christ, the coming of the Qá'im and such terms as 'resurrection', 'return' and 'day of judgement'.

He presents proofs of the divine character of the Báb's revelation and alludes to His own revelation, anticipating the opposition He Himself would face.

Shoghi Effendi described the *Kitáb-i-Íqán* as the 'foremost among the priceless treasures cast forth from the billowing ocean of Bahá'u-'lláh's Revelation',[18] and stated that it fulfilled the Báb's prophecy that the Promised One would complete the text of the Persian *Bayán*. It 'occupies a position unequalled by any work in the entire range of Bahá'í literature, except the *Kitáb-i-Aqdas*'.[19]

'Well may it be claimed that of all the books revealed by the Author of the Bahá'í Revelation, this Book alone, by sweeping away the age-long barriers that have so insurmountably separated the great religions of the world, has laid down a broad and unassailable foundation for the complete and permanent reconciliation of their followers.'[20]

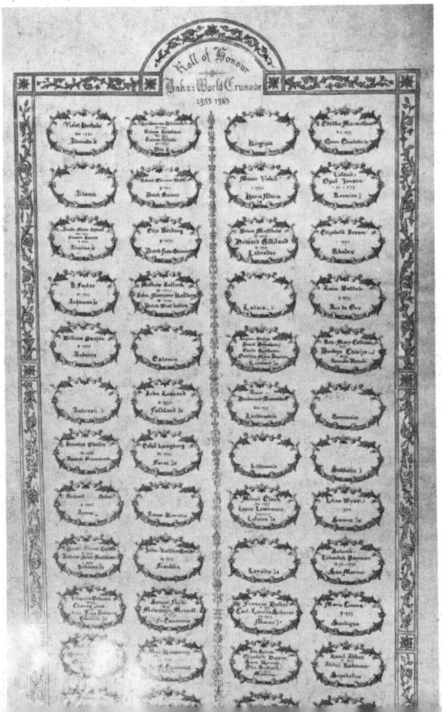

Part of the Roll of Honour listing the Knights of Bahá'u'lláh

Knight of Bahá'u'lláh Title initially given by Shoghi Effendi to those Bahá'ís who arose to open new territories to the Faith during the first year of the Ten Year Crusade and subsequently applied to those who first reached those still-unopened territories at a later date: 'I hail with feelings of joy and wonder the superb feats of the heroic company of the Knights of the Lord of Hosts in pursuance of their sublime mission for the spiritual conquest of the planet.'[21] 'The Concourse on High will continue to applaud the highly meritorious services rendered by future volunteers arising to reinforce the historic work so nobly initiated by the Knights of Bahá'u'lláh in the far-flung, newly opened territories.'[22] Shoghi Effendi kept a Roll of Honour of all the Knights of Bahá'u'lláh. A few more Knights of Bahá'u'lláh remain to be named, as there are a few territories not yet open to the Faith.

See also Ten Year Crusade.

Some of the Knights of Bahá'u'lláh who arose during the Ten Year Crusade

knowledge Understanding, awareness.

For Bahá'ís, 'true knowledge . . . is the knowledge of God, and this is none other than the recognition of His Manifestation in each Dispensation.'[23] The purpose of man's creation is to know God: 'I bear witness, O My God, that Thou hast created me to know Thee and to worship Thee.'[24]

The knowledge of oneself is a high station conferred upon man by God: 'Whatever duty Thou hast prescribed unto Thy servants of extolling to the utmost Thy majesty and glory is but a token of Thy grace unto them, that they may be enabled to ascend unto the station conferred upon their own inmost being, the station of the knowledge of their own selves.'[25] Further, Bahá'u'lláh links man's knowledge of himself with the ability to know God: 'Could ye apprehend with what wonders of My munificence and bounty I have willed to entrust your souls, ye would, of a truth, rid yourselves of attachment to all created things, and would gain a true knowledge of your own selves – a knowledge which is the same as the comprehension of Mine own Being.'[26]

The acquisition of knowledge – education – is an important Bahá'í principle: 'Knowledge is one of the wondrous gifts of God. It is incumbent upon everyone to acquire it.'[27] 'Knowledge is as wings to man's life, and a ladder for his ascent. Its acquisition is incumbent upon everyone. The knowledge of such sciences, however, should be acquired as can profit the peoples of the earth, and not those which begin with words and end with words . . . In truth, knowledge is a veritable treasure for man, and a source of glory, of bounty, of joy, of exaltation, of cheer and gladness unto him.'[28]

Koran *See* Qur'án.

A universal auxiliary language will help secur the unity of all people

Krishna In Hinduism, generally regarded to be the eighth or ninth avatar of the god Vishnu. 'Abdu'l-Bahá, in one of his talks, mentioned Krishna as one of the 'blessed souls' who 'were the cause of the illumination of the world of humanity'.[29] Shoghi Effendi has indicated that to Hindus Bahá'u'lláh is the reincarnation of Krishna.

Kull-i-Shay' (Kullu-Shay') [Ar] Literally, all things. In the Badí' or Bahá'í calendar, a period of 361 years composed of nineteen cycles (Váḥids) of nineteen years each. The numerical value of Kull-i-Shay' is 361.
See also calendar, Bahá'í.

L

láhút [Ar] Divinity; the inward or eternal aspect of reality.
See also násút.

Land of Mystery Adrianople.

language, universal auxiliary The establishment of an international language to be taught in all the schools of the world, in addition to the native tongue, is ordained by Bahá'u'lláh in the *Kitáb-i-Aqdas* and mentioned in various Tablets. Its achievement, Bahá'u'lláh has stated, would be one of the signs of the 'coming of age of the human race'.[1] 'We have enjoined upon the Trustees of the House of Justice either to choose one language from among those now existing or to adopt a new one, and in like manner to select a common script, both of which should be taught in all the schools of the world. Thus will the earth be regarded as one country and one home.'[2]

Law of God Commandments of God revealed by the Manifestations. There are two degrees of law: eternal laws, spiritual in nature, which never alter, such as the law requiring man to acknowledge and worship God, and the laws of unity, harmony and attraction; and social laws particular to the Dispensation, such as the law forbidding the eating of pork in the time of Moses and the laws governing marriage in the Dispensation of Bahá'u'lláh. Both are divine in origin and must be obeyed, but succeeding Manifestations may change or modify the social laws espoused by previous Manifestations.

lawḥ *See* Tablet.

Laylí In a Persian folktale, the beloved of Majnún, the classic loved one. Bahá'u'lláh uses the story of Laylí and Majnún as a symbol for the search of the true seeker for God and His Manifestation.

leaf (varaqih) A designation given by Bahá'u'lláh to the women of His family, but in some cases bestowed on persons not related to Him.
See also Bahíyyih Khánum *and* Navváb.

learned, the The appointed branch of the Bahá'í Administrative Order: 'Blessed are the rulers and the learned among the people of Bahá. They are My trustees among My servants and the manifestations of My commandments amidst My people.'[3]

The Institution of the 'learned' includes the Hands of the Cause, the Continental Boards of Counsellors and the Auxiliary Boards and their assistants. The function of the 'learned' within the Bahá'í Administrative Order is advisory and inspirational, in contrast to that of the elected branch, the 'rulers'. The members of this institution are appointed and function as individuals rather than as a body.

Lesser Peace *See* Peace, Great.

Lesser Plan of God *See* Minor Plan of God.

Letters of the Living (Ḥurúf-i-Ḥayy) The first eighteen followers of the Báb who independently searched for and found the Báb and became believers in His revelation. 'Ḥayy', meaning 'living', is numerically equal to eighteen. These eighteen are:

Mullá Ḥusayn-i-Bushrú'í
Muḥammad Ḥasan-i-Bushrú'í
Muḥammad-Báqir-i-Bushrú'í
Mullá 'Alíy-i-Basṭámí
Mullá Khudá-Bakhsh-i-Qúchání (later named Mullá 'Alí)
Mullá Ḥasan-i-Bajistání
Siyyid Ḥusayn-i-Yazdí
Mírzá Muḥammad Rawḍih-Khán-i-Yazdí
Sa'íd-i-Hindí
Mullá Maḥmúd-i-Khu'í
Mullá Jalíl-i-Urúmí
Mullá Aḥmad-i-Ibdál-i-Marághi'í
Mullá Báqir-i-Tabrízí
Mullá Yúsuf-i-Ardibílí
Mírzá Hádí
Mírzá Muḥammad-'Alíy-i-Qazvíní
Ṭáhirih
Quddús

liberty Freedom from constraint, the power to do as one pleases.
Bahá'u'lláh condemns the idea of absolute liberty for man. Freedom can only be exercised within the limits of the law, ultimately the law of God. 'Liberty must, in the end, lead to sedition, whose flames none can quench . . . That which beseemeth man is submission unto such restraints as will protect him from his own ignorance and guard him against the harm of the mischief-maker . . . True liberty consisteth in man's submission unto My commandments . . . Were men to observe that which We have sent down unto them from the Heaven of Revelation, they would, of a certainty, attain unto perfect liberty.'[4]

lifeblood of the Cause The Bahá'í funds.

Livá [Pers] Banner. Name given by 'Abdu'l-Bahá to Lua Getsinger.
See also Getsinger, Lua.

local spiritual assembly The local administrative body of the Bahá'í community. The nine members are directly elected from among the body of the believers in a community every Riḍván and serve for a period of one year. All adult believers in a given community are eligible for election to the local spiritual assembly. The assembly elects its own officers for the year and meets as often as it sees necessary. The local assembly oversees the teaching and other work of the Bahá'í community, conducts marriages and funerals, provides for the Bahá'í education of the children in its community, ensures the holding of the Bahá'í Holy Days and the Nineteen Day Feasts, and provides advice, guidance and assistance for those in difficulty. All its decisions are made after consultation.

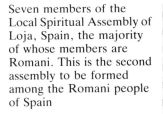

Seven members of the Local Spiritual Assembly of Loja, Spain, the majority of whose members are Romani. This is the second assembly to be formed among the Romani people of Spain

Six members of the Local Spiritual Assembly of Chusmiza, in the northern highlands of Chile. This is the first local assembly to be formed among the Aymara people of Chile

Bahá'u'lláh called for the creation of local spiritual assemblies in the *Kitáb-i-Aqdas*: 'The Lord hath ordained that in every city a House of Justice be established wherein shall gather counsellors to the number of Bahá (9) . . .'[5] The Local House of Justice is presently called the local spiritual assembly, but it is clear that the two institutions are the same: '. . . the Spiritual Assemblies of today will be replaced in time by the Houses of Justice, and are to all intents and purposes identical and not separate bodies . . .'[6] 'For reasons which are not difficult to discover, it has been found advisable to bestow upon the elected representatives of Bahá'í communities throughout the world the temporary appellation of Spiritual Assemblies . . .'[7]

Shoghi Effendi has characterized the local spiritual assemblies thus: 'instituted, without any exception, in every city, town, and village where nine or more adult believers are resident; annually and directly elected, on the first day of the greatest Bahá'í Festival [Riḍván] by all adult believers, man and woman alike; invested with an authority rendering them unanswerable for their acts and decisions to those who elect them; solemnly pledged to follow, under all conditions, the dictates of the "Most Great Justice" . . . charged with the responsibility of promoting at all times the best interests of the communities within their jurisdiction, of familiarizing them with their plans and activities, and of inviting them to offer any recommendations they might wish to make . . . supported by local funds to which all believers voluntarily contribute . . .'[8]

See also consultation, elections, House of Justice *and* national spiritual assembly.

Lord of the Age A title of the Imám Mahdí, whom Bahá'ís believe to be the Báb.

Lord of Hosts Bahá'u'lláh. 'Abdu'l-Bahá writes: 'The blessed Person of the Promised One is interpreted in the Holy Book as the Lord of Hosts – the heavenly armies. By heavenly armies those souls are intended who are entirely freed from the human world, transformed into celestial spirits and have become divine angels.'[9]

Lote Tree, Divine *See* Sadratu'l-Muntahá.

love The power of attraction, of magnetism.

Mankind was created through the love of God: 'Veiled in My immemorial being and in the ancient eternity of My essence, I knew My love for thee; therefore I created thee, have engraved on thee Mine image and revealed to Thee My beauty.'[10] 'I loved thy creation, hence I created thee.'[11]

All creation is based on love, on the attraction of atomic particles. Each level of creation – mineral, vegetable, animal and human – manifests this quality of cohesion, which 'Abdu'l-Bahá equates with love: 'The cause of the creation of the phenomenal world is love. All the Prophets have promulgated the law of love.'[12] '. . . the axis around which life revolves is love . . . if attraction did not exist between the atoms, the composite substance of matter would not be possible . . . This stone is the lowest degree of phenomena, but nevertheless within it a power of attraction is manifest without which the stone could not exist. This power of attraction in the mineral world is love, the only expression of love the stone can manifest.'[13]

Love is a divine attribute: 'That which is acceptable in the sight of God is love. Love is, in reality, the first effulgence of Divinity and the greatest splendour of God.'[14] 'The attributes of God are love and mercy . . . Wherever love is witnessed, know that there is a manifestation of God's mercy . . .'[15]

Man must love God and love others: 'Love Me, that I may love thee. If thou lovest Me not, My love can in no wise reach thee.'[16] 'In the garden of thy heart plant naught but the rose of love . . .'[17] 'Just as God loves all and is kind to all, so we must really love and be kind to everybody . . . We must strive day and night that love and amity may increase . . .'[18]

'Abdu'l-Bahá describes four kinds of love: 'The love of God towards the identity of God . . . The love of God for His children – for His servants. The love of man for God and the love of man for man. These four kinds of love originate from God.'[19]

M

madrisih [Ar] School, especially a religious school or seminary.

Máh-Kú (Mákú) Four-towered fortress near a village of the same name in northwestern Á<u>dh</u>arbáyján in which the Báb was imprisoned for nine months and named by Him Jabal-i-Basíṭ (the Open Mountain). Shoghi Effendi writes, 'No more than one companion and one attendant from among his followers were allowed to keep Him company in those bleak and inhospitable surroundings . . . So grievous was His plight while in that fortress that, in the Persian Bayán, He Himself has stated that at night-time He did not even have a lighted lamp, and that His solitary chamber, constructed of sun-baked bricks, lacked even a door, while, in His Tablet to Muḥammad <u>Sh</u>áh, He has complained that the inmates of the fortress were confined to two guards and four dogs.'[1]

See also <u>Ch</u>ihríq.

The Prison at Máh-Kú. The castle is at the base of the overhanging rock above the village

Maiden of Heaven (ḥúrí, or houri; literally, white one). A houri, according to Islam one of the maidens dwelling in Paradise who would consort with the souls of the blessed.

In Bahá'u'lláh's writings the houri, often described as clothed in white, is used as a symbol of the Spirit of God, a personification of the Spirit which descended upon Bahá'u'lláh. It was in the Síyáh-<u>Ch</u>ál prison in Ṭihrán that the Holy Spirit first appeared to Him in the form of a maiden: 'While engulfed in tribulations I heard a most wondrous, a most sweet voice, calling above My head. Turning My face, I beheld a Maiden – the embodiment of the remembrance of the name of My Lord – suspended in the air before Me. So rejoiced was she in her very soul that her countenance shone with the ornament of the good-pleasure of

God, and her cheeks glowed with the brightness of the All-Merciful. Betwixt earth and heaven she was raising a call which captivated the hearts and minds of men. She was imparting to both My inward and outer being tidings which rejoiced My soul, and the souls of God's honoured servants. Pointing with her finger unto My head, she addressed all who are in heaven and all who are on earth, saying: "By God! This is the Best-Beloved of the worlds, and yet ye comprehend not. This is the Beauty of God amongst you, and the power of His sovereignty within you, could ye but understand. This is the Mystery of God and His Treasure, the Cause of God and His glory unto all who are in the kingdoms of Revelation and of creation, if ye be of them that perceive."'[2]

See also Holy Spirit.

Majnún Insane. Name of the classical Persian lover who searches for his beloved Laylí. Bahá'u'lláh uses the symbol of Laylí and Majnún to demonstrate the patience and thoroughness the seeker must have when searching for God and His Manifestation.

See also Laylí.

Major Plan of God *See* Greater Plan of God.

malakút [Ar] Angelic realm.

Man-Yuẓhiruhu'lláh [Ar] Him Whom God Shall Make Manifest. The title given by the Báb to the Promised One Whose advent was imminent (Bahá'u'lláh).

Manifestation of God The great Prophets of God, His chosen Messengers, who appear in each age: 'He . . . hath caused those luminous Gems of Holiness to appear out of the realm of the spirit, in the noble form of the human temple, and be made manifest unto all men, that they may impart unto the world the mysteries of the unchangeable Being and tell of the subtleties of His imperishable Essence . . . All the Prophets of God, His well-favoured, His holy and chosen Messengers are, without exception, the bearers of His names and the embodiments of His attributes . . .'[3]

The Manifestations of God are not God descended to earth, but are rather perfect reflections of His attributes, just as a mirror reflects the sun but is not the sun itself: 'These Tabernacles of Holiness, these primal Mirrors which reflect the Light of unfading glory, are but expressions of Him Who is the Invisible of Invisibles.'[4] 'These sanctified Mirrors . . . are one and all the exponents on earth of Him Who is the central Orb of the universe, its essence and ultimate purpose. From

Him proceed their knowledge and power; from Him is derived their sovereignty. The beauty of their countenance is but a reflection of His image, and their revelation a sign of His deathless glory.'[5]

All the Manifestations have the same spirit, although their outward forms are different and they manifest different attributes of God relevant to the needs and circumstances of the age in which they appear: 'Inasmuch as these Birds of the celestial Throne are all sent down from the heaven of the Will of God, and as they all arise to proclaim His irresistible Faith, they therefore are regarded as one soul and the same person . . . They all abide in the same tabernacle, soar in the same heaven, are seated upon the same throne, utter the same speech, and proclaim the same Faith . . . They only differ in the intensity of their revelation and the comparative potency of their light . . . That a certain attribute of God hath not been outwardly manifested by these Essences of Detachment doth in no wise imply that they Who are the Day-Springs of God's attributes and the Treasuries of His holy names did not actually possess it.'[6]

The Bahá'í Writings identify several Manifestations, among them Abraham, Noah, Buddha, Zoroaster, Christ, Moses, Muḥammad, the Báb and Bahá'u'lláh. The Hindu figure of Krishna is also considered a Manifestation, although not much is known about Him. In the *Kitáb-i-Íqán* Bahá'u'lláh mentions other Prophets, such as Húd and Ṣáliḥ. Bahá'ís believe there have been other Manifestations but that there is no record of their names.[7]

Bahá'u'lláh has stated that another Manifestation will not arise before the lapse of a thousand years.

marḥabá [Ar] Exclamation used in the same sense as 'well done' or 'bravo!'

Marie, Queen (1875–1938) Queen of Rumania from 1914 to 1927, queen dowager from 1927 to 1938. Granddaughter of Queen Victoria, she was the first crowned head to be a supporter of the Bahá'í Faith. She learned of the Bahá'í Faith through Martha Root.

Queen Marie of Rumania

marriage According to the *Kitáb-i-Aqdas*, marriage is 'highly recommended but not obligatory'.[8] Plurality of wives is forbidden, both partners must be at least fifteen years of age and both parties must consent, as well as their parents. Bahá'ís must be married in a Bahá'í ceremony, witnessed by two representatives of a spiritual assembly. The only requirement for the Bahá'í ceremony is the recitation by bride and groom of the following verse which constitutes the Bahá'í marriage vow: 'We will all, verily, abide by the Will of God.'[9] The engagement period must not exceed ninety-five days. The *Kitáb-i-Aqdas* also specifies the payment of a dowry to be given by the man to the woman, but at present the provisions of the law relating to the engagement period and dowry are applied only to Iranians.

Back row Two Bahá'í couples on the occasion of their marriage on Tanna Island, Vanuatu, in January 1987. *Front row* The two witnesses to the marriage

When one partner is not a Bahá'í it is permissible to participate in the ceremony of another faith as long as it does not involve a declaration of faith in another religion and as long as the ceremony occurs in the same twenty-four-hour period as the Bahá'í ceremony.[10]

Bahá'u'lláh writes: 'And when He desired to manifest grace and beneficence to men, and to set the world in order, He revealed observances and created laws; among them He established the law of marriage, made it as a fortress for well-being and salvation, and

The first Bahá'í wedding in Kyushu, Japan

enjoined it upon us in that which was sent down out of the heaven of sanctity in His Most Holy Book. He saith, great is His glory: "Marry, O people, that from you may appear he who will remember Me amongst My servants; this is one of My commandments unto you; obey it as an assistance to yourselves."'[11]

'Abdu'l-Bahá described the nature of Bahá'í marriage: 'Bahá'í marriage is the commitment of the two parties one to the other, and their mutual attachment of mind and heart. Each must, however, exercise the utmost care to become thoroughly acquainted with the character of the other, that the binding covenant between them may be a tie that will endure forever. Their purpose must be this: to become loving companions and comrades and at one with each other for time and eternity . . . The true marriage of Bahá'ís is this, that the husband and wife should be united both physically and spiritually, that they may ever improve the spiritual life of each other, and may enjoy everlasting unity throughout all the worlds of God. This is Bahá'í marriage.'[12]

See also divorce *and* year of waiting.

martyr Originally (in both English and Arabic), witness: one who bears witness to a belief by submitting to death rather than renouncing one's faith.

The first martyr of the Bahá'í era was Mullá 'Alíy-i-Basṭámí. He was followed by, in the words of Shoghi Effendi, 'no less than twenty thousand martyrs' who gave their lives in the early days of the Bahá'í Era and who continue to do so to this day.

The designation of martyr has occasionally been given to others who have sacrificed their lives for the Faith, though not through death.

See also martyrdom.

martyrdom The giving up of one's life for the Cause of God.

In one of His Tablets Bahá'u'lláh explains that 'martyrdom is not confined to the shedding of blood', that it is possible to live and still be counted as a martyr in the sight of God.[13] After the martyrdom of Badí' Bahá'u'lláh advised the believers not to volunteer to give their lives: as Adib Taherzadeh notes, 'martyrdom in the path of God is undoubtedly the greatest bounty provided it takes place through circumstances beyond one's control'.[14] Bahá'u'lláh has further ordained that teaching the Cause is as meritorious as dying for the Cause.

Martyrdom of the Báb Bahá'í Holy Day observed on 9 July commemorating the day the Báb was martyred in the barracks square of Tabríz in 1850.

When Mírzá Taqí Khán, Grand Vizier of Náṣiri'd-Dín Sháh, found he was unable to stamp out the Bábí Faith, he determined to put the Báb to death. The Báb was taken to Tabríz and the Armenian regiment of Urúmíyyih, commanded by the Christian colonel Sám Khán, was ordered to carry out the execution. When the smoke cleared after the 750 rifles had fired, the Báb was nowhere to be seen and His companion, Mírzá Muḥammad 'Alí, was standing unharmed. The bullets had only cut the ropes that bound them. The Báb was found in the room He had occupied the night before, continuing a conversation with His amanuensis which had been interrupted. Sám Khán refused to carry out the execution a second time and ordered his regiment to leave the barracks. The colonel of the bodyguard, Áqá Ján Khán-i-Khamsih, volunteered to carry out the order and this time the bullets of his Náṣirí regiment killed the Báb. The anniversary of the Martyrdom of the Báb is observed at noon on 9 July. Work is suspended on this Holy Day.

See also Sám Khán.

The barracks square in Tabríz where the Báb was martyred. The spot where He and His disciple Anís were suspended before the firing squad is marked with an 'x'

Masá'il [Ar] Questions. The fifteenth month of the Bahá'í year (from sunset 11 December to sunset 30 December).

Mas<u>h</u>had (literally, place of martyrdom) Capital of <u>Kh</u>urásán, Iran, and shrine city of the Imám Riḍá, the eighth Imám.

Mas<u>h</u>íyyat [Ar] Will. The eleventh month of the Bahá'í year (from sunset 26 September to sunset 15 October).

Mas<u>h</u>riqu'l-A<u>dh</u>kár [Ar] Dawning-place of the praises or remembrances or mention of God. Generally, the Bahá'í House of Worship or Temple and the dependencies clustered around it.

Bahá'í Houses of Worship (Mas<u>h</u>riqu'l-A<u>dh</u>kár)

Wilmette, Illinois, USA

Kampala, Uganda

Frankfurt, Germany

Sydney, Australia

In the *Kitáb-i-Aqdas* Bahá'u'lláh reveals: 'Blessed is he who directeth his steps towards the Mashriqu'l-Adhkár at the hour of dawn, communing with Him, attuned to His remembrance, imploring His forgiveness. And having entered therein, let him sit in silence to hearken unto the verses of God . . . the Mashriqu'l-Adhkár is in truth any House raised in towns or villages, for mention of Me.'[15]

The term Mashriqu'l-Adhkár is used primarily to refer to buildings which conform to particular architectural requirements and which are reserved for devotions and reading from the revealed Word of God. However, the term Mashriqu'l-Adhkár is also used to refer to any building or room which is reserved for devotions; devotional meetings, particularly dawn prayers; and the heart of the sincere worshipper.[16]

Samoa

Panama

The Mashriqu'l-Adhkár is a nine-sided building surmounted by a dome. 'Abdu'l-Bahá delineated its general design: 'It has nine avenues, nine gardens, nine fountains, so it is nine on nine, all nines. . . . That is the way it should be.'[17] Bahá'u'lláh has forbidden the display of pictures or statues within its walls and the use of musical instruments. Only the human voice may be used to sing, chant or read the Word of God in the House of Worship.

New Delhi, India

'Abdu'l-Bahá stated that the House of Worship is 'also connected with a hospital, a drug dispensary, a travellers' hospice, a school for orphans, and a university for advanced studies. Every Mashriqu'l-Adhkár is connected with these five things.'[18]

Shoghi Effendi writes, 'From the Mashriqu'l-Adhkár . . . the representatives of Bahá'í communities, both local and national, together with the members of their respective committees, will as they gather daily within its walls at the hour of dawn, derive the necessary inspiration that will enable them to discharge . . . their duties and responsibilities . . .'[19]

masjid [Ar] (Literally, place of prostration) Mosque.

Master, the A title given by Bahá'u'lláh specially to 'Abdu'l-Bahá.
See also áqá.

materialism Excessive attachment to material goods and possessions; a preoccupation with material things: the belief that the highest values lie in material well-being.

Shoghi Effendi has stated that the world is 'enervated by a rampant and brutal materialism'.[20] 'The materialistic civilization of our age has so much absorbed the energy and interest of mankind that people in general do no longer feel the necessity of raising themselves above the forces and conditions of their daily material existence . . . The universal crisis affecting mankind is, therefore, essentially spiritual in its causes.'[21]

One of the primary evils of our world today is the 'crass materialism, which lays excessive and ever-increasing emphasis on material well-being, forgetful of those things of the spirit on which alone a sure and stable foundation can be laid for human society. It is this same cancerous materialism . . . which Bahá'u'lláh in unequivocal and emphatic language denounced in His Writings, comparing it to a devouring flame . . .'[22]

The Master
'Abdu'l-Bahá

maturity, age of The minimum age at which a person is expected to obey the laws of the *Kitáb-i-Aqdas* in regard to prayer, fasting, marriage, etc. Bahá'u'lláh has set this age at fifteen. Shoghi Effendi has explained that it does not apply to administrative functions, such as voting and serving on spiritual assemblies, the minimum age for which is, at present, set at twenty-one.

Children of Bahá'í parents under the age of fifteen are considered to be Bahá'ís and should observe the Bahá'í Holy Days, not attending school on these days if it can be arranged. A person may declare his belief in Bahá'u'lláh at any age; it is not necessary to wait until the age of fifteen. Some national assemblies require children to wait until they reach fifteen before enrolling in the Faith but this is not universal.
See also declaration *and* enrolment.

Maxwell, May Bolles Born in Englewood, New Jersey, USA, in January 1870. She heard of the Faith from Lua Getsinger while in Paris and was among the first party of Western pilgrims to meet 'Abdu'l-Bahá in 1898–9. 'Abdu'l-Bahá instructed her to remain in Paris and teach the Faith there. This she did, making Paris the first Bahá'í centre on the European continent. In 1902 she married Sutherland Maxwell, the architect of the Shrine of the Báb.

The Blue Mosque, Istanbul

May Maxwell served the Faith selflessly for forty years as a teacher and administrator. In 1940 she responded to an appeal of the Guardian for pioneers to go to South America and went to Buenos Aires where she died shortly after her arrival. Shoghi Effendi elevated her to the rank of a martyr on her death.

May Maxwell is the mother of Amatu'l-Bahá Rúḥíyyih Kh͟ánum.

maydán [Pers] Square, open place in a town or city.

Mázindarán Province in the north of Iran, bordering on the Caspian Sea. The ancestral home of Bahá'u'lláh is in Mázindarán.

May Maxwell

Mázindarán

The mansion of Mazra'ih at the turn of the century (Getsinger, early 1920s)

Mazra'ih (literally, farm) The country house or summer mansion at Mazra'ih, four miles north of 'Akká, once belonging to 'Abdu'lláh Páshá, which 'Abdu'l-Bahá rented and prepared for Bahá'u'lláh. It took the repeated pleadings of Shaykh 'Alíy-i-Mírí, the Muftí of 'Akká, to persuade Bahá'u'lláh, who was still technically a prisoner in the city of 'Akká, to take up residence at Mazra'ih in June 1877. Bahá'u'lláh lived there for two years, after which He moved to the Mansion of Bahjí.

meditation Quiet reflection, especially on a passage of Sacred Scripture: 'Do thou meditate on that which We have revealed unto thee,' writes Bahá'u'lláh, 'that thou mayest discover the purpose of God, thy Lord, and the Lord of all worlds. In these words the mysteries of Divine Wisdom have been treasured.'[23]

'Meditation is the key for opening the doors of mysteries,' 'Abdu'l-Bahá has said. '. . . in that state man withdraws himself from all outside objects; in that subjective mood he is immersed in the ocean of spiritual life and can unfold the secrets of things-in-themselves.'[24]

'The meditative faculty is akin to the mirror; if you put it before earthly objects it will reflect them . . . But if you turn the mirror of your spirits heavenwards, the heavenly constellations and the rays of the Sun of Reality will be reflected in your hearts, and the virtues of the Kingdom will be obtained.'[25]

There is no set form of meditation in the Bahá'í Writings and the manner of meditating is left entirely to the individual. Shoghi Effendi, in a letter written on his behalf, advised that 'it would be wiser for the Bahá'ís to use the Meditations given by Bahá'u'lláh, and not any set form of meditation recommended by someone else.'[26] Although individuals are free to seek 'their own level of communion with God' through the practice of meditation, they should 'guard against superstitious or foolish ideas creeping into it'.[27]

Messenger of God *See* Manifestation of God.

Mihdí (also, Mahdí) The Guided One. The Twelfth Imám, or Qá'im.

Mihdí, Mírzá The son of Bahá'u'lláh, surnamed by Him 'the Purest Branch', born in 1848. He accompanied His Father into exile and served Him as an amanuensis. In 1870, in the Most Great Prison in 'Akká, Mírzá Mihdí was pacing the roof, wrapped in devotions, when he fell through a skylight. Mortally wounded, his dying wish to his Father was that his life might be a ransom for those who were prevented from attaining Bahá'u'lláh's presence. In a prayer revealed by Bahá'u'lláh in Mírzá Mihdí's memory, Bahá'u'lláh speaks of the sacrifice of His son: 'I have, O my Lord, offered up that which Thou hast given Me, that Thy servants may be quickened, and all that dwell on earth be united.'[28]

Mírzá Mihdí, the Purest Branch

In another Tablet Bahá'u'lláh reveals: 'Blessed art thou, and blessed he that turneth unto thee, and visiteth thy grave, and draweth nigh, through thee, unto God . . . Thou art, verily, the trust of God and His treasure in this land. Erelong will God reveal through thee that which He hath desired . . . When thou wast laid to rest in the earth, the earth itself trembled in its longing to meet thee . . . Were we to recount the mysteries of thine ascension, they that are asleep would waken, and all beings would be set ablaze with the fire of the remembrance of My Name, the Mighty, the Loving.'[29]

Mírzá Mihdí was buried outside the city walls near a local shrine, but in 1939 Shoghi Effendi transferred his remains to the Monument Gardens on Mount Carmel near the Shrine of the Báb.

miḥráb [Ar] Prayer niche in a mosque showing the direction of Mecca. The imám leads the prayer from the mihráb.

Mi<u>sh</u>kín-Qalam

mind That which in the individual feels, thinks, perceives, wills and reasons.

'Abdu'l-Bahá has said that the 'human spirit which distinguishes man from the animal is the rational soul; and these two names – the human spirit and the rational soul – designate one thing . . . the mind is the power of the human spirit. Spirit is the lamp; mind is the light which shines from the lamp. Spirit is the tree, and mind is the fruit. Mind is the perfection of the spirit, and its essential quality, as the sun's rays are the essential necessity of the sun.'[30]

Minor Plan of God That process which will 'breathe life' into the unified body of mankind brought about by the Major Plan of God. 'The second process, the task of breathing life into this unified body – of creating true unity and spirituality culminating in the Most Great Peace – is that of the Bahá'ís, who are labouring consciously . . . to erect the fabric of the Kingdom of God on earth . . . The working out of God's Major Plan proceeds mysteriously in ways directed by Him alone, but the minor Plan that He has given us to execute, as our part in His grand design for the redemption of mankind, is clearly delineated.'[31] The teaching plans of Shoghi Effendi and the Universal House of Justice are the guidelines for the Minor Plan.

See also Greater Plan of God.

miracles Occurrences and events for which there is no apparent scientific explanation and which may indicate the intervention of God.

Bahá'ís do not deny the possibility of miracles occurring but believe that they are valuable proofs of the Manifestation of God only for those who witness them. What is more important is the inner significance of the miracle, its spiritual meaning. 'Abdu'l-Bahá states that Bahá'u'lláh performed numerous miracles and supernatural acts[32] and that all the Manifestations are able to perform them.[33] For Bahá'ís, however, the greatest miracle of the Manifestation is that He changes the hearts of people and creates a new civilization merely through the influence of His word.

Mi'ráj [Ar] The Ascent of Muḥammad, the mystic vision of His night journey in which He was transported from Mecca to Jerusalem and shown the signs of God.

mírzá [Pers] (from Amír-Zádih, 'son of a prince') A title which when placed before a name means 'Mister' and when placed after a name means 'prince'.

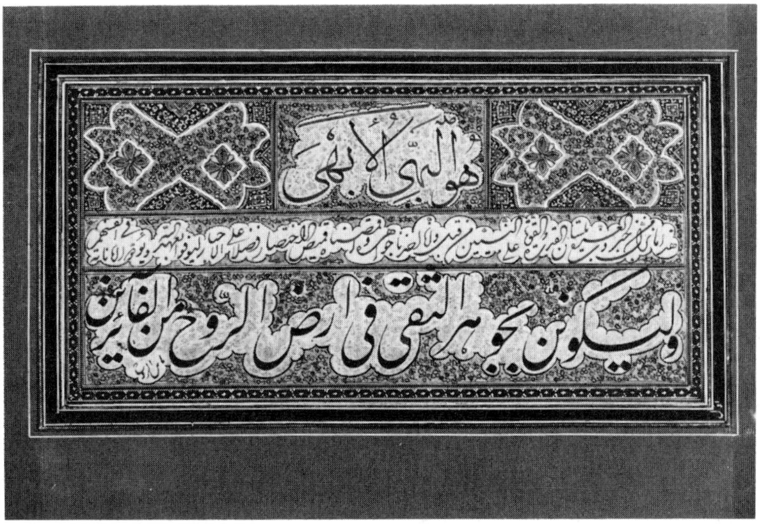

Calligraphy of Mishkín-Qalam

Mishkín-Qalam Musk-scented pen. Name by which Áqá Ḥusayn-i-Iṣfahání, a calligrapher of the first rank, was known. He first heard of the Faith in Iṣfáhán, but it was in Baghdád that he learned more about it. In Adrianople he met Bahá'u'lláh and became His follower. When Bahá'u'lláh and His companions were exiled to 'Akká, Mishkín-Qalam was sent to Cyprus. He was eventually freed and came to the Holy Land in 1886. After travelling in Egypt, Damascus and India, 'Abdu'l-Bahá asked him to come back to the Holy Land, where he passed away in about 1912.

It is Mishkín-Qalam's calligraphic rendering of the Greatest Name which Bahá'ís most commonly use as its symbol.

mi<u>th</u>qál A unit of weight used in Islamic countries for weighing gold and silver. It derives originally from the Roman unit of gold coinage. It is specified by the Báb and by Bahá'u'lláh in the *Kitáb-i-Aqdas* as the unit for determining certain required payments of gold and silver, including the dowry and Ḥuqúqu'lláh, and is set at a little over 3.5 grammes.

See also dowry *and* Ḥuqúqu'lláh.

months, Bahá'í The names of the months in the Bahá'í (Badi') calendar were given by the Báb, who drew them from the nineteen names of God invoked in a prayer said during the month of fasting in <u>Sh</u>í'ih Islam. They are

1	Bahá	Splendour	21 March – 8 April
2	Jalál	Glory	9 April – 27 April
3	Jamál	Beauty	28 April – 16 May
4	'Aẓamat	Grandeur	17 May – 4 June
5	Núr	Light	5 June – 23 June
6	Raḥmat	Mercy	24 June – 12 July
7	Kalimát	Words	13 July – 31 July
8	Kamál	Perfection	1 August – 19 August
9	Asmá'	Names	20 August – 7 September
10	'Izzat	Might	8 September – 26 September
11	Ma<u>sh</u>íyyat	Will	27 September – 15 October
12	'Ilm	Knowledge	16 October – 3 November
13	Qudrat	Power	4 November – 22 November
14	Qawl	Speech	23 November – 11 December
15	Masá'il	Questions	12 December – 30 December
16	<u>Sh</u>araf	Honour	31 December – 18 January
17	Sulṭán	Sovereignty	19 January – 6 February
18	Mulk	Dominion	7 February – 25 February
19	'Alá'	Loftiness	2 March – 20 March

Each of the days of the month is also given the name of one of the attributes of God. The names are the same as those of the nineteen months; thus, Naw-Rúz, the first day of the first month, would be considered the 'day of Bahá, of the month Bahá'. If it fell on a

Saturday, the first day of the Bahá'í week, it would also be the 'day of Jalál'.

See also calendar, Bahá'í; days of the week *and* years.

Monument Gardens Beautifully landscaped gardens in the vicinity of the Shrine of the Báb where beneath befitting monuments are buried the Greatest Holy Leaf, Navváb, the Purest Branch and the Holy Mother.

The Monument Gardens

Far right Twin tombs of the Purest Branch and his mother, Navváb

Tomb of the Greatest Holy Leaf

Tomb of Munírih Khánum

Moses Prophet of Judaism, born in Egypt, who led the people of Israel out of slavery to the Promised Land, and to whom, on Mount Sinai, God gave the Ten Commandments. Bahá'ís accept Moses as a Manifestation of God. In the Bahá'í Writings Moses is sometimes referred to as 'He Who conversed with God'.

The most challenging issue: racial prejudice must be overcome if world peace is to be established

most challenging issue, the Racial prejudice. In a letter written to the North American Bahá'ís in 1938 Shoghi Effendi identified it as 'the most vital and challenging issue confronting the Bahá'í community at the present stage of its evolution. The ceaseless exertions which this issue of paramount importance calls for, the sacrifices it must impose, the care and vigilance it demands, the moral courage and fortitude it requires, the tact and sympathy it necessitates, invest this problem, which the American believers are still far from having satisfactorily resolved, with an urgency and importance that cannot be overestimated.'[34]

'Freedom from racial prejudice, in any of its forms,' he further stated, 'should . . . be adopted as the watchword of the entire body of the American believers . . . It should be consistently demonstrated in every phase of their activity and life . . .'[35]

See also prejudice, elimination of all forms of.

Most Exalted Leaf A title given by Bahá'u'lláh to His wife Ásíyih Khánum and His daughter Bahíyyih Khánum, who is known in English as the Greatest Holy Leaf.

See also Bahíyyih Khánum *and* Navváb.

Most Great Branch (Ghuṣn-i-A'ẓam) A title given by Bahá'u'lláh to 'Abdu'l-Bahá in the *Kitáb-i-'Ahdí*. In the Tablet of the Branch (*Súriy-i-Ghuṣn*), Bahá'u'lláh describes the station of 'Abdu'l-Bahá in relation to Himself.

See also Tablet of the Branch.

Most Great House, the *See* House of Bahá'u'lláh in Baghdád.

Most Great Infallibility *See* infallibility.

Most Great Name *See* Greatest Name.

Most Great Peace *See* Peace, Most Great.

Most Great Prison The prison at 'Akká. Bahá'u'lláh has written: 'Know thou, that upon Our arrival at this Spot, We chose to designate it as the "Most Great Prison".'[36]

Most Holy Book *See Kitáb-i-Aqdas.*

Mother Book The archetype of the Holy Scriptures, the source of the revelation. In Islam, it is the original copy of the Book with Alláh in heaven, from which the revelations of the Qur'án come. The Mother Book of the Bábí Dispensation is the Persian *Bayán*; the Mother Book of the Bahá'í Dispensation is the *Kitáb-i-Aqdas*.[37]

Mother Temple The first Bahá'í House of Worship to be built in a particular geographical area. For example, the Temple in Wilmette, Illinois, USA, is the 'Mother Temple of the West' and the one near Frankfurt, Germany, is the 'Mother Temple of Europe'.

The Most Great Prison. The northwest building of the 'Akká prison complex seen from the inner moat. The two windows on the far right of the upper storey are in the cell of Bahá'u'lláh

mu'a<u>dh</u><u>dh</u>in [Ar] Muezzin; in Islam, the one who calls the faithful to prayer.

muftí In Sunní Islam, a consulting canon lawyer, who delivers legal opinions on points of Islamic law to the qáḍí (judge).

Muḥammad The Prophet-Founder of the religion of Islam, Muḥammad was born circa 570 AD in Mecca and died in 632 in Medina. His revelation is contained in the Qur'án. Bahá'ís accept Muḥammad as a Manifestation of God. As the 'Seal of the Prophets', Muḥammad's references to the 'Great Announcement', 'Day of Judgement' and Day on which 'thy Lord shall come and the angels rank on rank' refer to the coming of Bahá'u'lláh. In the Bahá'í Writings Muḥammad is sometimes referred to as the 'Friend of God' and 'the Apostle'.

Muḥammad, Ḥájí Mírzá Siyyid One of the maternal uncles of the Báb. It was in answer to his questions that Bahá'u'lláh revealed the *Kitáb-i-Íqán*. Ḥájí Mírzá Siyyid Muḥammad had not been entirely convinced that his nephew was the Promised Qá'im and, during a visit to Ba<u>gh</u>dád, asked Bahá'u'lláh to clarify how the traditions and prophecies were fulfilled by the Báb. Bahá'u'lláh told him to make a list of his questions. In the next two days and nights Bahá'u'lláh revealed the *Kitáb-i-Íqán* in answer. His doubts were dispelled, and he acknowledged the truth of both the Báb and Bahá'u'lláh.

Muḥammad-'Alí, Mírzá A son of Bahá'u'lláh and half-brother of 'Abdu'l-Bahá who became the Arch-Breaker of Bahá'u'lláh's Covenant.

Bahá'u'lláh had given Muḥammad-'Alí, called the 'Greater Branch' (<u>Gh</u>uṣn-i-Akbar), a rank second to 'Abdu'l-Bahá, but after Bahá'u'lláh's Will was read, the jealous Muḥammad-'Alí tried to discredit and subvert both the Will and its object, 'Abdu'l-Bahá. He began a campaign of lies, calumnies and forgery; he even plotted against 'Abdu'l-Bahá's life and intrigued to have 'Abdu'l-Bahá imprisoned again by the Turkish authorities. Those who followed Muḥammad-'Alí are considered Covenant-breakers. Muḥammad-'Alí died alone and unsupported, repudiated by the Bahá'í community, and was buried by Muslim rites in an unmarked grave.

See also Covenant of Bahá'u'lláh *and Kitáb-i-Ahdí.*

Muḥammad-'Alíy-i-Bárfurú<u>sh</u>í, Ḥájí Mullá *See* Quddús.

Muḥammad-'Alíy-i-Zunúzí Surnamed Anís. The youth who shared martyrdom with the Báb.

See also Martyrdom of the Báb.

Muḥammad-Báqir, Shaykh Named by Bahá'u'lláh 'The Wolf' (Dhi'b), a notorious divine of Iṣfáhán who pronounced the death sentence on two brothers known as the King of Martyrs and the Beloved of Martyrs. Bahá'u'lláh addressed his *Lawḥ-i-Burhán* (Tablet of the Proof) to Shaykh Muḥammad-Báqir. 'The Wolf' died alone and deserted in Iraq in 1884.

See also Muḥammad-Taqíy-i-Najafí, Shaykh.

Muḥammad-Ḥusayn, Mír *See* Raqshá.

Right Shaykh Muḥammad-Báqir

Far right Mírzá Muḥammad-Qulí

Muḥammad-i-Iṣfahání, Siyyid Known as the Antichrist of the Bahá'í Revelation, Siyyid Muḥammad of Iṣfáhán was a Bábí of unsavoury character and personal ambition who induced Mírzá Yaḥyá to oppose Bahá'u'lláh and to claim prophethood for himself. Although an Azalí, Siyyid Muḥammad was included by the Turkish authorities in the group of exiles sent to 'Akká with Bahá'u'lláh. There he continued to agitate and plot against Bahá'u'lláh. When he tried to instigate a mob attack against Bahá'u'lláh's house, seven of the Bahá'í exiles killed him, to the anguish of Bahá'u'lláh. This action placed Bahá'u'lláh in peril and caused Him to be subjected to imprisonment and interrogation.

Muḥammad-Qulí, Mírzá Faithful half-brother of Bahá'u'lláh who shared His exile.

Muḥammad Sh̲áh Sh̲áh of Persia (reigned 1834–48). After putting to death the Grand Vizier, the Qá'im Maqám, who had raised him to the throne (for which act the Sh̲áh was chastised by Bahá'u'lláh in the *Kalimát-i-Firdawsíyyih*), the Sh̲áh raised his tutor Ḥájí Mírzá Áqásí to that office. During his reign he left much of the government in Áqásí's hands, to the extreme detriment of the country.

Muḥammad Sh̲áh sent Siyyid Yaḥyáy-i-Dárábí (later known as Vaḥíd) to investigate the claims of the Báb, whereupon the latter became a fervent Bábí. The Sh̲áh summoned the Báb to the capital but allowed his Grand Vizier to order instead that the Báb be imprisoned in Máh-Kú, thus preventing their meeting. Muḥammad Sh̲áh died in 1848.

Far left Muḥammad Sh̲áh

Left Sh̲ayk̲h̲ Muḥammad-Taqíy-i-Najafí, the Son of the Wolf

Muḥammad-Taqí, Ḥájí Mírza (the Vakílu'd-Dawlih) A cousin of the Báb whom 'Abdu'l-Bahá assigned the task of raising the Mash̲riqu'l-Adh̲kár in 'Ish̲qábád.

Muḥammad-Taqíy-i-Najafí, Sh̲ayk̲h̲ Also known as Áqá Najafí, 'The Son of the Wolf'. Like his father, Sh̲ayk̲h̲ Muḥammad-Báqir, he was a notorious divine and an enemy of the Bahá'í Faith who brought about the persecution and martyrdom of Bahá'ís. Bahá'u'lláh addressed his last book, *Epistle to the Son of the Wolf,* to Sh̲ayk̲h̲ Muḥammad-Taqí. He died in 1914.

See also Muḥammad-Báqir, Sh̲ayk̲h̲ *and* Son of the Wolf.

Muḥammad-i-Zarandí, Mullá *See* Nabíl-i-A'ẓam.

Muḥarram [Ar] The first month of the Muslim year. The first ten days of Muḥarram are observed by Shí'ih Muslims as a period of mourning for the Imáms, ending on the tenth day with the Áshúrá, the commemoration of the martyrdom of the Imám Ḥusayn.

mujtahid Literally, 'one who strives'. In Shí'ih Islam, the highest rank of divine, with the right to make authoritative pronouncements and decisions on points of law in the name of the Hidden Imám.

Mulk Dominion. The eighteenth month of the Bahá'í year (from sunset 6 February to sunset 1 March).

Mullás

mullá Islamic cleric, theologian, judge.

Munírih Khánum The Holy Mother, wife of 'Abdu'l-Bahá. She was the daughter of Mírzá Muḥammad-'Alíy-i-Nahrí by his second wife.

Munírih Khánum

The first wife of Mírzá Muḥammad-'Alí had borne no children, and the second wife was also childless until the Báb intervened. At a banquet in honour of the Báb, the brother of Mírzá Muḥammad-'Alí asked the Báb to intercede on his brother's behalf so that the couple might have a child. The Báb took a portion of his food and directed that it be taken to Mírzá Muḥammad-'Alí and his wife. 'Let them partake of this; their wish will be fulfilled.' In due course a baby daughter was born to the couple, whom they named Fáṭimih. Bahá'u'lláh later on gave her the name Munírih (Illumined).[38] She married 'Abdu'l-Bahá in about 1873 and passed away in 1938.

Mírzá Músá

Far left Munírih Khánum, the Holy Mother

Músá, Mírzá Surnamed Áqáy-i-Kalím, a younger brother of Bahá'u-'lláh who remained devoted and faithful to Bahá'u'lláh and served Him to the end of his life. After the Martyrdom of the Báb, Mírzá Músá, at Bahá'u'lláh's instructions, hid the casket containing the remains of the Báb in the Shrine of Imám-Zádih Ḥasan in Ṭihrán. Mírzá Músá accompanied Bahá'u'lláh into exile and often served as His deputy in meeting with government officials and religious leaders, until 'Abdu'l-Bahá took on this function. Shoghi Effendi designated him one of the Nineteen Apostles of Bahá'u'lláh. Mírzá Músá died in 'Akká in 1887.

Mustagháth He Who Is Invoked. A reference to the appearance of the Promised One at the time specified by the Báb. The Báb had set the limit of time for the coming of the Promised One as Mustagháth, the numerical value of which, in the abjad system, is 2001.

Mystery of God (Sirru'lláh) A title given by Bahá'u'lláh to 'Abdu'l-Bahá. Shoghi Effendi states that this designation '. . . while it does not by any means justify us to assign to him ['Abdu'l-Bahá] the station of Prophethood, indicates how in the person of 'Abdu'l-Bahá the incompatible characteristics of a human nature and superhuman knowledge and perfection have been blended and are completely harmonized.'[39]

Mystery of Mysteries God.

N

Nabíl-i-A'ẓam

Nabíl [Ar] Noble, learned.

Nabíl-i-Akbar Hand of the Cause Muḥammad-i-Qá'iní, whose title was conferred on him by Bahá'u'lláh. Also known as Fáḍil-i-Qá'iní (the Learned One of Qá'in). He was arrested as a Bábí, a charge which he denied. The incident started him thinking, however, and he studied the writings of the Báb and became a believer. He became an eminent mujtahid and met Bahá'u'lláh. At first he did not recognize Bahá'u-'lláh's station, but after listening to a discourse of Bahá'u'lláh, he became a Bahá'í. He taught the Faith widely and was arrested three times. It was to Nabíl-i-Akbar that Bahá'u'lláh's Tablet of Wisdom (*Lawḥ-i-Hikmat*) was addressed. He died in Bukhárá in 1892. 'Abdu'l-Bahá designated him a Hand of the Cause and Shoghi Effendi included him among the Apostles of Bahá'u'lláh.

Nabíl-i-A'ẓam Surname of Mullá Muḥammad-i-Zarandí who wrote the lengthy history of the Faith, *The Dawn-Breakers*. He became a Bábí, and after the martyrdom of the Báb put forward a claim to the leadership of the Bábí community. When he later visited Baghdád, he recognized the station of Bahá'u'lláh and put aside his own claims. From Baghdád and Adrianople he was sent to Iran by Bahá'u'lláh to alert the Bábís of the advent of 'Him Whom God shall make manifest'. On the passing of Bahá'u'lláh he was so overcome with grief that he ended his own life by throwing himself into the sea and drowning.

Najaf Shrine city in Iraq, one of the two holiest shrines for Shí'ihs.

Najíbíyyih *See* Riḍván, Garden of (Najíbíyyih).

Na'mayn *See* Riḍván, Garden of (Na'mayn).

Náṣiri'd-Dín Sh̲áh Sh̲áh of Iran 1848–96. During his reign, and under his orders, the Báb was executed and Bahá'u'lláh was imprisoned and exiled. He vowed to strangle the Faith in Iran. Bahá'u'lláh called him the 'Prince of Oppressors'. He was assassinated on the eve of his jubilee in 1896.

Náṣiri'd-Dín-Sh̲áh

násút [Ar] Humanity; the outward aspect of reality.
See also láhút.

national spiritual assembly The national administrative body of the Bahá'í Faith. 'Abdu'l-Bahá in His Will and Testament wrote: 'in all countries a secondary House of Justice must be instituted, and these secondary Houses of Justice must elect the members of the Universal one.'[1] The secondary House of Justice is for the present called the national spiritual assembly.

Shoghi Effendi has outlined the election, work and responsibilities of the national spiritual assemblies: 'In countries where the local Bahá'í communities had sufficiently advanced in number and in influence measures were taken for the initiation of National Assemblies, the pivots round which all national undertakings must revolve. Designated by 'Abdu'l-Bahá in His Will as the "Secondary House of Justice", they constitute the electoral bodies in the formation of the International House of Justice, and are empowered to direct, unify, coordinate and stimulate the activities of individuals as well as local Assemblies within their jurisdiction. Resting on the broad base of organized local communities, themselves pillars sustaining the institution which must be regarded as the apex of the Bahá'í Administrative Order, these Assemblies are elected, according to the principle of proportional representation, by delegates representative of Bahá'í local communities assembled at Convention during the period of the Riḍván Festival; are possessed of the necessary authority to enable them to insure the harmonious and efficient development of Bahá'í activity within their respective spheres; are freed from all direct responsibility for their policies and decisions to their electorates; are charged with the sacred duty of consulting the views, of inviting the recommendations and of securing the confidence and cooperation of the delegates and of acquainting them with their plans, problems and actions; and are supported by the resources of national funds to which all ranks of the faithful are urged to contribute.'[2]

In 1988 there were 148 national spiritual assemblies.

See also convention, elections, House of Justice *and* local spiritual assembly.

The first National Spiritual Assembly of South West Africa/Namibia

National Spiritual Assembly of the United States, 1953

nationalism Loyalty and devotion to a nation; especially a sense of national consciousness exalting one nation above all others and placing primary emphasis on the promotion of its culture and interests as opposed to those of other nations or supranational groups.

The attitude of the Bahá'ís to nationalism 'implies neither the slightest indifference to the cause and interests of their own country, nor involves any insubordination on their part to the authority of recognized and established governments. Nor does it constitute a repudiation of their sacred obligation to promote, in the most effective manner, the best interests of their government and people. It indicates the desire cherished by every true and loyal follower of Bahá'u'lláh to serve, in an unselfish, unostentatious and patriotic fashion, the highest interests of the country to which he belongs, and in a way that would entail no departure from the high standards of integrity and truthfulness associated with the teachings of his Faith.'[3]

Shoghi Effendi writes that 'the fury of a capricious and militant nationalism' must be 'transmuted into an abiding consciousness of world citizenship'.[4] The purpose of the world order of Bahá'u'lláh is not, however, 'to stifle the flame of a sane and intelligent patriotism in men's hearts, nor to abolish the system of national autonomy so essential if the evils of excessive centralization are to be avoided . . . It calls for a wider loyalty . . . It insists upon the subordination of national impulses and interests to the imperative claims of a unified world.'[5]

Navváb The wife of Bahá'u'lláh, Ásíyih Khánum, entitled by Him the 'Most Exalted Leaf'. Navváb shared Bahá'u'lláh's exile for nearly forty years and was the mother of 'Abdu'l-Bahá, the Greatest Holy Leaf and the Purest Branch. She evinced a 'fortitude, a piety, a devotion and a nobility of soul which earned her from the pen of her Lord the posthumous and unrivalled tribute of having been made His "perpetual consort in all the worlds of God"'.[6] She passed away in 1886. Shoghi Effendi transferred the remains of Navváb from the cemetery in 'Akká to the Monument Gardens of Haifa in 1939.

Naw-Rúz (literally, New Day) The Bahá'í New Year. Like the ancient Persian New Year, it occurs on the spring equinox, which generally falls on 21 March. If the equinox falls after sunset on 21 March, Naw-Rúz is celebrated on 22 March, since the Bahá'í day begins at sunset. For the present, however, the celebration of Naw-Rúz is fixed on 21 March. In the Bahá'í calendar, Naw-Rúz falls on the day of Bahá of the month of Bahá.

The Festival of Naw-Rúz marks the end of the month of fasting and is a joyous time of celebration. It is a Bahá'í Holy Day on which work is to be suspended.

Nayríz Village in the southwest of Iran in the province of Fárs. Following the visit of Vaḥíd there in 1850 many people became Bábís, provoking opposition from the government. An upheaval followed, resulting in the martyrdom of many Bábís, including Vaḥíd.

new era The present stage of mankind's spiritual and social development ushered in by Bahá'u'lláh.

New Era School Bahá'í school in Panchgani, Maharashtra, India, open to children from all national, racial and religious backgrounds.

new race of men People whose personal characters have been transformed in conformity with the spiritual values taught by the Manifestation of God. 'Is it not the object of every Revelation to effect a transformation in the whole character of mankind, a transformation that shall manifest itself, both outwardly and inwardly, that shall affect both its inner life and external conditions? For if the character of mankind be not changed, the futility of God's universal Manifestation would be apparent.'[7]

'A race of men, incomparable in character, shall be raised up which, with the feet of detachment, will tread under all who are in heaven and on earth, and will cast the sleeve of holiness over all that hath been created from water and clay.'[8] '. . . the supreme and distinguishing function of His Revelation . . . is none other than the calling into being of a new race of men . . .'[9]

new world order *See* World Order of Bahá'u'lláh.

nightingale One of a variety of thrushes known for the sweetness of its nocturnal song. Used in the Bahá'í Writings to symbolize the Manifestation of God, particularly Bahá'u'lláh.

Nine Year Plan *See* plans, teaching.

numerical values *See* abjad.

nuqṭih [Ar] Point.

Nuqṭiy-i-Úlá *See* Primal Point.

Núr [Ar] Light. The fifth month of the Bahá'í year (from sunset 4 June to sunset 23 June).

Núr A district of Mázindarán in northern Iran, the ancestral home of Bahá'u'lláh.

O

obelisk A monumental pillar, commissioned by Shoghi Effendi, designed and fashioned in Italy, and erected by the Universal House of Justice in August 1971 on the site of the Mashriqu'l-Adhkár which one day will stand on Mount Carmel.

The obelisk on Mount Carmel

obligatory prayer *See* prayer, obligatory.

Olinga, Enoch Hand of the Cause born in 1926 in the village of Abaango, Uganda – Africa's only native Hand of the Cause. He became a Bahá'í in 1952, the third Ugandan to accept Bahá'u'lláh and the first of the Teso tribe. He taught the Faith widely, particularly among his own tribe. He pioneered to Cameroon during the Ten Year Crusade, thus becoming a Knight of Bahá'u'lláh. For his work in confirming 300 new believers and founding five spiritual assemblies Shoghi Effendi named him 'Abu'l-Futúḥ – the Father of Victories. Enoch Olinga was appointed a Hand of the Cause in October 1957. He and several members of his family were brutally murdered by gunmen in their Kampala home in 1979.

oneness of mankind The central principle of the Bahá'í Faith: 'The earth is but one country and mankind its citizens.' It is the 'pivot round which all the teachings of Bahá'u'lláh revolve'.[1]

'Its appeal is not to be merely identified with a reawakening of the spirit of brotherhood and good-will among men, nor does it aim solely at the fostering of harmonious cooperation among individual peoples and nations . . . It implies an organic change in the structure of present-day society . . . It calls for the reconstruction and demilitarization of the whole civilized world – a world organically unified in all the essential aspects of its life, its political machinery, its spiritual aspiration, its trade and finance, its script and language, and yet infinite in the diversity of the national characteristics of its federated units. It represents the consummation of human evolution . . .'[2] The oneness of mankind is the foundation upon which all the other social principles and teachings of Bahá'u'lláh are based.

P

paradise Literally, a place of bliss, happiness or delight; heaven. Paradise is not a place but a spiritual state of nearness to God: 'They say: "Where is Paradise, and where is Hell?" Say: "The one is reunion with Me; the other thine own self . . ."'[1]

Bahá'u'lláh in the Tablet to Vafá reveals, 'As to Paradise: It is a reality and there can be no doubt about it, and now in this world it is realized through love of Me and My good-pleasure. Whosoever attaineth unto it God will aid him in this world below, and after death He will enable him to gain admittance into Paradise whose vastness is as that of heaven and earth.'[2]

'Abdu'l-Bahá said that earth can be a paradise: 'The Lord of all mankind hath fashioned this human realm to be a Garden of Eden, an earthly paradise. If, as it must, it findeth the way to harmony and peace, to love and mutual trust, it will become a true abode of bliss, a place of manifold blessings and unending delights. Therein shall be revealed the excellence of humankind, therein shall the rays of the Sun of Truth shine forth on every hand.'[3]

See also Abhá Kingdom *and* heaven and hell.

pá<u>sh</u>á [Turk] Title given in former times to high-ranking officers in Turkey.

peace A state of tranquillity; freedom from disturbance; harmony in personal relations. Bahá'ís believe peace must be established within every level of human society: the individual, the family, the community, the nation and the world.

See also Peace, Great *and* Peace, Most Great.

The destruction and misery of war will be eliminated when the rulers of the world 'hold fast' to the Lesser Peace

Peace, Great (Translated in some Bahá'í literature as the 'Lesser Peace' to distinguish it from the 'Most Great Peace'). A political peace to be established by the nations of the world in order to bring about an end to war. In the nineteenth century, when the kings and rulers addressed by Bahá'u'lláh did not heed his summons, which could have brought the Most Great Peace, he advised them to 'hold ye fast unto this, the Lesser Peace, that haply ye may in some degree better your own condition and that of your dependants'.[4] Its establishment will prepare the way for the Most Great Peace. In 1985, in a statement to the peoples of the world, *The Promise of World Peace*, the Universal House of Justice called upon the nations of the world to bring about this 'Great Peace'.

See also Peace, Most Great *and Promise of World Peace, The.*

Peace, Lesser *See* Peace, Great.

Peace, Most Great A condition of permanent peace and world unity to be founded on the spiritual principles and institutions of the World Order of Bahá'u'lláh. Its establishment shall follow the 'Lesser Peace', and unlike that purely political peace, brought about to avoid war, the Most Great Peace will be the 'consequence of the spiritualization of the world and the fusion of its races, creeds, classes and nations',[5] based on the teachings of Bahá'u'lláh and the establishment of His World Order. The Most Great Peace, signalizing mankind's coming of age, shall fulfil the promises of the past concerning the establishment of 'the Kingdom of the Father', a reign of sustained peace on earth, and shall be the Golden Age of the Bahá'í Era.

Peace, United Nations International Day of A special event day observed by Bahá'í communities in the United States and elsewhere to call attention to the need for world peace. In 1985 the observance of UN International Day of Peace replaced World Peace Day, which had been observed by Bahá'í communities in the United States since 1959. UN International Day of Peace is observed on the third Tuesday in September.

peace, world A fundamental principle of Bahá'í social teaching, the achievement of which, through the establishment of the World Order of Bahá'u'lláh, is the primary mission of the Bahá'í Faith. According to Bahá'u'lláh, the achievement of world peace shall occur in stages, first through the political peace to be brought about by the nations of the world, followed by the Most Great Peace, founded on the unification of the planet through the spiritual principles of Bahá'u'lláh.
See also Peace, Great *and* Peace, Most Great.

People of Bahá The followers of Bahá'u'lláh, Bahá'ís.

People of the Bayán The followers of the Báb, Bábís.

People of the Book (Ahlu'l-Kitáb) An Islamic term denoting the followers of any of the Prophets of God who revealed a Holy Book. Usually refers to Jews and Christians, as well as to the Muslims themselves.

People of the Son The followers of Christ, Christians.

persecution The harassment of individuals or a group with a view to causing injury, grief, affliction or death; specifically, to cause such individuals or groups to suffer because of their beliefs.

Bahá'ís in several parts of the world, particularly the Middle East and most notably Iran, have suffered persecution. The Bahá'ís, and before them the Bábís, in Iran have been persecuted by succeeding governments from the beginning of their history. The latest persecutions in Iran began with the Islamic Revolution in 1979 and have prevented Bahá'ís from working, from receiving pensions, and from attending school and university, with extreme forms of persecution being imprisonment, torture and execution.

Evidence of persecution, destruction of the House of the Báb in Shíráz, 1979

Persia Iran.

pilgrim One who travels to a holy shrine or place, specifically with the intention of paying one's respects or worshipping there.

In the Bahá'í Faith, a pilgrim is one who visits the House of Bahá'u'lláh in Baghdád, the House of the Báb in Shíráz or the Holy Shrines and places in the Holy Land. Early Bahá'í pilgrims visited Bahá'u'lláh and 'Abdu'l-Bahá.

Pilgrim House The houses near the Shrines of the Báb and Bahá'u'lláh where pilgrims gather for rest and refreshment during their visits to these Shrines.

Pilgrims with 'Abdu'l-Bahá

A caravanserai in 'Akká, the Khán-i-'Avámíd, was the first place used by pilgrims as a pilgrim house. Two of its rooms were frequently used by pilgrims who had travelled to the Holy Land to meet Bahá'u'lláh.

About 1892 'Abdu'l-Bahá rented the house at Bahjí which is now known as the Pilgrim House. The property was acquired about 1956 from the Israeli Government in exchange for other land owned by the Bahá'ís in Ein Gev. This house is now used by pilgrims visiting the Shrine of Bahá'u'lláh.

The Pilgrim House at Bahjí
(Baker, *circa* 1930)

Pilgrim House

Soon after 'Abdu'l-Bahá interred the remains of the Báb on Mount Carmel, Mírzá Ja'far Raḥmání of 'Ishqábád asked 'Abdu'l-Bahá to allow him to build a pilgrim house near the Shrine of the Báb. 'Abdu'l-Bahá agreed and this believer personally supervised its construction and paid all the expenses. It is a stone building which for decades housed the pilgrims from Iran, hence its name 'Eastern Pilgrim House'. A pilgrim house for the use of pilgrims from the West was begun in 1919 on land donated by a Persian believer and partly paid for by William Harry Randall. Amelia Collins provided the funds for the rest of the building in 1923 and when it was finished a few years later it became the Western Pilgrim House. In 1951 it became the seat of the International Bahá'í Council, later the first Seat of the Universal House of Justice, and is now the temporary seat of the International Teaching Centre.

Pilgrims gather outside the Pilgrim House on Mount Carmel

pilgrimage A journey made to a shrine or holy place.

In the *Kitáb-i-Aqdas* Bahá'u'lláh ordains pilgrimage for Bahá'ís to the Most Great House in Baghdád and to the House of the Báb in Shíráz. After the passing of Bahá'u'lláh 'Abdu'l-Bahá added to these the Shrine of Bahá'u'lláh at Bahjí. For Bahá'ís, pilgrimage to these three places is, 'Abdu'l-Bahá has stated, 'obligatory if one can afford it and is able to do so, and if no obstacle stands in one's way'.[6]

In a Tablet to a believer 'Abdu'l-Bahá wrote concerning pilgrimages: 'You have asked about visiting holy places and the observance of marked reverence toward these resplendent spots. Holy places are undoubtedly centres of the outpouring of Divine grace, because on entering the illumined sites associated with martyrs and holy souls, and by observing reverence, both physical and spiritual, one's heart is moved with great tenderness. But there is no obligation for everyone to visit such places, other than the three, namely: the Most Holy Shrine, the Blessed House in Baghdád and the venerated House of the Báb in Shíráz. To visit these is obligatory if one can afford it and is able to do so, and if no obstacle stands in one's way . . . These three Holy Places are consecrated to pilgrimage. But as to the other resting places of martyrs and holy souls, it is pleasing and acceptabe in the sight of God if a person desires to draw nigh unto Him by visiting them; this, however, is not a binding obligation.'[7] Under present circumstances, Bahá'ís are able to make pilgrimage only to the Shrine of Bahá'u'lláh. The only person to have performed completely the obligation of Bahá'í pilgrimage to all the designated places in accordance with all of the instructions pertaining thereto was Nabíl-i-A'ẓam.

pioneer 'Any believer who arises and leaves his home to journey to another country for the purpose of teaching the Cause is a pioneer.'[8] 'The duties of teaching and pioneering are enjoined upon all believers . . . Any Bahá'í who spreads the Message of Bahá'u'lláh is a teacher, any Bahá'í who moves to another area to spread the Faith is a pioneer. No special training is required for a pioneer.'[9]

Bahá'ís preparing to become pioneers

Plan of God *See* Greater Plan of God *and* Minor Plan of God.

plans, teaching Organized campaigns, local, national or international in their scope, in which Bahá'ís are encouraged to take the Bahá'í message to particular countries, territories or peoples, to translate the Bahá'í literature into various languages, and to develop certain aspects of Bahá'í community life. All such teaching plans are based on, and are supplementary to, the Divine Plan outlined by 'Abdu'l-Bahá in *The Tablets of the Divine Plan*.

The first plan was developed by Shoghi Effendi for the North American Bahá'ís. Called the First Seven Year Plan (1937–44), it had three elements: to complete the exterior ornamentation of the Wilmette House of Worship, to establish one local spiritual assembly in every state of the United States and every province of Canada, and to create one centre in each Latin American republic.

After the inauguration of the First Seven Year Plan, plans were developed in various parts of the world at different times: a Six Year Plan in Britain, a Five Year Plan in Germany and Austria, a Nineteen Month Plan, Two Year, Three Year, Forty-Five Month, Four-and-a-half Year, and other plans.

After the successful completion of the First Seven Year Plan, Shoghi Effendi launched the Second Seven Year Plan (1946–53), again assigned to the North American believers. The objectives of this Plan were: consolidation of the work throughout the Americas; the completion of the interior ornamentation of the Wilmette House of Worship; the election of three national spiritual assemblies in Canada, Central and South America; and a systematic teaching campaign in Europe aimed at establishing spiritual assemblies in the Iberian Peninsula, the Low Countries, Scandinavia and Italy. The British, in conjunction with the United States, Egypt and Iran, were called upon to undertake a two-year Africa campaign (1951–3).

In 1953 Shoghi Effendi launched the Ten Year World Crusade, with tasks assigned to each of the twelve national spiritual assemblies then in existence. Of it Shoghi Effendi wrote: 'The avowed, the primary aim of this Spiritual Crusade is none other than the conquest of the citadels of men's hearts. The theatre of its operations is the entire planet. Its duration a whole decade.'[10] This Plan had four objectives: development of the institutions at the Bahá'í World Centre, consolidation of the home fronts of the twelve participating national assemblies, consolidation of the territories already opened to the Faith, and the opening of the remaining chief territories of the planet. Shoghi Effendi passed away in 1957, before the midpoint of the Plan; nevertheless, the Hands of the Cause directed the national spiritual assemblies to the successful completion of the plan in 1963 and supervised the election of the Universal House of Justice in that year.

The Universal House of Justice has continued the work begun by Shoghi Effendi. In 1964 it launched a Nine Year Plan, in 1974 a Five Year Plan, in 1979 a Seven Year Plan, and in 1986 a Six Year Plan. Each of these has resulted in a further geographic spread of the Bahá'í Faith, the development of the Bahá'í World Centre, the translation of more literature, the inauguration of various social and economic development projects and an increase in the number of Bahá'ís.

Point of the Bayán The Báb.

See also Primal Point.

politics The art or science of government, of winning and holding control over a government, particularly the competition between different groups or individuals for power and leadership.

The Bahá'í Faith is, in the words of Shoghi Effendi, 'essentially non-political, supranational in character, rigidly non-partisan, and entirely dissociated from nationalistic ambitions, pursuits, and purposes'.[11]

Bahá'ís are prohibited from participating in partisan politics: 'Let them refrain', Shoghi Effendi wrote, 'from associating themselves, whether by word or by deed, with the political pursuits of their respective nations, with the policies of their governments and the schemes and programmes of parties and factions. In such controversies they should assign no blame, take no side, further no design, and identify themselves with no system prejudicial to the best interests of that worldwide Fellowship which it is their aim to guard and foster.'[12]

As to voting in political elections, in a letter written on behalf of Shoghi Effendi, it is stated: 'The friends may vote, if they can do it without identifying themselves with one party or another . . . It remains for the individuals so to use their right to vote as to keep aloof from party politics, and always bear in mind that they are voting on the merits of the individual, rather than because he belongs to one party or another.'[13]

Shoghi Effendi has stated, however, that Bahá'ís may hold government posts which are not political or linked to partisan politics: 'It is their duty to strive to distinguish as clearly as they possibly can . . . such posts and functions as are either diplomatic or political from those that are purely administrative in character, and which under no circumstances are affected by the changes and chances that political activities and party government, in every land, must necessarily involve.'[14]

The Bahá'í attitude to politics 'implies neither the slightest indifference to the cause and interests of their own country, nor involves any insubordination on their part to the authority of recognized and established governments. Nor does it constitute a repudiation of their sacred obligation to promote, in the most effective manner, the best interests of their government and people. It indicates the desire cherished by every true and loyal follower of Bahá'u'lláh to serve, in an unselfish, unostentatious and patriotic fashion, the highest interests of the country to which he belongs . . .'[15]

See also government, obedience to.

'Tell the rich of the midnight sighing of the poor . . .'

poor, the Those without material wealth.

Bahá'u'lláh explains the Bahá'í attitude towards wealth and poverty: 'O Ye that Pride Yourselves on Mortal Riches! Know ye in truth that wealth is a mighty barrier between the seeker and his desire, the lover and his beloved. The rich, but for a few, shall in no wise attain the court of His presence nor enter the city of content and resignation. Well is it then with him, who, being rich, is not hindered by his riches from the eternal kingdom.'[16] 'Be not troubled in poverty nor confident in riches, for poverty is followed by riches, and riches are followed by poverty. Yet to be poor in all save God is a wondrous gift, belittle not the value thereof, for in the end it will make thee rich in God . . .'[17] 'Cleanse thyself from the defilement of riches and in perfect peace advance into the realm of poverty; that from the well-spring of detachment thou mayest quaff the wine of immortal life.'[18]

The attitude of the more prosperous person to the poor is described by Bahá'u'lláh: 'Vaunt not thyself over the poor, for I lead him on his way and behold thee in thy evil plight and confound thee for evermore.'[19] 'O Ye Rich Ones on Earth! The poor in your midst are My trust; guard ye My trust, and be not intent only on your own ease.'[20]

Further, Bahá'ís are expected to assist the poor: 'Bestow My wealth upon My poor, that in heaven thou mayest draw from stores of unfading splendour and treasures of imperishable glory.'[21] 'Tell the rich of the midnight sighing of the poor, lest heedlessness lead them into the path of destruction, and deprive them of the Tree of Wealth. To give and to be generous are attributes of Mine; well is it with him that adorneth himself with My virtues.'[22] 'Be generous in prosperity, and thankful in adversity . . . Be a treasure to the poor, an admonisher to the rich, an answerer of the cry of the needy . . .'[23]

See also wealth and poverty, elimination of extremes of.

prayer Supplication to, or communion with, God.

In the *Kitáb-i-Aqdas* Bahá'u'lláh sets out the law of prayer: 'We have commanded you to pray and fast from the beginning of maturity; this is ordained by God, your Lord and the Lord of your forefathers.'[24] Bahá'ís are enjoined by Bahá'u'lláh to pray every morning and evening: 'Recite ye the verses of God every morning and evening. Whoso reciteth them not hath truly failed to fulfil his pledge to the Covenant of God . . .'[25] Bahá'u'lláh and 'Abdu'l-Bahá revealed many prayers which Bahá'ís are encouraged to use. Bahá'ís may also use their own words in private prayer. In addition to these personal prayers, Bahá'u'lláh has stipulated that Bahá'ís should recite one of three obligatory prayers every day.

However, Bahá'u'lláh states that one should not pray to excess: 'Take heed lest excessive reading and too many acts of piety in the daytime and in the nightseason make you vainglorious. Should a person recite but a single verse from the Holy Writings in a spirit of joy and radiance, this would be better for him than reciting wearily all the Scriptures of God, the Help in Peril, the Self-Subsisting. Recite ye the verses of God in such measure that ye be not overtaken with fatigue or boredom. Burden not your souls so as to cause them exhaustion and weigh them down, but rather endeavour to lighten them, that they may soar on the wings of revealed Verse unto the dawning-place of His signs. This is conducive to nearer access unto God, were ye to comprehend.'[26]

Prayers are usually said in private or with one's family, although there are occasions when community worship is appropriate, such as in the devotional part of the Nineteen Day Feast or at the observances of

Bahá'í Holy Days. Special gatherings for prayers may also be held but are not obligatory. 'One of the characteristics of the Bahá'í society will be the gathering of the believers each day during the hours between dawn and two hours after sunrise to listen to the reading and chanting of the Holy Word.'[27] Prayers are also offered in the Mashriqu'l-Adhkár and at the Holy Shrines. It is a common practice among Bahá'ís to begin and end meetings with prayers, but this also is not obligatory. Except for the obligatory prayers, there are no special gestures or positions one must take up for prayer. Prayers may be read, recited, chanted or sung. There is no congregational prayer in the Bahá'í Faith, except for the prayer for the dead, when the prayer is recited by one person while all others present stand. Bahá'ís do not generally recite prayers in unison, although the singing of a short prayer by a small group of believers is not forbidden.[28]

Bahá'ís may pray directly to God or through Bahá'u'lláh. Bahá'ís may also pray to other departed souls to intercede on their behalf.

See also intercession; Mashriqu'l-Adhkár; meditation; *and* prayer, obligatory.

prayer, obligatory The daily recital of one of three specific prayers revealed by Bahá'u'lláh is binding on Bahá'ís from the age of maturity, which is fifteen years. The believer is free to choose one of the three prayers, to be said privately. The short obligatory prayer is to be recited once a day at noon (between noon and sunset), the medium obligatory prayer three times daily, and the long obligatory prayer once in twenty-four hours. The *Kitáb-i-Aqdas* specifies other requirements and exceptions related to the obligatory prayers, including the performance of ablutions and facing the Qiblih while praying.

prejudice, elimination of all forms of A basic principle of Bahá'í social teaching. 'Prejudice and fanaticism,' 'Abdu'l-Bahá explained, 'whether sectarian, denominational, patriotic or political – are destructive to the foundation of human solidarity; therefore man should release himself from such bonds in order that the oneness of the world of humanity may become manifest.'[29]

'Abdu'l-Bahá has condemned prejudice of all sorts as a major cause of war: '. . . as to religious, racial, national and political bias: all these prejudices strike at the very root of human life; one and all they beget bloodshed, and the ruination of the world. So long as these prejudices survive, there will be continuous and fearsome wars.'[30]

Further, 'Abdu'l-Bahá described how prejudices can be eliminated: 'there is need of a superior power to overcome human prejudices, a power which nothing in the world of mankind can withstand and which will overshadow the effect of all other forces at work in human

conditions. That irresistible power is the love of God.'[31]
See also most challenging issue.

Pride of Martyrs *See* Badí'.

Primal Point (Nuqṭiy-i-Úlá) ('from which have been generated all things'[32]) The Báb. In Persian mysticism, all writing is said to originate from a 'nuqṭih', a point or dot.

Primitive Age *See* Heroic Age.

principles, Bahá'í A term used for those fundamental tenets of Bahá'í social teaching excerpted from the Writings of Bahá'u'lláh and expounded by 'Abdu'l-Bahá during His talks in Europe and America in 1911–13, as recorded in *The Promulgation of Universal Peace* and other books. These include the following:

The oneness of mankind
The common foundation of all religions
Religion's obligation to be the cause of unity and harmony
The protection and guidance of the Holy Spirit
The accord of religion with science and reason
The non-interference of religion with politics
The independent investigation of truth
The establishment of justice
The equality of men and women
The equality of all men before the law
The elimination of all kinds of prejudice
The elimination of the extremes of wealth and poverty
World peace
World government
A universal auxiliary language
An international tribunal
Universal education
A spiritual solution to economic problems

These principles, 'Abdu'l-Bahá said, 'embody the divine spirit of the age and are applicable to this period of maturity in the life of the human world.'[33]

He further states, 'the teachings of Bahá'u'lláh are the very healing of the sick world, the remedy for every need and condition. In them may be found the realization of every desire and aspiration, the cause of the happiness of the world of humanity, the stimulus and illumination of mentality, the impulse for advancement and uplift, the basis of unity for all nations, the fountain source of love amongst mankind, the centre of agreement, the means of peace and harmony, the one bond which will unite the East and the West.'[34]

proclamation Term used to describe the initial presentation of the Bahá'í teachings to those unfamiliar with them. Proclamation activities may include the holding of public meetings, advertising, participation in fêtes and parades, mounting exhibitions, donating Bahá'í books to libraries, and presenting Bahá'í literature to dignitaries, often at special dinners. The intention of proclamation is to introduce the Bahá'í Faith to new people, after which it is left to those individuals who are interested to seek further information from the Bahá'ís.

See also proselytizing *and* teaching.

Proclamation of Bahá'u'lláh, The *See* Kings, Tablets to the.

progressive revelation The concept that Divine Revelation is not final, but continuing.

The concept of progressive revelation is founded on the belief that all the Greater Prophets of the past were Manifestations of God who appeared in different ages with teachings appropriate to the needs of the time: 'in every Dispensation', writes Bahá'u'lláh, 'the light of Divine Revelation hath been vouchsafed unto men in direct proportion to their spiritual capacity.'[35] Each succeeding Revelation is greater than the one that preceded it, as the capacity of the people to comprehend increases. With each dispensation social evolution has advanced, as the scope of man's sense of loyalty to a group has become wider – from the family to the clan, tribe, city-state, nation and ultimately to the recognition of the oneness of mankind, the distinguishing feature of the

Bahá'ís of Port Blair, Andaman and Nicobar Islands proclaim the Faith with an arch erected to welcome the Prime Minister of India to the country

The Promise of World Peace has been translated into many languages

revelation of Bahá'u'lláh. Bahá'ís believe the great religions of the past were all 'different stages in the eternal history and constant evolution of one religion, Divine and indivisible,'[36] and that in not less than a thousand years, another prophet will appear, to bring further divine guidance to mankind. Concerning future Manifestations, 'Abdu'l-Bahá said, 'in so far as their relation to the source of their inspiration is concerned they are under the shadow of the Ancient Beauty [Bahá'u-'lláh]. In their relation, however, to the age in which they appear, each and every one of them "doeth whatsoever He willeth".'[37]

See also Adamic Cycle *and* Bahá'í Cycle.

Promise of World Peace, The Statement addressed to the peoples of the world, issued by the Universal House of Justice in 1985 in response to Bahá'u'lláh's injunction to its members to promote the Lesser Peace and as its contribution to the UN Year of Peace (1986). It states that peace is inevitable: it will be established either after 'unimaginable horrors' or as a result of 'an act of consultative will'.[38]

The Promise of World Peace outlines the favourable signs for peace;

The Promise of World Peace is presented to President Ronald Reagan by Representatives of the National Spiritual Assembly of the United States

defines the role of religion as a source of order; examines the root causes of war; sets out the obstacles to peace such as racism, the inordinate disparity between rich and poor, unbridled nationalism and the lack of full equality between the sexes; states that world order can be founded only on a consciousness of the oneness of mankind, offers the Bahá'í community as a model of the unity necessary for peace, and calls for the holding of a 'mighty convocation' of the leaders of all nations that will lay the foundations of universal peace.

The Promise of World Peace has been presented to heads of state and government in most countries, as well as to other national and civic leaders. By 1988 it had been presented to over one million people.

Promised One, the The Promised One of the Bayán, 'Him Whom God Shall Make Manifest': Bahá'u'lláh. The Promised One of Islam, the Qá'im: the Báb. Generally, the Promised One of all religions: Bahá'u'lláh.

Prince Khuzulwandle of Swaziland receives *The Promise of World Peace* in October 1985

Prophets, Greater The independent Prophets, or Manifestations, who are the 'lawgivers and the founders of a new cycle . . . They are like the sun which is luminous in itself; the light is its essential necessity; it does not receive light from any other star.'[39] They are also termed 'Prophets endowed with constancy'.[40]

Prophets, Lesser Followers, promoters of the Greater Prophet. They are not independent: 'they receive the bounty of the independent Prophets, and they profit from the light of the Guidance of the universal Prophets. They are like the moon, which is not luminous and radiant in itself, but receives its light from the sun.'[41] The prophets of Israel and the Old Testament, such as Solomon, David, Isaiah, Jeremiah and Ezekiel, are not regarded as Manifestations "endowed with constancy".'[42]

prophets endowed with constancy *See* Prophets, Greater.

proselytizing To make someone convert from one religion or belief to another.

Proselytizing, or trying to induce someone to become a believer, is not permitted. Bahá'ís are enjoined to teach their Faith, but with 'tolerance, love, kindness, patience, a goodly character, and holy deeds'.[43] 'Do not argue with anyone,' 'Abdu'l-Bahá writes, 'and be wary of disputation. Speak out the truth. If your hearer accepteth, the aim is achieved. If he is obdurate, you should leave him to himself and place your trust in God.'[44]

Publishing Trust The publishing arm of national spiritual assemblies and working under their direction. The Publishing Trusts are primarily responsible for the publication and dissemination of Bahá'í Scripture but they also publish books of commentary, biography and so on.

Purest Branch, the *See* Mírzá Mihdí.

The United Kingdom Bahá'í Publishing Trust exhibit at the London Book Fair 1988

Q

qáḍí In Islam, a religious judge.

Qá'im (Qá'im-i-Ál-i-Muḥammad) He who shall arise (of the family of Muḥammad). The Twelfth Imám, the Mihdí, awaited by Shí'ih Muslims, who was to return in the fullness of time and bring a reign of righteousness to the world. The Báb declared Himself to be the Qá'im and also the Gate (Báb) to a greater divine messenger, 'Him Whom God Shall Make Manifest'.

Qá'im-Maqám In Iran, a local governor.

Qájár Turkoman tribe which gained the Iranian throne in 1795 and reigned throughout the lifetimes of the Báb, Bahá'u'lláh and 'Abdu'l-Bahá until it was itself overthrown in 1925.

Qará-Guhar The name given to one of two dreaded chains (the other was Salásil) by which Bahá'u'lláh was fettered in the Síyáh-Chál dungeon in 1852. In *Epistle to the Son of the Wolf* Bahá'u'lláh states that He was 'tormented and chained by one or the other of them'[1] for the four months He was imprisoned in that subterranean gaol.

Qawl [Ar] Speech. The fourteenth month of the Bahá'í year (from sunset 22 November to sunset 11 December).

Qayyúm [Ar] Bahá'u'lláh. Siyyid Káẓim foretold the coming of the Qayyúm: 'Verily I say, after the Qá'im [the Báb] the Qayyúm will be made manifest. For when the star of the Former has set, the sun of the beauty of Ḥusayn will rise . . .'[2]

Qayyúmu'l-Asmá' The Báb's commentary on the Súrih of Joseph, the first chapter of which was revealed in the presence of Mullá Ḥusayn on the evening of 22 May 1844. The *Qayyúmu'l-Asmá'* was, according to Bahá'u'lláh, 'the first, the greatest, and mightiest of all books' of the Báb.[3]

Written in Arabic, the *Qayyúmu'l-Asmá'* is composed of over 9300 verses divided into 111 chapters, each of which is a commentary on one verse of the Súrih of Joseph. Its fundamental purpose, Shoghi Effendi has written, 'was to forecast what the true Joseph (Bahá'u'lláh) would, in a succeeding Dispensation, endure at the hands of one who was at once His arch-enemy and blood brother.'[4]

The Bábís regarded the *Qayyúmu'l-Asmá'* as their 'Qur'án'. Some of its pages were taken to Bahá'u'lláh by Mullá Ḥusayn, whereupon Bahá'u'lláh immediately became a follower of the Báb. In contrast,

Shoghi Effendi writes, the book 'inflamed the hostility of Ḥusayn Khán and precipitated the initial outbreak of persecution in Shíráz . . .'[5] The entire text was translated into Persian by Ṭáhirih.
See also Súrih of Joseph.

Qiblih [Ar] The Point of Adoration; the direction in which people turn when praying. The Kaaba in Mecca is the Qiblih for Muslims; the Shrine of Bahá'u'lláh at Bahjí is the Qiblih for Bahá'ís.

Quddús The Most Holy. Title given by the Báb to Ḥájí Muḥammad-'Alíy-i-Bárfurúshí, the last Letter of the Living, 'the beloved disciple whose primacy was unquestioned'.[6] He accompanied the Báb to Mecca and attended the Conference of Badasht. He joined the Bábís in the fort at Shaykh Ṭabarsí and was taken from there to his native town at Bárfurúsh. There he was tortured, and in May 1849 in the public square, he was struck down with an axe, dismembered and burnt.

Qudrat [Ar] Power. The thirteenth month of the Bahá'í year (from sunset 3 November to sunset 22 November).

Questions and Answers An explanatory appendix to the *Kitáb-i-Aqdas*, composed of the questions posed by Jináb-i-Zaynu'l-Muqarrabín to Bahá'u'lláh regarding the text of the *Kitáb-i-Aqdas*, along with Bahá'u'lláh's replies.

Qur'án The sacred book of Islam, containing the collected revelations of Muḥammad.

The Qur'án comprises 114 chapters called 'súrihs' or 'súras', each of which represents a separate revelation. Shoghi Effendi urged the Bahá'ís to 'make a thorough study of the Qur'án as the knowledge of this Sacred Scripture is absolutely indispensable for every believer who wishes to adequately understand and intelligently read the Writings of Bahá'u'lláh.'[7]

Qurratu'l-'Ayn *See* Ṭáhirih.

R

Rabbání [Pers] Divine. 'Abdu'l-Bahá gave this surname to Shoghi Effendi in the early years of his study in Haifa so that he would no longer be confused with his cousins, as they were all called Afnán. This name was also used by Shoghi Effendi's brothers and sisters.[1]

Race Unity Day In the United States, a special event day initiated by the National Spiritual Assembly and observed on the second Sunday in June to focus attention on the 'most vital and challenging issue' facing America, racial prejudice, and to proclaim the principle of the oneness of mankind.

racism A belief that human values are determined by race, that one race has supremacy over another; prejudice or discrimination based on race.

The Universal House of Justice has stated: 'Racism, one of the most baneful and persistent evils, is a major barrier to peace. Its practice perpetrates too outrageous a violation of the dignity of human beings to be countenanced under any pretext. Racism retards the unfoldment of the boundless potentialities of its victims, corrupts its perpetrators, and blights human progress. Recognition of the oneness of mankind, implemented by appropriate legal measures, must be universally upheld if this problem is to be overcome.'[2]

The elimination of racism is essential for world peace

Radio Bahá'í Local radio stations established initially to enable Bahá'ís in remote areas to keep in touch with one another, to deepen in their Faith through specially designed broadcasts, and to teach the Bahá'í Faith. Through their broadcasting of local news, indigenous music, and relevant agricultural information, the stations rapidly became a major influence in the lives of indigenous people in their broadcast areas.

The first such station, Radio Bahá'í Ecuador, began full-time broadcasting in Otavalo, Ecuador, in 1977. It was followed by radio stations in Peru, Bolivia, Ecuador, Chile, Panama, South Carolina and Liberia.

Children perform at the Folklore Festival sponsored annually by Radio Bahá'í Ecuador

Raḥmat [Ar] Mercy. The sixth month of the Bahá'í year (from sunset 23 June to sunset 12 July).

Raqshá She-Serpent. In *Epistle to the Son of the Wolf*, Bahá'u'lláh addresses the Imám-Jum'ih of Iṣfáhán, Mír Muḥammad-Ḥusayn, as Raqshá. He is condemned for his instigation of the martyrdom of the King and Beloved of Martyrs, to whom he owed a sum of money. He died in 1881 of a disease so loathsome that even his family would not touch him.

See also King of Martyrs and Beloved of Martyrs; Muḥammad-Báqir, Shaykh; *and* Muḥammad-Taqíy-i-Najafí, Shaykh.

rawḍih-khání [Pers] In Shí'ih Islam, the traditional recital of the sufferings of the martyred Imám Ḥusayn.

rectitude of conduct Moral uprightness enjoined on Bahá'ís, particularly, though not exclusively, on their elected representatives. 'This rectitude of conduct, with its implications of justice, equity, truthfulness, honesty, fair-mindedness, reliability, and trustworthiness, must distinguish every phase of the life of the Bahá'í community.'[3]

religion 'Religion is the outer expression of the divine reality.'[4]

'Religion . . . is not a series of beliefs, a set of customs; religion is the teachings of the Lord God, teachings which constitute the very life of humankind, which urge high thoughts upon the mind, refine the character, and lay the groundwork for man's everlasting honour.'[5]

Religion has two main purposes: the personal spiritual development of the individual and to establish order in the world: '. . . the fundamental purpose of all religions . . . is to bring man closer to God, and to change his character . . .'[6] 'Religion is verily the chief instrument for the establishment of order in the world and of tranquillity amongst its peoples.'[7]

Bahá'u'lláh writes, 'The purpose of religion as revealed from the heaven of God's holy Will is to establish unity and concord amongst the peoples of the world . . . Religion bestoweth upon man the most precious of all gifts, offereth the cup of prosperity, imparteth eternal life, and showereth imperishable benefits upon mankind.'[8]

'. . . in truth, religion is a radiant light and an impregnable stronghold for the protection and welfare of the peoples of the world, for the fear of God impelleth man to hold fast to that which is good, and shun all evil. Should the lamp of religion be obscured, chaos and confusion will ensue, and the lights of fairness and justice, of tranquillity and peace cease to shine.'[9]

religion, as a cause of harmony A fundamental principle of Bahá'í social teaching, that 'religion must be the cause of unity, harmony and agreement among mankind. If it is the cause of discord and hostility, if it leads to separation and creates conflict, the absence of religion would be preferable in the world.'[10]

religion, unity of One of the basic principles of the Bahá'í Faith. All religions are divine in origin and teach the same great spiritual truths. 'The religion of God is one religion . . .'[11] The recognition of this principle by all the people is necessary for the happiness and progress of the world: 'That which the Lord hath ordained as the sovereign remedy and mightiest instrument for the healing of all the world is the union of all its peoples in one universal Cause, one common Faith.'[12]

Remnant of God *See* Baqíyyatu'lláh.

Remote Prison Adrianople.

Resting Place of Shoghi Effendi Shoghi Effendi is buried in the New Southgate Cemetery (previously the Great Northern Cemetery) in north London. His grave is built of white Carrara marble. It consists of a marble column, crowned by a corinthian capital surmounted by a globe, with the map of Africa facing forward. On this globe is a large

Revelation writing. A Tablet of Bahá'u'lláh in the hand of Mírzá Áqá Ján

Resting Place of Shoghi Effendi

gilded bronze eagle, a reproduction of a Japanese sculpture he much admired. Many Bahá'ís visit the resting place of Shoghi Effendi to say prayers.

resurrection In Islam and Christianity, the raising of the dead on the Day of Judgement. Bahá'ís interpret this event spiritually as the coming of the Manifestation of God.

As to the resurrection of Christ, 'Abdu'l-Bahá has explained its meaning: 'the disciples were troubled and agitated after the martyrdom of Christ. The Reality of Christ, which signifies his teachings, his bounties, his perfections, and his spiritual power, was hidden and concealed for two or three days after his martyrdom, and was not resplendent and manifest . . . The Cause of Christ was like a lifeless body; and, when after three days the disciples became assured and steadfast, and began to serve the Cause of Christ, and resolved to spread the divine teachings, putting his counsels into practice, and arising to serve him, the Reality of Christ became resplendent and his bounty appeared; his religion found life, his teachings and his admonitions became evident and visible.'[13]

See also Judgement, Day of.

revelation The laws, teachings or message of God transmitted through His Manifestations to mankind.

A Bahá'í scholar has commented, 'The mystical intercourse between God, as the Father, and His chosen Mouthpiece, the Prophet, as the Mother, gives birth to Divine Revelation which in turn brings forth the Word of God. It is not possible for man to understand the nature of this sacred relationship, a relationship through which God is linked with His manifestation . . . The revealed Word has an inner spirit and an outer form. The innermost spirit is limitless in its potentialities; it belongs to the world of the uncreated and is generated by the Holy Spirit of God. The outer form of the Word of God acts as a channel through which the stream of God's Holy Spirit flows.'[14]

Revelation of Bahá'u'lláh The writings of Bahá'u'lláh and His recorded sayings. May also refer to the Bahá'í Faith and the Dispensation of Bahá'u'lláh.

revelation writing When Bahá'u'lláh revealed Tablets, the speed of revelation was so fast that the handwriting of his amanuensis, Mírzá Áqá Ján, was almost illegible. Only Mírzá Áqá Ján could decipher this revelation writing, and he occasionally had to seek the help of Bahá'u'lláh before it could be transcribed. After approving these Tablets Bahá'u'lláh sometimes authenticated them with one of His seals.

Riḍá-Qulí, Mírzá Half-brother of Bahá'u'lláh who kept apart from Bahá'u'lláh and who tried to conceal the fact of their relationship.

Mírzá Riḍá-Qulí

Riḍván [Ar] Paradise. Name given by Bahá'u'lláh to the Najíbíyyih Garden at Baghdád, the Garden of Na'mayn near 'Akká, and the twelve-day festival commemorating Bahá'u'lláh's Declaration of His mission to His companions in 1863.

See below.

Riḍván, Feast or Festival of The twelve-day festival commemorating Bahá'u'lláh's Declaration of His mission to His companions and celebrated annually from 21 April through 2 May. Bahá'u'lláh acclaimed Riḍván as the 'Most Great Festival', the 'King of Festivals', the 'Festival of God' and has referred to it as the Day whereon 'the breezes of forgiveness were wafted over the entire creation'.[15]

'Of the exact circumstances attending that epoch-making Declaration we, alas, are but scantily informed. The words Bahá'u'lláh actually uttered on that occasion, the manner of His Declaration, the reaction it produced, its impact on Mírzá Yaḥyá, the identity of those who were privileged to hear Him, are shrouded in an obscurity which future historians will find it difficult to penetrate.'[16]

The first, ninth and twelfth days of Riḍván are celebrated as Holy Days on which work is suspended. Local spiritual assemblies are elected annually on the first day of Riḍván while national spiritual assemblies are elected during the Riḍván period. The Universal House of Justice is elected every five years during the Riḍván period.

Riḍván, Garden of (Najíbíyyih) The garden of Najíb Páshá, situated on the outskirts of Baghdád, across the River Tigris from the House of Bahá'u'lláh. In April–May 1863 Bahá'u'lláh spent twelve days in the Najíbíyyih Garden immediately before His exile from Baghdád to Constantinople. It was here that He made the public declaration of His mission. The Garden subsequently became known among Bahá'ís as the Garden of Riḍván.

Riḍván, Garden of (Na'mayn) A 'verdant knoll',[17] less than a kilometre from the walls of 'Akká, around which the Na'mayn River divides before it empties into the sea. It is located at the southeast corner of the Tell of 'Akká at Shahuta (the Place Apart). 'Abdu'l-Bahá rented this island in 1875 for Bahá'u'lláh as a place of rest and beauty for Him. Bahá'u'lláh named it Riḍván (Paradise), and called it the 'New Jerusalem' and 'Our Verdant Isle'.[18]

Bahá'u'lláh may have first visited the garden in June 1877 when He left the city of 'Akká for Mazra'ih. Afterwards He visited it frequently and it became one of His 'favourite retreats'.[19] In 1881 it was purchased

The Riḍván Garden near 'Akká

in His name.

In the *Tablet of Ṭarázát* He relates: 'One day of days We repaired unto Our Green Island. Upon Our arrival, We beheld its streams flowing, and its trees luxuriant, and the sunlight playing in their midst. Turning Our face to the right, We beheld what the pen is powerless to describe; nor can it set forth that which the eye of the Lord of Mankind witnessed in that most sanctified, that most sublime, that blest, and most exalted Spot.'[20]

The garden was described by Lady Blomfield in *The Chosen Highway*: 'The Riḍván is a beautiful garden, which the Master had planted in a plot of land which He had acquired. It is on the bank of a brook. There is a large mulberry tree with seats round its trunk. Many beautiful blossoming trees are now flourishing there, also flowers innumerable, and sweet-smelling herbs; it is a blaze of glorious colour and wonderful beauty. The scent of attar roses, of rosemary, bergamot, mint and thyme and balm, lemon-scented verbena, and musk makes the air sweet with their wealth of various fragrances. Scented white and scarlet and rose-coloured geraniums are there in wild luxuriance, and trees of pomegranate with their large, brilliant scarlet blossoms, also other lovely blooming shrubs . . . a particular white rose was a favourite flower of Bahá'u'lláh's. This rose, single with golden centre, brownish stalks, shiny leaves, and a peculiarly delightful scent, is now flourishing at the Riḍván. Many bushes of these beautiful roses are in full bloom; the waxen cream and gold of their blossoms, and their burnished leaves, make a pure and peaceful note in the love-laden harmony of the glory of that garden.'[21]

rik'at [Ar] Prostration in prayer.

ringstone symbol A form of the Greatest Name, designed by 'Abdu'l-Bahá, used on Bahá'í rings. Bahá'ís are not obliged to wear a ring carrying this emblem, as there is no specific law of Bahá'u'lláh's requiring it. However, 'Abdu'l-Bahá told the friends in the West that the ring should be placed on the right hand, which is a perpetuation of an Islamic law.

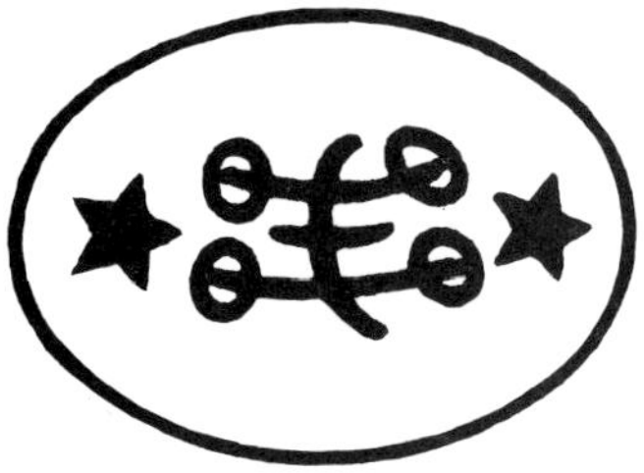
Ringstone symbol

The symbol has two elements: the design itself and the letters it contains. As to the design, the three horizontal strokes represent, from the top, the world of God, the Creator; the world of the Manifestation, the Cause or Command; and the world of man, the creation. The vertical line is a repeat of the second horizontal line, the world of the Manifestation, thus joining the world of the Creator to that of His creation. The two stars represent the human body, as well as the two Manifestations, the Báb and Bahá'u'lláh, for this day.

As to the letters of the symbol, these are 'b' and 'h'. 'B' stands for the name 'Bahá' and 'h' for the name 'Báb'.[22]

ritual An action performed according to a prescribed manner.

Bahá'u'lláh eliminated elaborate religious rites, although He prescribed certain simple ones such as the marriage ceremony and the observances connected with burial and the obligatory prayers. Shoghi Effendi, through his secretary, explained: 'Bahá'u'lláh has reduced all ritual and form to an absolute minimum in His Faith. The few forms that there are – like those associated with the two longer obligatory prayers, are only symbols of the inner attitude.'[23]

Root, Martha Hand of the Cause, whom, in 1942, Shoghi Effendi called 'that archetype of Bahá'í itinerant teachers and the foremost Hand raised by Bahá'u'lláh since 'Abdu'l-Bahá's passing' and to whom he awarded the title of 'Leading Ambassadress of His Faith and Pride of Bahá'í teachers, whether men or women, in both the East and the West'.[24]

Martha Root was the first to arise in response to the call of 'Abdu'l-Bahá in *The Tablets of the Divine Plan*. She travelled around the world four times over a period of twenty years, travelling four times to China and Japan, three times to India, and visiting every major city in South America. She spoke of the Bahá'í Faith to 'kings, queens, princes and princesses, presidents of republics, ministers and statesmen, publicists, professors, clergymen and poets, as well as a vast number of people in various walks of life, and contacted, both officially and informally, religious congresses, peace societies, Esperanto associations, socialist congresses, Theosophical societies, women's clubs and other kindred organizations . . .'[25] Her eight successive audiences with Queen Marie of Rumania resulted in the Queen becoming a Bahá'í. Her death in Honolulu in September 1939 'brought to a close a life which may well be regarded as the fairest fruit as yet yielded by the Formative Age of the Dispensation of Bahá'u'lláh.'[26]

Rúḥíyyih Khánum *See* Amatu'l-Bahá Rúḥíyyih Khánum.

Rúḥu'lláh The twelve-year-old son of Mírzá 'Alí-Muḥammad (Varqá), who was martyred in Iran after the assassination of Náṣiri'd-Dín Sháh. Even after Rúḥu'lláh had been made to watch the brutal murder of his father, the boy refused to renounce his Faith and was strangled by the executioner.

See also Varqá.

rulers The elected branch of the Bahá'í Administrative Order which includes the 'Local, National and International Houses of Justice' (local and national spiritual assemblies and the Universal House of Justice). The function of the institution of the 'rulers', in contrast to that of the 'learned', is decision-making and legislative.

See also learned *and* Kings, Tablets to the.

Right Martha Root
Far right Rúḥu'lláh Varqá

S

sacrifice To give up, suffer the loss of, or renounce something for the sake of God, an ideal or belief.

'This is the reason why the universal Manifestations of God unveil Their countenances to man, and endure every calamity and sore affliction, and lay down Their lives as a ransom; it is to make these very people, the ready ones, the ones who have capacity, to become dawning points of light, and to bestow upon them the life that fadeth never. This is the true sacrifice: the offering of oneself, even as did Christ, as a ransom for the life of the world.'[1]

'In one of His Tablets, 'Abdu'l-Bahá explains that not until a seed completely disintegrates under the soil can it produce a tree. It is then that the object as insignificant as a seed, by sacrificing itself completely, will be transformed into a mighty tree with branches, fruits and flowers. It is the same when man sacrifices something of his own.'[2]

'Self-sacrifice means to subordinate this lower nature and its desires to the more Godly and noble side of ourselves. Ultimately, in its highest sense, self-sacrifice means to give our will and our all to God to do with as He pleases. Then He purifies and glorifies our true self until it becomes a shining and wonderful reality.'[3]

Sadratu'l-Muntahá [Ar] The 'Tree beyond which there is no passing'.[4] Originally the tree which, in ancient times, the Arabs planted to mark the end of a road. In the Bahá'í Writings, a symbol of the Manifestation of God, the 'Tree beyond which neither men nor angels can pass'; specifically, Bahá'u'lláh. Sometimes called the Divine or Sacred Lote Tree. 'Twin Lote Trees': the Báb and Bahá'u'lláh.

sadrih [Ar] Tree.

Ṣáḥibu'z-Zamán The Lord of the Age. A title of the Qá'im.

Salásil One of two chains (the other was Qará-Guhar) by which Bahá'u'lláh was chained in the Síyáh-Chál in 1852.

Ṣáliḥ Prophet of God who appeared before Abraham and who was sent to the tribe of Thamúd in Arabia. He exhorted the people to believe in God and to stop worshipping idols, and warned them that if they did not respond to his message, they would be struck by a calamity and would be punished by God. Eventually an earthquake wiped out the whole tribe except Ṣáliḥ and his followers.

Sám Khán The colonel who commanded the Armenian regiment of Urúmíyyih which was ordered to execute the Báb in the barracks square of Tabríz in July 1850. Sám Khán was so impressed by the Báb and affected by the treatment He had received that he feared the wrath of God if he shed the Báb's blood. He told the Báb that he was a Christian and held no ill will against Him, and asked to be freed from the obligation to execute Him. The Báb instructed him to follow his orders, and if his intentions were sincere, God would relieve his perplexity. When the bullets of the regiment's 750 rifles failed to harm the Báb or His companion, Sám Khán ordered his regiment to leave the barracks and vowed not to proceed with the executions, even if it cost him his life.

See also Martyrdom of the Báb.

Sarkár-Áqá [Ar] The Honourable Master. A title of 'Abdu'l-Bahá.

Satan, satanic In the Bahá'í Writings, the terms 'Satan' and 'satanic' are used metaphorically to refer to the lower, base, selfish side of human beings, in contrast to their higher, virtuous, selfless side. Bahá'ís do not believe evil originates in a creature called Satan but that the capacity for 'satanic' actions, like the capacity for good, exists within man himself. Bahá'u'lláh explains: 'Know verily that Knowledge is of two kinds: Divine and Satanic. The one welleth out from the fountain of divine inspiration; the other is but a reflection of vain and obscure thoughts. The source of the former is God Himself; the motive-force of the latter the whisperings of selfish desire.'[5]

scholarship Advanced study of specific subjects; the character, qualities or attainments of one who has undertaken advanced studies in a special field; a fund of knowledge and learning.

The need for scholars of the Bahá'í Faith was indicated in a letter written on behalf of Shoghi Effendi in 1932 and in a letter written in 1949: 'Shoghi Effendi surely hopes that before long the Cause would produce scholars that would write books which would be far deeper and more universal in scope [than Esslemont's *Bahá'u'lláh and the New Era*].' 'It seems what we need now is a more profound and coordinated Bahá'í scholarship . . .' In 1979 the Universal House of Justice stated in a letter addressed to participants in a Bahá'í Studies Seminar at Cambridge, England, that it regarded Bahá'í scholarship of 'great potential importance for the development and consolidation of the Bahá'í community as it emerges from obscurity'.

A major function of Bahá'í scholarship is to enable Bahá'ís to apply the teachings of their Faith to contemporary problems. In a letter written on his behalf in 1949, Shoghi Effendi stated: 'We need Bahá'í scholars, not only people far, far more deeply aware of what our teachings really are, but also well-read and educated people capable of correlating our teachings to the current thoughts of the leaders of society.' Another function is to assist in the defence of the Bahá'í community from verbal and written attacks by building and drawing upon the body of knowledge necessary to refute arguments. In 1942, Shoghi Effendi, in a letter written on his behalf, stated: 'There is an answer in the teachings for everything; unfortunately, the majority of Bahá'ís, however intensely devoted and sincere they may be, lack for the most part the necessary scholarship and wisdom to reply to and refute the claims and attacks of people with some education and standing . . .'

Serious, critical examination of the Bahá'í Faith by Bahá'í and other scholars was limited for many years as the Bahá'ís concentrated on developing the administrative institutions of the Faith. However, during an earlier period several Bahá'í scholars did emerge, notably Mírzá Abu'l-Faḍl.

A renewed interest in Bahá'í studies developed in the Bahá'í community in the early 1970s, and informal groups of Bahá'ís with an academic interest in the Faith emerged, encouraged by the writings of Hand of the Cause H. M. Balyuzi. Increasingly Bahá'ís undertook academic research into the Bábí and Bahá'í religions and several post-graduate theses were written.

Further impetus for this trend was given by the Universal House of Justice when in 1974 it called upon the Canadian Bahá'í community to 'cultivate opportunities for formal presentations, courses and lectureships on the Bahá'í Faith in Canadian universities and other institutions of higher learning'. As a result, the Canadian National Spiritual Assembly established the Canadian Association for Studies on the Bahá'í Faith. Branches of the Association with similar aims were established in several countries and in 1981 the name was changed to the Association for Bahá'í Studies, reflecting the international membership and activities of the Association.

In an article in *The Bahá'í World: 1979–1983*, Gerald Filson writes that the Association is designed to 'provide a suitable means of approach to intellectuals and universities and bring to these circles an awareness of the Faith and an acquaintance with the academic resources which are available to facilitate formal study of it'. The Association holds annual international conferences, several regional conferences and special theme conferences all of which provide a forum for intellectual and spiritual development. Special interest groups cater for such subjects as education, social and economic development and so on. An affiliated organization, the Bahá'í International Health Agency, was launched in 1982.

The Association publishes the papers of the annual and theme conferences in its periodical *Bahá'í Studies Notebook*. In addition to this the Association has published *Bahá'í Studies*, a periodical examining different themes such as marriage, poetry as a response to the revelation of Bahá'u'lláh, and the establishment of a violence-free society. In 1988 the Association inaugurated *The Journal of Bahá'í Studies*, a quarterly journal making available the results of current studies into the Bahá'í Faith.

science In the Bahá'í teachings, the study of sciences must have as its goal the welfare and benefit of mankind. Bahá'u'lláh writes, 'Knowledge is as wings to man's life, and a ladder for his ascent. Its acquisition is incumbent upon everyone. The knowledge of such sciences, however, should be acquired as can profit the peoples of the earth, and not those which begin with words and end with words. Great indeed is the claim of scientists and craftsmen on the peoples of the world . . . In truth, knowledge is a veritable treasure for man, and a source of glory, of bounty, of joy, of exaltation, of cheer and gladness unto him.'[6]

'It is permissible to study sciences and arts, but such sciences as are useful and would redound to the progress and advancement of the people.'[7]

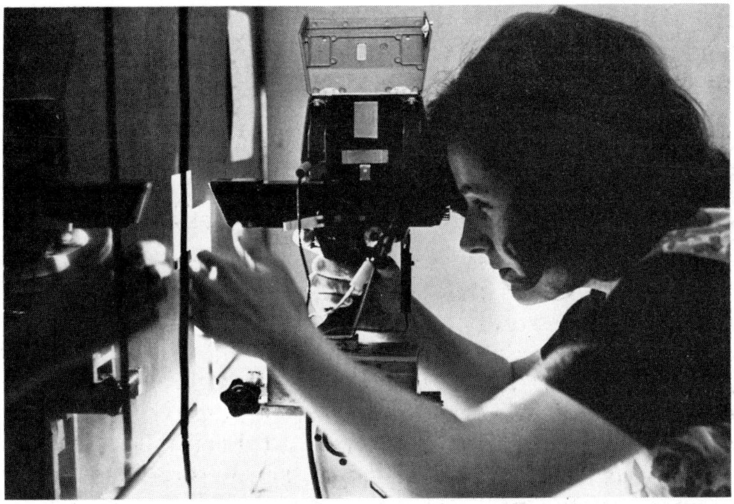

The goal of the study of sciences must be the welfare of mankind

science and religion, harmony of A fundamental principle of Bahá'í social teaching. 'Abdu'l-Bahá explained: '. . . Religion and science are in complete agreement. Every religion which is not in accordance with established science is superstition. Religion must be reasonable. If it does not square with reason, it is superstition and without foundation. It is like a mirage, which deceives man by leading him to think it is a body of water. God has endowed man with reason that he may perceive what is true. If we insist that such and such a subject is not to be reasoned out and tested according to the established logical modes of the intellect, what is the use of the reason which God has given man?'[8]

Scriptures, Holy The Holy Books of all the Manifestations of God, such as the Old and New Testaments, the Qur'án and the *Bayán*. All the Writings of Bahá'u'lláh and of 'Abdu'l-Bahá are Holy Scripture.

Seal of the Prophets Muḥammad. Muḥammad was the last of the Manifestations to prophesy the coming of Bahá'u'lláh, and His Dispensation the last of the prophetic cycle of religion. With the appearance of the Báb, this cycle closed. The Báb's Mission was not to foretell the Day of God but to announce it.[9]

Seat of the Universal House of Justice The building on the Arc of Mount Carmel which houses the council chamber and offices of the Universal House of Justice. The Universal House of Justice wrote that the Seat 'will not only serve the practical needs of a steadily consolidating administrative centre but will, for centuries to come, stand as a visible expression of the majesty of the divinely ordained institutions of the Administrative Order of Bahá'u'lláh.'[10]

Some volumes of Bahá'í Holy Scripture with other Bahá'í books

Seat of the Universal House of Justice

The building, designed by architect Husayn Amanat, was begun in 1972 and completed in 1982. Its design is classical with a marble exterior and a colonnade of fifty-eight pillars. The interior is 'simple, open, and adaptable to the evolving functions of a long future in service to the Faith.'[11]

Secondary House of Justice *See* national spiritual assembly.

Servant of Bahá 'Abdu'l-Bahá.

service Helpful or useful act, helping others.

To become a servant of God, one must serve mankind. Bahá'u'lláh has stated: 'That one indeed is a man who, today, dedicateth himself to the service of the entire human race. The Great Being saith: Blessed and happy is he that ariseth to promote the best interests of the peoples and kindreds of the earth.'[12]

'In His Teaching Bahá'u'lláh has made it clear that there are only three stations in this world of existence. First, the station of God which is beyond our comprehension, then the station of the Manifestation of God which is exalted above the world of humanity, and lastly the station of man which is that of servitude.'[13]

See also work.

Seven Martyrs of Ṭihrán *See* Ṭihrán, Seven Martyrs of.

Seven Valleys* and *The Four Valleys, The Two mystical works revealed by Bahá'u'lláh in Baghdád after He returned from Sulaymáníyyih.

The Seven Valleys was written to answer the questions of Shaykh Muḥyí'd-Dín, a Ṣúfí. It describes the seven stages of the journey of the soul towards God, as set forth by the 12th-century Ṣúfí poet 'Aṭṭár in his poem 'Language of the Birds'. Bahá'u'lláh speaks of these stages as the valleys of Search, Love, Knowledge, Unity, Contentment, Wonderment, and True Poverty and Absolute Nothingness.

The Four Valleys was written to Shaykh 'Abdu'r-Raḥmán of Karkúk who had become an admirer of Bahá'u'lláh in Sulaymáníyyih. This work also describes in mystical language the journey towards the divine goal, in four stages or valleys.

Seven Year Plan *See* plans, teaching.

sex The Bahá'í concept of sex is explained by Shoghi Effendi as being 'based on the belief that chastity should be strictly practised by both sexes, not only because it is in itself highly commendable ethically, but also due to its being the only way to a happy and successful marital life. Sex relationships of any form, outside marriage, are not permissible therefore, and whoso violates this rule will not only be responsible to God, but will incur the necessary punishment from society.

'The Bahá'í Faith recognizes the value of the sex impulse, but condemns its illegitimate and improper expressions, such as free love, companionate marriage and others, all of which it considers positively harmful to man and to the society in which he lives. The proper use of the sex instinct is the natural right of every individual, and it is precisely for this purpose that the institution of marriage has been established. Bahá'ís do not believe in the suppression of the sex impulse but in its regulation and control.'[14] He further explained that 'Homosexuality, according to the Writings of Bahá'u'lláh, is spiritually condemned. This does not mean that people so afflicted must not be helped and advised and sympathized with. It does mean that we do not believe that it is a permissible way of life . . .'[15]

Shíráz

sháh [Pers] King, especially of Iran.

Sháh-Bahrám The World Saviour promised by the prophet Zoroaster. He foretold that 3,000 years of conflict would precede the coming of the Sháh-Bahrám, who would triumph over Ahriman, the personification of evil, and bring an era of blessedness and peace. Bahá'ís believe this prophecy refers to the coming of Bahá'u'lláh.

Sharaf [Ar] Honour. The sixteenth month of the Bahá'í year (from sunset 30 December to sunset 18 January).

Sharí'at (also, sharí'a) Islamic religious law including parts of the Qur'án as well as other laws. The Sharí'at was abrogated by the laws revealed by the Báb and Bahá'u'lláh.

shaykh [Ar] A title of respect which was generally given to an old man, denoting reverence, especially referring to one who is a venerated teacher or the head of an order of ṣúfís.

Shaykhí A follower of Shaykh Aḥmad-i-Aḥsá'í and his successor Siyyid Káẓim-i-Rashtí, who taught that the resurrection, Muḥammad's Night Journey, and the signs accompanying the coming of the Qá'im, were allegorical events with a spiritual meaning rather than physical occurrences, and that the time of the coming of the Qá'im was near.

Shaykhu'l-Islám In Shí'ih Islam, a leading Muslim divine; the head of a religious court, a position appointed by the sháh though sometimes passed from father to son. When the Báb was interrogated by the divines of Tabríz, it was the Shaykhu'l-Islám himself, Ḥájí Mírzá 'Alí Aṣghar, who inflicted the bastinado on Him when the guards refused to do so.

She-Serpent *See* Raqshá.

Shí'ih (Shí'í, Shí'ah, Shi'ite) One of the two major branches of Islam. Shí'ih Muslims believe in the succession of 'Alí after Muḥammad and in the Imamate, and many are waiting for the appearance of the Twelfth or Hidden Imám. The Shí'ih Muslims are regarded by the Báb and Bahá'u'lláh as the followers of the true sect of Islam.
See also Sunní.

Shíráz The city in Iran which saw the opening of the Bahá'í Era with the Declaration of the Báb to Mullá Ḥusayn in the House of the Báb in Shíráz on the evening of 22 May 1844.

Shoghi Effendi

Shoghi Effendi The Guardian of the Bahá'í Faith, born on 1 March 1897 in 'Akká, the son of Ḍíyá'íyyih <u>Kh</u>ánum, the eldest daughter of 'Abdu'l-Bahá, and Mírzá Hádí <u>Sh</u>írází, a relative of the Báb. He was educated at the American University at Beirut and Balliol College, Oxford.

While at Oxford, Shoghi Effendi was informed of the passing of 'Abdu'l-Bahá and hurried back to Haifa, where he learned that he had been appointed Guardian of the Cause of God in 'Abdu'l-Bahá's Will and Testament: 'After the passing away of this wronged one, it is incumbent upon the A<u>gh</u>ṣán, the Afnán of the Sacred Lote-Tree, the Hands of the Cause of God and the loved ones of the Abhá Beauty to turn unto Shoghi Effendi . . . as he is the sign of God, the chosen branch, the guardian of the Cause of God . . . He is the expounder of the words of God . . .'[16]

Unable to bear his grief over the passing of 'Abdu'l-Bahá and crushed by the weight of the responsibilities so unexpectedly thrust upon him, Shoghi Effendi retired for some time from Haifa leaving Bahíyyih <u>Kh</u>ánum in charge. After about a year he returned to take up his office. He married Mary Maxwell, Amatu'l-Bahá Rúḥíyyih <u>Kh</u>ánum, in 1937.

Shoghi Effendi in 1922

Among the achievements of his ministry, the following stand out as the most notable: the establishment of the Administrative Order of the Bahá'í Faith (both its elected bodies and the appointed side of the administration); the spread of the Faith to all parts of the globe in a series of organized Plans; the elaboration of many aspects of the Faith and the guidance of the world Bahá'í community through the writing of numerous letters; the defence of the Faith from the actions of the Covenant-breakers; the translation of numerous passages from the Writings of Bahá'u'lláh; the writing of books such as *God Passes By* and the translation of *Nabíl's Narrative*; the acquisition of land and the planning and supervision of the laying out of the Bahá'í gardens in the Haifa–'Akká area; the supervision of the building of the Shrine of the Báb and the International Archives building.

Shoghi Effendi passed away on 5 November 1957 while in London and is buried in the New Southgate Cemetery there.

See also Guardian *and* Guardianship.

Shrine of 'Abdu'l-Bahá The three rooms on the north side of the Shrine of the Báb presently serve as the Shrine of 'Abdu'l-Bahá until such time as His own Shrine can be built. 'Abdu'l-Bahá is buried in the central room, while the western and eastern antechambers are places of prayer and visitation.

Shrine of the Báb Nine-roomed monument built on Mount Carmel, overlooking the Bay of Haifa, in the central room of which the remains of the Báb are buried.

In 1891 Bahá'u'lláh pointed out to 'Abdu'l-Bahá the site where the remains of the Báb were to be placed. In 1898 'Abdu'l-Bahá instructed that the remains of the Báb be brought from their hiding place in Ṭihrán to the Holy Land; they arrived in 'Akká in January 1899. In that same year 'Abdu'l-Bahá laid the foundation-stone of the edifice, and a

The Shrine of the Báb

few months later construction began. About the same time, the marble sarcophagus designed to receive the body of the Báb, a gift from the Bahá'ís of Rangoon, was shipped to Haifa.

There were many difficulties in completing the building of the Shrine: long negotiations with the owner of the building site; the exorbitant price at first demanded for the opening of a road leading to the site; the objections raised by officials; the false accusations brought by the Covenant-breakers as to the purpose of the building; 'Abdu'l-Bahá's enforced absences from Haifa and His consequent inability to supervise the building work.

The initial six-roomed building was completed in 1909 and on the first of Naw-Rúz in that year 'Abdu'l-Bahá had the sarcophagus transported to the vault prepared for it. In the evening he laid within it the wooden casket containing the remains of the Báb. This done, 'Abdu'l-Bahá cast aside His turban, removed His shoes, threw off His cloak, and bent low over the open sarcophagus. He rested His forehead on the border of the wooden casket and wept aloud.

Shoghi Effendi had a further three rooms built onto the Shrine, which now also housed the remains of 'Abdu'l-Bahá. In 1942 Shoghi Effendi asked architect Sutherland Maxwell to design a superstructure for the Shrine. The design was developed in close collaboration with the Guardian and in May 1944 a model was displayed for the first time. In April 1948 contracts were placed in Italy for the granite columns and the work of preparing the foundations was begun. In 1949 construction began and in October 1953 the work was completed.

The superstructure consists of a colonnade and arcade, an octagon above, the drum of the dome with eighteen lancet windows honouring the Letters of the Living, and finally the crown and dome with golden tiles and lantern. Around the Shrine Shoghi Effendi designed beautiful gardens.

Shoghi Effendi saw the Shrine of the Báb and the remains of the Báb within it as the focus of a planetary spiritual system: 'The outermost circle in this vast system . . . is none other than the entire planet. Within the heart of this planet lies the 'Most Holy Land' . . . Within this Most Holy Land rises the Mountain of God of immemorial sanctity . . . Reposing on the breast of this holy mountain are the extensive properties permanently dedicated to, and constituting the sacred precincts of, the Báb's holy Sepulchre. In the midst of these properties . . . is situated the most holy court, an enclosure comprising gardens and terraces . . . Embosomed in these lovely and verdant surroundings stands in all its exquisite beauty the mausoleum of the Báb, the shell designed to preserve and adorn the original structure raised by 'Abdu'l-Bahá . . . Within this shell is enshrined the Pearl of Great Price, the holy of holies, those chambers which constitute the tomb itself, and which were constructed by 'Abdu'l-Bahá. Within the heart of this holy of holies is the tabernacle, the vault wherein reposes the most holy casket. Within this vault rests the alabaster sarcophagus in which is deposited that inestimable jewel, the Báb's holy dust.'[17] 'Abdu'l-Bahá acclaimed the tomb housing the dust of the Báb as the 'spot round which the Concourse on high circle in adoration'.[18]

Shrine of Bahá'u'lláh The resting place of Bahá'u'lláh's mortal remains. On the day of Bahá'u'lláh's Ascension, 29 May 1892, He was laid to rest beneath the floor of a room in the house adjacent to the Mansion of Bahjí. The Shrine of Bahá'u'lláh is the holiest spot on earth to Bahá'ís, a place of pilgrimage and the Qiblih of the Bahá'í Faith.
See also Ḥaram-i-Aqdas.

The Shrine of Bahá'u'lláh

Six Year Plan *See* plans, teaching.

Síyáh-Chál The Black Pit. The subterranean dungeon in Ṭihrán where Bahá'u'lláh was imprisoned along with many other Bábís in the summer of 1852 following an attempt on the life of the Sháh by misguided Bábís. Bahá'u'lláh described it: 'Upon Our arrival We were first conducted along a pitch-black corridor, from whence We descended three steep flights of stairs to the place of confinement assigned to Us. The dungeon was wrapped in thick darkness, and Our fellow-prisoners numbered nearly a hundred and fifty souls; thieves, assassins and highwaymen . . . No pen can depict that place, nor any tongue describe its loathsome smell. Most of these men had neither clothes nor bedding to lie on. God alone knoweth what befell Us in that most foul-smelling and gloomy place!'[19] The Bábís were chained to one another and each day one would be taken out and killed. It was here in the Síyáh-Chál that Bahá'u'lláh received His divine revelation when the Holy Spirit appeared to Him in the form of a Maiden of Heaven.

siyyid A descendant of the Prophet Muḥammad through his daughter Fáṭimih, with the right to wear the green turban distinguishing his ancestry. A title prefixed to a man's name, denoting descent from the Prophet. The Báb was a siyyid.

Siyyid-i-Báb Name by which Iranians referred to the Báb.

Siyyid-i-Dhikr Lord of Remembrance. A designation of the Báb.

smoking Although the practice of smoking is not specifically prohibited in the Bahá'í Faith, it is strongly discouraged: 'Some . . . prohibitions were absolute, and binding upon all . . .' 'Abdu'l-Bahá explained. 'But there are other forbidden things which do not cause immediate harm, and the injurious effects of which are only gradually produced: such acts are also repugnant to the Lord, and blameworthy in His sight, and repellent. The absolute unlawfulness of these, however, hath not been expressly set forth in the Text, but their avoidance is necessary to purity, cleanliness, the preservation of health, and freedom from addiction.

'Among these latter is smoking tobacco, which is dirty, smelly, offensive – an evil habit, and one the harmfulness of which gradually becometh apparent to all. Every qualified physician hath ruled – and this hath also been proved by tests – that one of the components of tobacco is a deadly poison, and that the smoker is vulnerable to many and various diseases. This is why smoking hath been plainly set forth as repugnant from the standpoint of hygiene.'[20]

social and economic development *See* development, social and economic.

Some Answered Questions A volume first published in 1908 comprising questions posed to 'Abdu'l-Bahá by Laura Clifford Barney during several visits to 'Akká in 1904–6, along with 'Abdu'l-Bahá's answers and explanations. Topics touched upon include God, His Prophets, various Christian subjects, evolution, the soul, immortality, healing, the non-existence of evil and reincarnation. Shoghi Effendi termed Laura Clifford Barney's effort in compiling the volume 'imperishable'[21] and frequently mentioned this book as one of those which 'should be mastered by every Bahá'í'.[22]

Son of God Christ.

Son of the Wolf Shaykh Muḥammad-Taqí, known as Áqá Najafí, the son of Shaykh Muḥammad-Báqir, who was stigmatized by Bahá'u'lláh as the 'Wolf'. Áqá Najafí was an opponent of the Cause of Bahá'u'lláh, evil-minded and vicious. He collaborated with his father in the policy of murdering the Bahá'ís, and it was through his instigation that the great upheavals against the Bahá'ís occurred in Iṣfáhán and Yazd.

soul The inner and essential reality of man which is not composed of physical matter and thus continues to exist after death.

In the Bahá'í Writings the soul has been compared to a rider where the body is only the steed; to a light, independent of the lamp within which it shines; and to a caged bird which continues to exist after the cage is broken. Just as the bird, when released, is freed from constraints, the power of the soul is stronger without the intermediary of the body. While distinct from the body and its physical limitations, the soul is affected by occurrences and itself can affect the body physically.

As in the embryonic world the physical being acquires what is needed for life in the world, so in the physical world the soul must prepare itself for the next existence by acquiring spiritual virtues through knowledge and love of God, philanthropic deeds and self-sacrifice. After death the soul retains the spiritual attributes it has acquired during life in the physical body, and after it is freed from the body it progresses according to the mercy of God. Through the intercession and prayers of other human souls, or through charity performed in its name, it continues to progress until it attains the presence of God.

See also death, life after *and* death, nature of.

special event days In the United States and elsewhere, certain days, apart from the Bahá'í Holy Days, set aside (1) for proclamation or (2) to support United Nations observances. Bahá'í-initiated special event days such as World Religion Day (third Sunday in January) and Race Unity Day (second Sunday in June) are observed with the purpose of proclaiming the Faith and encouraging local government bodies to recognize the importance of these issues.

United Nations-sponsored and -initiated days supported by Bahá'í communities include United Nations Day (24 October), Human Rights

Day (10 December) and International Day of Peace (third Tuesday in September) which in 1985 replaced the Bahá'í-initiated World Peace Day. UN special event days are observed to show support for UN activities, not to seek direct Bahá'í proclamation.

See also Bahá'í International Community.

Spirit of God (Ar, Rúḥu'lláh) Jesus. The name by which He is mentioned in the Qur'án and in the Bahá'í Writings.

spiritual assembly *See* local spiritual assembly *and* national spiritual assembly.

Star of the West First Bahá'í magazine in the Western world, published in North America from 1910 to April 1924.

Bound volumes of *Star of the West*

study classes Meetings organized for the study of the Bahá'í Writings and literature. Bahá'ís are urged to make a thorough and profound study of the history, tenets and Sacred Writings of the Faith.

See also deepening.

Ṣubḥ-i-Azal *See* Yaḥyá, Mírzá.

Sublime Porte The Ottoman court, the government of the Turkish Empire. Taken from the gate or 'porte' of the Sulṭán's palace where in ancient times justice was dispensed. Generally refers to Constantinople (Istanbul).

Ṣúfí A member of a Muslim mystical order.

Sulaymáníyyih A town in Kurdish Iraq; it was in the mountains surrounding Sulaymáníyyih that Bahá'u'lláh resided from April 1854 to 1856.

As a result of the dissension among the Bábís in Baghdád and the sedition of Mírzá Yaḥyá, Bahá'u'lláh had decided to retire to the wilderness and left Baghdád, living in seclusion on a mountain called Sar-Galú. During this period, Áqá Abu'l-Qásim-i-Hamadání was His only companion. To conceal His identity, Bahá'u'lláh dressed as a dervish and took the name Darvísh Muḥammad-i-Íráníʼ. The inhabitants of the area came to revere Him, particularly the local ṣúfís, who sought Him out for explanations of mystical works. At their request He composed the poem called *Qaṣídiy-i-'Izz-i-Varqá'íyyih*, which originally consisted of 2000 couplets, only 127 of which Bahá'u'lláh allowed to be preserved.

Sulṭán [Ar] Sovereignty. The seventeenth month of the Bahá'í year (from sunset 18 January to sunset 6 February).

summer schools, Bahá'í Instructional sessions, often of a week or longer, during which Bahá'ís learn more about their Faith and have an opportunity to live together for a short time in accordance with Bahá'í ideals. Many summer schools are residential and some are owned by the Bahá'ís.

The subjects studied include Bahá'í history, Bahá'í administration, the moral and spiritual teachings of Bahá'u'lláh and Bahá'í law. Shoghi Effendi has said that they will develop into the universities of the future.

Summer school in Singapore

Sunní The majority sect of Islam, which accepts the caliphs as the deputies of Muḥammad and heads of Islam, denying the authority to succession claimed by the hereditary Imáms.
See also Shí'ih.

Supreme Concourse Also 'Concourse on High', 'Celestial Concourse'. The 'hosts of the Supreme Concourse of heaven'. The gathering of the Prophets and holy souls in the next world or spiritual realm.

Supreme Pen Title of Bahá'u'lláh.

súrih (also, súra) [Ar] Literally, a row or series. In Islam, the chapters of the Qur'án. In certain Writings of Bahá'u'lláh it denotes 'Tablet'.

Súriy-i-Ghuṣn *See* Tablet of the Branch.

Súriy-i-Haykal Tablet of the Temple. In this Tablet Bahá'u'lláh reveals the majesty and glory of the Temple, which is His own Self, and unveils new facets of God's revelation. Bahá'u'lláh ordered this Súrih, together with the Tablets to the Kings, to be copied in the form of a pentacle symbolizing the human-temple.

Súrih of Joseph A chapter of the Qur'án relating the story, from Genesis, of Jacob's son Joseph, who was sold into slavery by his brother but was elevated by Pharaoh to rule over Egypt. The Súrih of Joseph is said to have been revealed by Muḥammad in order to prove the truth of His Mission, in response to a challenge. Before setting out in search of the Promised One, Mullá Ḥusayn had decided that one of the proofs by which he would judge any man who might claim to be the awaited Messenger would be his ability to reveal without hesitation a commentary on the Súrih of Joseph. On the evening of 22 May 1844, when Mullá Ḥusayn was in the presence of the Báb, the Báb revealed, unasked, His commentary on that subject. It is known as the *Qayyúmu'l-Asmá'*.

Súrih of Kawthar A súrih of the Qur'án. Muḥammad Sháh sent Siyyid Yaḥyáy-i-Dárábí, a prominent Muslim divine, to investigate the claim of the Báb. After two interviews with the Báb, Siyyid Yaḥyá determined to set a test for the Báb which he thought impossible: if the Báb, unasked, would reveal a commentary on the súrih which the Siyyid had in mind (the Súrih of Kawthar) in a style different from the commentators of the time, Siyyid Yaḥyá would accept the Báb's claim. When the Báb did so, Siyyid Yaḥyá, overwhelmed, immediately became a Bábí.
See also Vaḥíd.

Súriy-i-Mulúk Tablet of Kings. Revealed by Bahá'u'lláh in Arabic while He was in Adrianople, the *Súriy-i-Mulúk* is addressed to the kings of the world collectively. It proclaims the station of Bahá'u'lláh and puts forward His claims as the Manifestation of God for this age.

Súriy-i-Ra'ís Tablet by Bahá'u'lláh revealed in honour of Ḥájí Muḥammad Ismá'il-i-Káshání and addressed to 'Alí Páshá, the Grand Vizier of Turkey. Bahá'u'lláh rebukes 'Alí Páshá and bids him hearken to the voice of God. He affirms that the tribulations and sufferings inflicted upon the believers will act as oil for the lamp of the Cause of God and add to its radiance and glory.

T

Ṭá, Land of Ṭihrán, so referred to in the Writings of Bahá'u'lláh. 'Ṭá' is the letter ṭ.

Ṭabarsí, Fort of Shaykh Shrine of Shaykh Aḥmad ibn-i-Abí-Ṭálib-i-Ṭabarsí about fourteen miles southeast of Bárfurúsh, Iran, which in October 1848 the Bábís, under the supervision of Mullá Ḥusayn, built a fortress around to use as a safe camp. 313 Bábís were encamped at Shaykh Ṭabarsí. The clergy of Bárfurúsh, and later the government, sent army after army to reduce their numbers, but the Bábís held out against them from 12 October 1848 until 9 May 1849. Mullá Ḥusayn was killed in February 1849 on a sortie from the fort and was buried inside the shrine. The pressure on the Bábís increased, food became scarce, and the defenders had to eat grass, the leaves of trees, the skin and ground bone of their slaughtered horses and the boiled leather of

Part of the Fort of Shaykh Ṭabarsí

their saddles. The siege ended when the commander of the attacking forces, Prince Mihdí-Qulí Mírzá, swore a false oath on the Qur'án that the lives and property of the Bábís would be inviolate should they come out of the fort and disperse. A horse was sent for Quddús to take him to the camp of the Prince, but once the Bábís came out of the fort, they were massacred, the fortress pillaged and razed to the ground. Quddús was taken to Bárfurúsh, tortured and killed.

See also Ḥusayn-i-Bushrú'í, Mullá *and* Quddús.

A Tablet of Bahá'u'lláh in the hand of 'Abdu'l-Bahá

Tablet (lawḥ) Divinely revealed scripture. Originally, the tables, or tablets, of the Law brought down from Mount Sinai by Moses. In Bahá'í scripture the term is used in the title of certain Writings revealed by Bahá'u'lláh and 'Abdu'l-Bahá. It is also used generally to refer to their written works.

Tablet of the Branch (*Súriy-i-Ghuṣn*) A Tablet of Bahá'u'lláh revealed in Adrianople, addressed to Mírzá 'Alí-Riḍáy-i-Mustawfí, a Bahá'í of Khurásán. It describes the station of 'Abdu'l-Bahá, to Whom Bahá'u-'lláh had given the title of Most Great Branch (Ghuṣn-i-A'ẓam). In this Tablet Bahá'u'lláh writes: 'Verily the Limb of the Law of God hath sprung forth from this Root which God hath firmly implanted in the Ground of His Will, and Whose Branch hath been so uplifted as to encompass the whole of creation . . . Whoso turneth towards Him hath turned towards God, and whoso turneth away from Him hath turned away from My Beauty, hath repudiated My Proof, and transgressed against Me . . . They who deprive themselves of the shadow of the Branch, are lost in the wilderness of error, are consumed by the heat of worldly desires, and are of those who will assuredly perish.'[1]

Tablet of Carmel *(Lawḥ-i-Karmil)* Tablet revealed in Arabic by

Bahá'u'lláh on Mount Carmel, probably on His fourth visit to that spot in 1891. It is considered to be one of the most momentous revealed during His ministry. The Tablet contains significant allusions to the establishment of the World Centre of the Bahá'í Faith and is stated by Shoghi Effendi to be its charter.

Tablets of the Divine Plan Fourteen Tablets revealed by 'Abdu'l-Bahá during the First World War, addressed to the Bahá'ís in North America and received by them in 1919, which Shoghi Effendi has called the 'mandate' and 'the supreme charter for teaching'.[2] They are addressed either to the Bahá'ís of the United States and Canada as one body or to one of five regional areas of North America.

The 'mandate' was to carry the 'fame of the Cause of God' to the East and to the West and to spread the Glad Tidings of the coming of Bahá'u'lláh throughout the five continents of the world.[3] In all, 'Abdu'l-Bahá mentioned some 120 territories and islands to which the message of Bahá'u'lláh was to be carried.

The first eight Tablets were revealed between 26 March and 22 April 1916, and the final six between 2 February and 8 March 1917. Of the first group, five Tablets reached America and were published in the 8 September 1916 issue of *Star of the West*. After that, communication with the Holy Land was cut off and the rest of the Tablets remained in the vault under the Shrine of the Báb until the end of the war. They were dispatched to America and unveiled in a ceremony during the 'Convention of the Covenant' held at the Hotel McAlpin in New York in April 1919.

An immediate response to the Tablets was made by Martha Root, who began her world travels, and by Mr and Mrs Hyde Dunn, who arose to move to Australia. However, it was not until 1937, when Shoghi Effendi gave the American believers the First Seven Year Plan, that the Divine Plan began to be generally implemented.

Tabríz Capital of Á<u>dh</u>arbáyján, Iran, where the Báb was kept forty days before being incarcerated in Máh-Kú. He was taken there again in

Tabríz

July 1848 to be interrogated by the ‘ulamá and Crown Prince Náṣiri’d-Dín, and afterwards subjected to the bastinado. It was in Tabríz that the Báb was martyred before a firing squad in the barracks square on 9 July 1850.

Ṭáhirih The Pure One. Title given by the Báb to Fáṭimih Umm-Salamih, also known by the titles Qurratu’l-‘Ayn (Solace of the Eyes) and Zarrín-Táj (Crown of Gold). Ṭáhirih was the only woman Letter of the Living. At the Conference of Badasht she cast aside her veil, proclaiming the new day.

Ṭáhirih was ‘born in the same year as Bahá’u’lláh; regarded from her childhood . . . as a prodigy, alike in her intelligence and beauty; highly esteemed even by some of the most haughty and learned ‘ulamá of her country, prior to her conversion, for the brilliancy and novelty of the views she propounded . . . she had, through a dream . . . established her first contact with a Faith which she continued to propagate to her last breath, and in its hour of greatest peril, with all the ardour of her unsubduable spirit.’[4] She was martyred in the Ílkhání garden, strangled with her own silken kerchief which she had reserved for the purpose. ‘Her body was lowered into a well, which was then filled with earth and stones, in the manner she herself had desired. Thus ended the life of this great Bábí heroine, the first woman suffrage martyr, who, at her death, turning to the one in whose custody she had been placed, had boldly declared: “You can kill me as soon as you like, but you cannot stop the emancipation of women.”’[5]

Ṭáhirih’s handwriting

Táj of Bahá'u'lláh

Mírzá Taqí Khán

táj Crown or diadem. A tall felt hat often worn by the leader of a religious (Ṣúfí) order. On the first day of the Festival of Riḍván, Bahá'u'lláh set out from His home in Baghdád for the Garden of Riḍván wearing a finely embroidered táj instead of His usual headgear. It was noted as a symbolic sign of His divine authority.

Tajallíyát Effulgences. A Tablet of Bahá'u'lláh revealed in honour of Ustád 'Alí-Akbar, a martyr of Yazd. The four 'Tajallíyát' it expounds are the knowledge of God, which is attainable only through His Manifestation; steadfastness in the Cause of God through faith in His wisdom; the value of those arts and sciences which profit mankind, 'not those which begin with words and end with words'[6]; and recognition of Divinity in its Manifestation.

Tákur Village in the district of Núr, in the province of Mázindarán, Iran, where Bahá'u'lláh's ancestral home was located.

Taqí Khán-i-Faráhání, Mírzá Grand Vizier of Náṣiri'd-Dín Sháh, known as Amír Kabír (the Great Emir). He was a great reformer but a bitter enemy of the Bábí Faith. Mírzá Taqí Khán wielded power while the Sháh was a boy and determined to stamp out the Faith of the Báb. He was involved in the lengthy persecution of Bábís at Fort Ṭabarsí, Nayríz and Zanján; the murder of the Seven Martyrs of Ṭihrán; and he gave the order for the execution of the Báb. Mírzá Taqí Khán eventually lost his position and the Sháh, jealous of his power, ordered him to be murdered.

Taqíyyih [Pers] Dissembling, giving lip-denial of one's faith. This was permitted by Shí'ih Islam in time of peril, but it is forbidden to Bahá'ís.

Ṭarázát (Ornaments) A Tablet of Bahá'u'lláh containing six passages, each called a 'Ṭaráz', on such subjects as self-knowledge, consorting 'with the followers of all religions in a spirit of friendliness and fellowship',[7] good character, trustworthiness, the appreciation of arts and crafts, truthfulness and accuracy. It includes an injunction to the people of the Bayán and to Hádí Dawlat-Ábádí, a mullá of Iṣfáhán who became a Bábí but later recanted his faith.

Tarbíyat Schools Highly acclaimed schools, one for boys and one for girls, founded in Ṭihrán. The boys' school was established in 1898, while the girls' school was founded by Dr Susan Moody after her arrival in Ṭihrán in 1909. Both schools were owned and managed entirely by Bahá'ís, although children of all religions attended, particularly the children of government and civic officials.

The Tarbíyat School for Boys, Ṭihrán

The schools had always closed on the nine Bahá'í holy days but on the pretext that the Bahá'ís belonged to a denomination not officially recognized in Iran, the Ministry of Education in 1934 demanded that the schools remain open for these days. Shoghi Effendi refused to allow this and ordered the schools to close on the anniversary of the martyrdom of the Báb. As he would not let the Bahá'ís deny their Faith, nor allow the schools to remain open on holy days, the government refused permission for the schools to re-open after the holy day. The Tarbíyat Schools remain closed to this day.

ṭaríqat [Pers] Way, path; especially the way taken by the mystic wayfarer on the journey of spiritual enlightenment.

Tea House of 'Abdu'l-Bahá A 'three-room, single-storey structure just outside the northern wall of the Bayḍún estate, at the southern edge of the Bahá'í property at Bahjí'.[8] It was owned by a Persian family and was converted to its present state by Shoghi Effendi. During the time of 'Abdu'l-Bahá, when the Covenant-breakers had possession of Bahjí, this building and the one now known as the Pilgrim House were the only two properties at Bahjí in the possession of the Bahá'ís.

Tea House of 'Abdu'l-Bahá

teaching Sharing the Bahá'í message with others.

Bahá'u'lláh has stated: 'Teach thou the Cause of God with an utterance which will cause the bushes to be enkindled, and the call "Verily, there is no God but Me, the All-Mighty, the Unconstrained" to be raised therefrom.'[9] 'Abdu'l-Bahá says, 'Of all the gifts of God the greatest is the gift of teaching.'[10]

Bahá'ís are enjoined to teach their Faith with kindness and good-will: 'Should any one among you be incapable of grasping a certain truth, or be striving to comprehend it, show forth, when conversing with him, a spirit of extreme kindliness and good-will. Help him to see and recognize the truth, without esteeming yourself to be, in the least, superior to him, or to be possessed of greater endowments.'[11] 'Abdu'l-Bahá describes the qualities a Bahá'í teacher must possess: 'If thou wishest to guide the souls, it is incumbent on thee to be firm, to be good and to be imbued with praiseworthy attributes and divine qualities under all circumstances. Be a sign of love, a manifestation of mercy, a fountain of tenderness, kind-hearted, good to all and gentle to the servants of God, and especially to those who bear relation to thee, both men and women.'[12]

Members of the first local all-girl teaching team of Papua New Guinea, 1982

temple *See* Ma<u>sh</u>riqu'l-A<u>dh</u>kár.

Temple Unity, Bahá'í *See* Bahá'í Temple Unity.

Templers Members of the Society of the Temple, founded in Württemberg, Germany, in the mid-1800s by Christoph Hoffman, Georg David

Hardegg and Christoph Paulus, who believed that the second coming of Christ would occur sometime soon. When their prediction of the second coming of Christ apparently failed, they focused instead on the idea of a Christian community living together in Jerusalem following the true precepts of Christ.

The first and largest settlement of Templers was in Haifa, established under Hardegg's leadership in 1868–9. The houses of the Templers with their distinctive red-tiled roofs can be seen at the foot of Mount Carmel, many bearing pious quotations carved into the lintels over their doorways.

Bahá'u'lláh stayed some nights in one of the Templer buildings, now called Oliphant House, and 'Abdu'l-Bahá had cordial relations with the Templers. The Templer Wilhelm Deiss planted the cypresses behind the Shrine of the Báb and became gardener to 'Abdu'l-Bahá.

The Templer colony at the foot of Mount Carmel

Ten Year Crusade Ten-year teaching Plan initiated by Shoghi Effendi in 1953 and culminating at Riḍván 1963 with the election of the Universal House of Justice. Shoghi Effendi passed away before the midpoint of the Plan, and the remaining work was supervised and coordinated by the Hands of the Cause.

Shoghi Effendi said of the Crusade: 'The avowed, the primary aim of this Spiritual Crusade is none other than the conquest of the citadels of men's hearts. The theatre of its operations is the entire planet. Its duration a whole decade. Its commencement synchronizes with the Centenary of the birth of Bahá'u'lláh's Mission. Its culmination will coincide with the Centenary of the Declaration of that same mission.'[13]

The four-fold objectives of the Crusade were: the development of the institutions at the World Centre; the consolidation of the communities of the participating national spiritual assemblies; the consolidation of all territories already opened to the Faith; and the opening of the main unopened territories.

See also Knights of Bahá'u'lláh *and* plans, teaching.

Thámud Said to be a descendant of Noah. The people of Thámud were a tribe in Southern Arabia who were the successors to the culture and civilization of the people of 'Ád. Tradition says that they were a younger branch of the same tribe and lived in the same regions of the Arabian peninsula. They were idolators and skilful carvers of stone. The prophet Ṣáliḥ was sent to them by God to exhort them to believe in God and stop worshipping idols. When they ignored him, the people of Thamúd were wiped out by an earthquake.[14]

See also 'Ád, Húd and Ṣáliḥ.

Ṭihrán (also, Tehran) Capital of Iran, location of the Síyáh-Chál, the underground prison where Bahá'u'lláh was imprisoned in 1852 and where He received His Revelation.

Ṭihrán, Seven Martyrs of Seven followers of the Báb, prominent and distinguished men, who were arrested in 1850 on the false charges of plotting against the life of the Grand Vizier. Despite offers to spare their lives if they recanted their faith, they refused to do so. They were beheaded and their corpses left three days in the public square to endure the desecration of the Shí'ih mobs. The Seven Martyrs were Ḥájí Mírzá Siyyid 'Alí, maternal uncle of the Báb; Mírzá Qurbán-'Alí, a leading figure of a dervish order; Ḥájí Mullá Ismá'íl-i-Qumí, a former disciple of Siyyid Káẓim; Siyyid Ḥusayn-i-Turshízí, an esteemed mujtahid; Ḥájí Muḥammad-Taqíy-i-Kirmání, a leading merchant; Siyyid Murtaḍá, a noted merchant of Zanján; and Muḥammad-Ḥusayn-i-Marághi'í. The last three were so eager to be martyrs that each pleaded with the executioner to be allowed to die first. The executioner's answer was to behead them together.

Ṭihrán

Townshend, George Hand of the Cause, born in Dublin and educated at Oxford. Townshend was ordained as an Anglican priest in 1906 in the United States. He first heard of the Bahá'í Faith after his return to Ireland when a friend wrote to him from the United States. He soon began to work for the Faith although it was not until 1947 that he formally resigned his orders and became a full member of the Bahá'í community. He was among the first group of Hands of the Cause named by Shoghi Effendi in 1951. He wrote a number of books, the most well-known being *The Promise of all Ages* (1934), *The Heart of the Gospel* (1939), and *Christ and Bahá'u'lláh* (1957). He died 25 March 1957.

Hand of the Cause George Townshend

Transitional Age *See* Formative Age.

transliteration Putting the letters of one alphabet into the letters of another. The system of transliterating Arabic and Persian into English used by Shoghi Effendi and the Bahá'ís in general is based on the one adopted at the tenth International Congress of Orientalists held at Geneva in 1894.

On 12 March 1923 Shoghi Effendi requested the Bahá'ís to 'avoid confusion in the future' by faithfully adhering to a uniform spelling. In November 1923 he wrote: 'I am confident that the friends will not feel their energy and patience taxed by a scrupulous adherence to what is an authoritative and universal, though arbitrary code for the spelling of Oriental terms.'[15]

Traveller's Narrative, A A volume by 'Abdu'l-Bahá, the manuscript of which was given to E. G. Browne, who published it with his translation in 1891. It was not known until many years later that the book had been written by 'Abdu'l-Bahá. It outlines events in the history of the Báb and His followers, as well as the exile of Bahá'u'lláh, quoting from Bahá'u'lláh's Writings.

Tree, Blessed *See* Sadratu'l-Muntahá.

tribunal, international The formation of an international tribunal to rule on international disputes is cited as one of the basic principles of Bahá'í social teaching. It is only one of the international institutions envisioned by Bahá'ís as part of the future world civilization.

See also World Order of Bahá'u'lláh.

true seeker One who is detached and sincerely searching for knowledge of God and His Manifestation.[16]

Bahá'u'lláh in the *Kitáb-i-Íqán* outlines the conditions one must fulfil to be a true seeker: '. . . he must, before all else, cleanse and purify his heart . . . from the obscuring dust of all acquired knowledge, and the allusion of the embodiments of satanic fancy. He must purge his breast . . . of every defilement, and sanctify his soul from all that pertaineth to water and clay, from all shadowy and ephemeral attachments. He must so cleanse his heart that no remnant of either love or hate may linger therein, lest that love blindly incline him to error, or that hate repel him away from the truth . . . That seeker must at all times put his trust in God, must renounce the peoples of the earth, detach himself from the world of dust, and cleave unto Him who is the Lord of Lords. He must never seek to exalt himself above any one, must wash away from the tablet of his heart every trace of pride and vainglory, must cling unto patience and resignation, observe silence, and refrain from idle talk . . . That seeker should also regard backbiting as grievous error, and keep himself aloof from its dominion . . . He should be content with little, and freed from all inordinate desire. He should treasure the companionship of those that have renounced the world, and regard avoidance of boastful and worldly people a precious benefit. At the dawn of every day he should commune with God . . . He should succour the dispossessed. He should show kindness to animals, how much more unto his fellow-man . . . He should not hesitate to offer up his life for his Beloved, nor allow the censure of the people to turn him away from the Truth. He should not wish for others that which he doth not wish for himself, nor promise that which he doth not fulfil. With all his heart should the seeker avoid evil doers, and pray for the remission of their sins. He should forgive the sinful, and never despise his low estate, for none knoweth what his own end shall be.'[17]

trustworthiness Being worthy of trust; dependability. Bahá'u'lláh calls trustworthiness 'the supreme instrument for the prosperity of the world, and the horizon of assurance unto all beings.'[18]

Turner, Robert The first Black on the American continent to become a Bahá'í. He was the butler of Phoebe Hearst and among the first party of Western pilgrims to meet 'Abdu'l-Bahá.

Twelfth Imám Also, Hidden Imám. According to Sh͟híʻih Islam, the last of twelve successors of the Prophet Muḥammad. The Twelfth Imám, who was named Muḥammad, disappeared in the ninth century AD. He is believed to have gone into concealment but to have continued to communicate with his followers through intermediaries called 'bábs' (gates). Neither the Twelfth Imám nor the last báb named a successor, and the tradition arose that at the time appointed by God, the Twelfth Imám would appear once again, sent by God to guide mankind. He is

Twelfth Imám

also called the Mihdí (or Mahdí – The Guided One), Ḥujjat (the Proof), Baqíyyatu'lláh (the Remnant of God) and the Qá'im (He Who Shall Arise).

Twigs *See* Afnán.

U

'ulamá [Ar] Plural of 'álim. Learned scholars; Muslim divines. The Bábí and Bahá'í Faiths found their most devoted believers, heroes and martyrs, as well as their bitterest enemies, among the 'ulamá of nineteenth-century Iran.

Umm-i-Salamih *See* Ṭáhirih.

Ummu'l-Kitáb *See* Mother Book.

United Nations, Bahá'ís and the *See* Bahá'í International Community.

United Nations Day A UN-sponsored special event day observed on 24 October to mark the anniversary of the founding of the United Nations.

Unity Oneness, wholeness, togetherness, solidarity.

Unity is the hallmark of the teachings of Bahá'u'lláh. He calls for the unity of mankind, for the recognition of the unity of the Godhead and of the Manifestations, for unity of the sexes, and for unity of action after a decision has been made. It is the Covenant which provides the unity of the Bahá'í Faith itself.

Bahá'u'lláh has written: 'The purpose of religion as revealed from the heaven of God's holy Will is to establish unity and concord amongst the peoples of the world . . .'[1] 'So powerful is the light of unity that it can illuminate the whole earth.'[2] 'The purpose of justice is the appearance of unity among men . . . Verily I say, whatever is sent down from the heaven of the Will of God is the means for the establishment of order in the world and the instrument for promoting unity and fellowship among its peoples.'[3]

'Abdu'l-Bahá said, 'Unity is necessary to existence. Love is the very cause of life; on the other hand, separation brings death. In the world of material creation . . . all things owe their actual life to unity. The elements which compose wood, mineral, or stone, are held together by the law of attraction . . . So it is with the great body of humanity.'[4]

'Most important of all is that love and unity should prevail in the Bahá'í community, as this is what people are most longing for in the present dark state of the world.'[5]

See also oneness of mankind; religion, unity of; *and* unity of God.

Unity, Seven Candles of A passage by 'Abdu'l-Bahá in which He describes how in this 'century of light' world unity shall come about, like the illumination of candles, one by one (although not necessarily in this order): 'The first candle is unity in the political realm, the early glimmerings of which can now be discerned. The second candle is unity of thought in world undertakings, the consummation of which will ere long be witnessed. The third candle is unity in freedom which will surely come to pass. The fourth candle is unity in religion which is the corner-stone of the foundation itself, and which, by the power of God, will be revealed in all its splendour. The fifth candle is the unity of nations – a unity which in this century will be securely established, causing all the peoples of the world to regard themselves as citizens of one common fatherland. The sixth candle is unity of races, making of all that dwell on earth peoples and kindreds of one race. The seventh candle is unity of language, i.e. the choice of a universal tongue in which all peoples will be instructed and converse. Each and every one of these will inevitably come to pass, inasmuch as the power of the Kingdom of God will aid and assist in their realization.'[6]

unity in diversity The concept that unity does not imply or require uniformity of culture, taste, thought, race, nationality or custom: 'The diversity in the human family should be the cause of love and harmony, as it is in music where many different notes blend together in the making of a perfect chord.'[7]

'Abdu'l-Bahá explained the concept of unity in diversity as follows: 'A critic may object [to the notion of the unity of mankind], saying that peoples, races, tribes and communities of the world are of different and varied customs, habits, tastes, character, inclinations and ideas, that opinions and thoughts are contrary to one another, and how, therefore, is it possible for real unity to be revealed and perfect accord among human souls to exist?

'In answer we may say that differences are of two kinds. One is the cause of annihilation . . . The other kind which is a token of diversity is the essence of perfection and the cause of the appearance of the bestowals of the Most Glorious Lord.

'Consider the flowers of a garden: though differing in kind, colour, form and shape, yet inasmuch as they are refreshed by the waters of one spring, revived by the breath of one wind, invigorated by the rays

'The diversity in the human race should be the cause of love . . .'

of one sun, this diversity increaseth their charm, and addeth unto their beauty. Thus when that unifying force, the penetrating influence of the Word of God, taketh effect, the difference of customs, manners, habits, ideas, opinions and dispositions embellisheth the world of humanity . . .

'How unpleasing to the eye if all the flowers and plants, the leaves and blossoms, the fruits, the branches and the trees of that garden were all of the same shape and colour! Diversity of hues, form and shape, enricheth and adorneth the garden, and heighteneth the effect thereof. In like manner, when divers shades of thought, temperament and character, are brought together under the power and influence of one central agency, the beauty and glory of human perfection will be revealed and made manifest. Naught but the celestial potency of the Word of God . . . is capable of harmonizing the divergent thoughts, sentiments, ideas, and convictions of the children of men.'[8]

Unity Feast Gatherings of Bahá'ís and, often, their friends for devotions and fellowship and the promotion of unity. The unity feast is usually based on the format of the Nineteen Day Feast, but has no administrative status or function. The consultative part of the Feast is either omitted in the unity feast or replaced with some other activity, such as a study of the Writings or a fireside. A Nineteen Day Feast where a non-Bahá'í is present, and where consequently the consultative and administrative part of the Feast is excluded, is often referred to as a unity feast.

unity of God The concept that there is only one God, without peer or likeness: 'It is clearly established and evident to thee that the divine Essence is highly exalted above all comparison and likeness and that His inmost Reality is sanctified from any peer or partner. This is the station of true unity and of veritable singleness.'[9]

'He is the true believer in Divine unity who, far from confusing duality with oneness, refuseth to allow any notion of multiplicity to becloud his conception of the singleness of God, who will regard the Divine being as One Who, by His very nature, transcendeth the limitations of numbers. The essence of belief in Divine unity consisteth in regarding Him Who is the Manifestation of God and Him Who is the invisible, the inaccessible, the unknowable Essence as one and the same. By this is meant that whatever pertaineth to the former, all His acts and doings, whatever He ordaineth or forbiddeth, should be considered, in all their aspects, and under all circumstances, and without any reservation, as identical with the Will of God Himself. This is the loftiest station to which a true believer in the unity of God can ever hope to attain.'[10]

unity of mankind *See* oneness of mankind.

unity of religion *See* religion, unity of.

universal cycle A long period of time during which several Manifestations appear, each with his own laws and commandments which prevail for a certain time or cycle. When a universal cycle is completed, 'important events and great occurrences will take place which entirely efface every trace and every record of the past; then a new universal cycle begins in the world'.[11]

See also Universal Manifestation.

Universal House of Justice Supreme administrative body of the Bahá'í Faith, ordained by Bahá'u'lláh in the *Kitáb-i-Aqdas*. Its membership is confined to men, at present fixed at nine. The Universal House of Justice is elected every five years by the members of the national spiritual assemblies who gather at an International Convention for the purpose. The Universal House of Justice is infallible.

In the Tablet of Carmel Bahá'u'lláh refers to the Ark which will sail upon Mount Carmel. Shoghi Effendi states, 'Bahá'u'lláh refers to an

Members of the first Universal House of Justice, 1963

"Ark", whose dwellers are the men of the Supreme House of Justice . . . The "sailing of the Ark" of His laws is a reference to the establishment of the Universal House of Justice.'[12]

In His *Will and Testament* 'Abdu'l-Bahá states that the Universal House of Justice, with the Guardian, is 'under the care and protection of the Abhá Beauty, under the shelter and unerring guidance of His Holiness, the Exalted One . . . Whatsoever they decide is of God. Whoso obeyeth him not, neither obeyeth them, hath not obeyed God; whoso rebelleth against him and against them hath rebelled against God; whoso opposeth him hath opposed God; whoso contendeth with them hath contended with God . . .'[13] The Universal House of Justice is the 'source of all good and freed from all error'.[14] Everything which is not expressly recorded in the Writings 'must be referred to the Universal House of Justice. That which this body, whether unanimously or by a majority doth carry, that is verily the Truth and the Purpose of God himself.'[15] The Universal House of Justice has 'power to enact laws that are not expressly recorded in the Book' and 'power to repeal the same . . . The House of Justice is both the Initiator and the Abrogator of its own laws.'[16]

The Universal House of Justice was elected for the first time in 1963 with the following membership: Hugh Chance, Hushmand Fatheazam, Amoz Gibson, Luṭfu'lláh Ḥakím, David Hofman, H. Borrah Kavelin,

'Alí Nakhjavání, Ian Semple and Charles Wolcott. Its constitution was adopted in 1973 and it assumed its permanent Seat on Mount Carmel in 1982.

See also House of Justice *and* Seat of the Universal House of Justice.

universal language *See* language, universal auxiliary.

Universal Manifestation A Manifestation appearing during a universal cycle whose appearance 'causes the world to attain to maturity, and the extension of his cycle is very great. Afterwards other Manifestations will arise under his shadow.'[17] Bahá'u'lláh is the Universal Manifestation for this universal cycle.

See also Manifestation.

universal participation The 'dedicated effort of every believer in teaching, living the Bahá'í life, in contributing to the Fund, and particularly in the persistent effort to understand more and more the significance of Bahá'u'lláh's Revelation.'[18] 'The real secret of universal participation lies in the Master's oft-expressed wish that the friends should love each other, constantly encourage each other, work together, be as one soul in one body, and in doing so become a true, organic, healthy body animated and illumined by the spirit.'[19]

Unknowable Essence God.

'Urvatu'l-Vuthqá [Ar] The Sure Handle. 'Abdu'l-Bahá has written: 'Know thou that the "Sure Handle" mentioned from the foundation of the world in the Books, the Tablets and the Scriptures of old is naught else but the Covenant and the Testament.'[20]

Úshídar-Máh The Promised One referred to in the Zoroastrian Scriptures and fulfilled by the Báb.[21]

ustád [Ar] Professor; master.

V

Váḥid [Ar] Unity. Váḥid symbolizes the unity of God. The numerical value of the letters of this word is nineteen.

Váḥid Each cycle of nineteen years in the Badí' calendar.

See also calendar, Bahá'í.

Váḥid of the *Bayán* Sections of the Persian *Bayán*. The Persian *Bayán* consists of nine Váḥids of nineteen chapters each, except for the last which has ten chapters.

Vaḥíd Title given to Siyyid Yaḥyáy-i-Dárábí, a prominent follower of the Báb who led the Bábís during the Nayríz upheaval.
See also Surih of Kawthar.

Varaqatu'l-'Ulyá (also, Varaqiy-i-'Ulyá) *See* Greatest Holy Leaf.

Varqá [Ar] Dove. Surname given by Bahá'u'lláh to the Bahá'í teacher and poet Mírzá 'Ali-Muḥammad who was named a Hand of the Cause by 'Abdu'l-Bahá and an Apostle of Bahá'u'lláh by Shoghi Effendi. The assassination of Náṣiri'd-Dín Sháh was initially laid at the door of the Bahá'ís, and Varqá and his son Rúḥu'lláh were put to death in revenge. Varqá was cut to pieces before the eyes of his twelve-year-old son who, refusing to recant, was then strangled with a rope.

Visitation, Tablets of Tablets or prayers to be recited when visiting a shrine or burial site.

One Tablet of Visitation is recited particularly when visiting the Shrines of the Báb and Bahá'u'lláh or at observances commemorating the Ascension of Bahá'u'lláh and the Martyrdom of the Báb.[1] The Tablet is actually a compilation of passages chosen by Nabíl-i-A'ẓam at the instruction of 'Abdu'l-Bahá and includes selections from Tablets of Bahá'u'lláh to several individuals, including Khadíjih-Bagum, the wife of the Báb.

A second Tablet of Visitation is a prayer revealed by 'Abdu'l-Bahá which is recited at His Shrine, on the anniversary of His Ascension and also used in private prayer.[2]

The Báb, Bahá'u'lláh and 'Abdu'l-Bahá all revealed Tablets of Visitation to be read at the graves of a number of prominent believers.

Hand of the Cause Varqá and his son Rúḥu'lláh

vizír (also, vazír) [Ar, Pers] Vizier. In Irán and the Ottoman Empire, the prime minister or minister of state.

See also 'Álí Pá<u>sh</u>á; Aqásí, Ḥájí Mírzá; *and* Taqí <u>Kh</u>án-i-Faráhání, Mírzá.

voting rights *See* administrative rights.

W

wealth and poverty, elimination of extremes of One of the basic social teachings of Bahá'u'lláh. Shoghi Effendi has stated: 'Social inequality is the inevitable outcome of the natural inequality of man. Human beings are different in ability and should, therefore, be different in their social and economic standing. Extremes of wealth and poverty should, however, be abolished . . .'[1]

'Abdu'l-Bahá stated, when in America, 'Each one of you must have great consideration for the poor and render them assistance. Organize in an effort to help them and prevent increase in poverty. The greatest means for prevention is that whereby the laws of the community will be so framed and enacted that it will not be possible for a few to be millionaires and many destitute. One of Bahá'u'lláh's teachings is the adjustment of means of livelihood in human society. Under this adjustment there can be no extremes in human conditions as regards wealth and sustenance. For the community needs financier, farmer, merchant and labourer just as an army must be composed of commander, officers and privates. All cannot be commanders; all cannot be officers or privates. Each in his station in the social fabric must be competent – each in his function according to ability but with justness of opportunity for all.'[2]

See also poor, the.

A shanty town in Madras, India. The extremes of wealth and poverty must be abolished.

Will and Testament of 'Abdu'l-Bahá Document, written entirely in the hand of 'Abdu'l-Bahá and sealed by Him, which constitutes the 'charter' of the Administrative Order. It was written in three parts over the seven-year period 1901–8. In its first part Shoghi Effendi is appointed Guardian of the Cause, although he was only eight years old when that section of the Will was written.

The Will and Testament, among other things, proclaims 'the fundamental beliefs of the followers of the Faith of Bahá'u'lláh; reveals . . . the two-fold character of the Mission of the Báb; discloses the full station of the Author of the Bahá'í Revelation . . . stresses the importance of the *Kitáb-i-Aqdas*; establishes the institution of the Guardianship as a hereditary office and outlines its essential functions; provides the measures for the election of the International House of Justice, defines its scope and sets forth its relationship to that Institution; prescribes the obligations, and emphasizes the responsibilities, of the Hands of the Cause of God; and extols the virtues of the indestructible Covenant established by Bahá'u'lláh.'[3]

wills The writing of a will and testament is enjoined upon all Bahá'ís. They are free to make bequests as they wish but if they leave no will, the *Kitáb-i-Aqdas* specifies the division of inheritance among relatives and includes a provision for inheritance by teachers. The ordinances regarding inheritance have not yet been put into general effect.

wine Although the drinking of alcohol is forbidden in the *Kitáb-i-Aqdas*, wine is often used as a metaphor in Bahá'í scriptures: 'The seal of the choice Wine of His Revelation hath, in this Day and in His Name, the Self-Sufficing, been broken. Its grace is being poured out upon men. Fill thy cup, and drink it in His Name, the Most Holy, the All-Praised.'[4]

See also drugs and alcohol.

wisdom Knowledge; the ability to discern inner qualities and relationships, insight; good judgement.

'Above all else, the greatest gift and the most wondrous blessing hath ever been and will continue to be wisdom. It is man's unfailing protector. It aideth him and strengtheneth him. Wisdom is God's emissary and the revealer of His Name the Omniscient. Through it the loftiness of man's station is made manifest and evident. It is all-knowing and the foremost teacher in the school of existence. It is the guide and is invested with high distinction.'[5]

Wolf, the *See* Muḥammad-Báqir, S̲h̲ayk̲h̲.

women, status of Bahá'u'lláh has raised the status of women: 'The status of woman in former times was exceedingly deplorable, for it was the belief of the Orient that it was best for woman to be ignorant. It was considered preferable that she should not know reading or writing in order that she might not be informed of events in the world. Woman was considered to be created for rearing children and attending to the duties of the household. If she pursued educational courses, it was deemed contrary to chastity; hence women were made prisoners of the household . . . Bahá'u'lláh destroyed these ideas and proclaimed the equality of man and woman. He made woman respected by commanding that all women be educated, that there be no difference in the education of the two sexes and that man and woman share the same rights. In the estimation of God there is no distinction of sex. One whose thought is pure, whose education is superior, whose scientific attainments are greater, whose deeds of philanthropy excel, be that one man or woman, white or coloured, is entitled to full rights and recognition; there is no differentiation whatsoever.'[6]

One Bahá'í principle which demonstrates the high status of women is that women have priority of education over men: '. . . the education of woman is more necessary and important than that of man, for woman is the trainer of the child from its infancy . . . The mothers are the first educators of mankind; if they be imperfect, alas for the condition and future of the race . . .'[7] 'Devote ye particular attention to the school for girls, for the greatness of this wondrous Age will be manifested as a result of progress in the world of women.'[8]

One result of providing women with an education is that peace will be established: 'War and its ravages have blighted the world; the education of woman will be a mighty step toward its abolition and ending, for she will use her whole influence against war. She will refuse to give her sons for sacrifice upon the field of battle. In truth, she will be the greatest factor in establishing universal peace and international arbitration. Assuredly, woman will abolish warfare among mankind.'[9]

Bahá'u'lláh has raised the status of women

women, status of

The Bahá'í Faith does not teach that men and women are the same, but rather that they have different but equal qualities which complement each other. One of the major obstacles to peace is that the qualities of the female are not fully realized in the world at large: '. . . men and women have basic and distinct qualities. The solution provided in the teachings of Bahá'u'lláh is not . . . for men to become women, and for women to become men. 'Abdu'l-Bahá gave us the key to the problem when He taught that the qualities and functions of men and women "complement" each other. He further elucidated this point when He said the "new age" will be "an age in which the masculine and feminine elements of civilization will be more properly balanced."'[10]

See also equality of men and women.

Work done in the spirit of service to humanity is accounted as worship

work In the *Kitáb-i-Aqdas* work is made obligatory. All must engage in some useful trade, craft or profession that benefits mankind. Such work is elevated to the station of worship.

In the *Bishárát* Bahá'u'lláh states: 'It is enjoined upon every one of you to engage in some form of occupation, such as crafts, trades and the like. We have graciously exalted your engagement in such work to the rank of worship unto God, the True One . . . Waste not your time in idleness and sloth. Occupy yourselves with that which profiteth yourselves and others . . . When anyone occupieth himself in a craft or trade, such occupation itself is regarded in the estimation of God as an act of worship . . .'[11]

'Abdu'l-Bahá further explains, 'arts, sciences and all crafts are [counted as] worship. The man who makes a piece of notepaper to the best of his ability, conscientiously, concentrating all his forces on perfecting it, is giving praise to God. Briefly, all effort and exertion put forth by man from the fullness of his heart is worship, if it is prompted by the highest motives and the will to do service to humanity.'[12]

See also service.

World Centre, Bahá'í The spiritual and administrative centre of the Bahá'í Faith at Haifa, Israel, comprising the Holy Places in the Haifa–'Akká area and the administrative institutions located on Mount Carmel, situated along an arc around the holy shrines of the Monument Gardens. The edifices to be constructed here will serve as the Seat of the World Bahá'í Administrative Order. They include the International Archives, the Seat of the Universal House of Justice, the International Teaching Centre, the International Bahá'í Library and the Centre for the Study of the Sacred Texts.

World Commonwealth A world community of nations governed by a world federation to which all national governments will be accountable: 'The unity of the human race, as envisaged by Bahá'u'lláh, implies the establishment of a world commonwealth in which all nations, races, creeds and classes are closely and permanently united, and in which the autonomy of its state members and the personal freedom and initiative of the individuals that compose them are definitely and completely safeguarded.'[13]

Bahá'í World Centre, Haifa

World Commonwealth

'Some form of world Super-State must needs be evolved, in whose favour all the nations of the world will have willingly ceded every claim to make war, certain rights to impose taxation and all rights to maintain armaments, except for purposes of maintaining internal order within their respective dominions. Such a State will have to include within its orbit an International Executive . . . a World Parliament whose members shall be elected by the people in their respective countries and whose election shall be confirmed by their respective governments; and a Supreme Tribunal . . .'[14]

World Congress Large gathering of Bahá'ís from all parts of the world called to commemorate special events. The first World Congress was called by Shoghi Effendi in his cable of October 1952 outlining the Ten Year Crusade: 'Convocation World Bahá'í Congress vicinity Garden of Riḍván, Ba<u>gh</u>dád, third holiest city Bahá'í world, on the occasion of the world-wide celebrations of the Most Great Jubilee [Riḍván 1963], commemorating the Centenary of the Ascension of Bahá'u'lláh to the Throne of His Sovereignty.'[15] However, the situation in Iraq in 1963 made it impossible for the Congress to be held there, and the venue was changed to the Royal Albert Hall, London. The second World Congress was called by the Universal House of Justice and is due to be held at New York in May 1992 to commemorate the Centenary of the Passing of Bahá'u'lláh and the completion of the Six Year Plan.

First Bahá'í World Congress, Royal Albert Hall, London, 1963

World Order of Bahá'u'lláh The future 'Divine Civilization, the establishment of which is the primary mission of the Bahá'í Faith',[16] whose foundations – laws, institutions and principles of 'Divine Economy' – were laid down by Bahá'u'lláh in the *Kitáb-i-Aqdas* and further defined by 'Abdu'l-Bahá in his Will and Testament and whose distinguishing features are described by Shoghi Effendi in his series of eleven letters published in the volume entitled *The World Order of Bahá'u'lláh*. These documents constitute 'a pattern for future society, a supreme instrument for the establishment of the Most Great Peace, and the one agency for the unification of the world, and the proclamation of the reign of righteousness and justice upon the earth.'[17] The guiding principle of the World Order of Bahá'u'lláh is the unity of mankind. Based on this principle, a world federation, or commonwealth, is to be established uniting the nations, races, creeds and classes, while preserving the autonomy of its states and individual personal freedom. This world community will be characterized by recognition and preservation of the diversity of nations and peoples while sharing a wider loyalty as citizens of the planet. Its achievement will represent, in the words of Shoghi Effendi, 'the consummation of human evolution'[18] and will signal the Golden Age of the Bahá'í Era. Before it can be achieved, however, humanity will suffer a period of world catastrophe and calamity.

World Order of Bahá'u'lláh The A volume of general letters written by Shoghi Effendi to the Bahá'ís of the West between 1929 and 1938. In it he describes the character and structure of the divine civilization designed by Bahá'u'lláh and known as the World Order of Bahá'u'lláh, its sources and authority in Bahá'í Scripture and its institutions. He recounts the disintegrating forces at work in civilization during the 1930s and describes the guiding principle of the unity of mankind and the future world commonwealth; affirms the non-involvement of Bahá'ís in partisan politics; reviews the history of the Faith in America and its spiritual destiny; elucidates the nature of the Dispensation of Bahá'u'lláh, the revelations of the past and the stations of the Báb and 'Abdu'l-Bahá; cites the scriptural authority of the Administrative Order; outlines the relationship of the Guardianship and the Universal House of Justice; and describes the process of the unfoldment of world civilization and the decline of the old world order.

World Parliament of Religions Conference held in Chicago in 1893 in conjunction with the Columbian Exposition. A paper written by Rev. Henry H. Jessup and read by Rev. George A. Ford provided the first mention of the Faith in the West: '. . . it was announced that "a famous Persian Sage", "the Babi Saint", had recently died in 'Akká, and that two years previous to His ascension "a Cambridge scholar" had visited Him, to whom He had expressed "sentiments so noble, so Christ-like" that the author of the paper, in his "closing words", wished to share them with his audience.'[19]

world peace *See* peace, world.

World Peace Day In the United States, a special event day begun in 1959 by the National Spiritual Assembly of the United States to call attention to the need for the establishment of a lasting peace among the nations of the world. It was replaced in 1985 by the United Nations International Day of Peace, which is observed on the third Tuesday in September.

World Religion Day In the United States, a special event day observed on the third Sunday in January. World Religion Day was begun in 1950 to associate the term 'world religion' with the Bahá'í Faith as well as to proclaim the Faith and to stress the theme that religion is the basis of unity and that world religion is the basis of world unity.

worship To honour and praise God.

There is no fixed form of worship service in the Bahá'í Faith. Bahá'ís worship God through prayer, through the action of daily life lived according to the Bahá'í teachings and through work performed in the spirit of service.

The Mashriqu'l-Adhkár is reserved as a place of worship although Bahá'ís are not confined to worshipping in it.

See also Mashriqu'l-Adhkár.

Writings Term generally used to refer to the written works of Bahá'u'lláh, the Báb and 'Abdu'l-Bahá. In the *Kitáb-i-Aqdas* Bahá'u-'lláh exhorts the believers 'to recite the holy verses at morn and at eventide', to read from the Writings twice each day.

Y

Yá Bahá'u'l-Abhá [Ar] (O Glory of Glories, or O Glory of the All-Glorious) A form of the Greatest Name, used as an invocation. The calligraphic rendering of this invocation by Mishkín-Qalam, the foremost Bahá'í calligrapher, is often framed and displayed in a position of honour in Bahá'í homes.

Yaḥyá, Mírzá Ṣubḥ-i-Azal (Morning of Eternity). The younger half-brother of Bahá'u'lláh who turned against Him. He had been named by the Báb as the nominal head of the Bábí community but after the exile of Bahá'u'lláh, Mírzá Yaḥyá fled Iran in disguise and joined the exiles in Baghdád. At the instigation of Siyyid Muḥammad-i-Iṣfahání, Mírzá Yaḥyá claimed to be the successor of the Báb and broke with his brother Bahá'u'lláh, even attempting to have Him murdered. When Bahá'u'lláh openly declared Himself to be the Promised One, Mírzá Yaḥyá refused to support Him and put forward his own claim to prophethood as Ṣubḥ-i-Azal. He was rejected by all but a handful of followers, who became known as Azalís. He and his band, in spite of their small numbers, continued to cause trouble and suffering to Bahá'u'lláh through their plots and intrigues. In Adrianople Mírzá Yaḥyá accused Bahá'u'lláh of plotting against the Turkish government, which led to Bahá'u'lláh's banishment and imprisonment in 'Akká. Yaḥyá was exiled to Cyprus, where he died in 1912.

Yaḥyáy-i-Dárábí, Siyyid *See* Vaḥíd *and* Súrih of Kawthar.

year of waiting (*or* year of patience) The period of separation that must be observed before a divorce can be granted under Bahá'í law: 'The purpose of the year of waiting is to attempt the saving of a marital relationship which was originally accepted as valid in the eyes of the Bahá'ís, and is now in jeopardy.'[1]

A couple wishing a divorce must inform the spiritual assembly which 'has the duty of trying to reconcile the parties before setting the date for the beginning of the year of patience. If no reconciliation is possible, and actual repugnance is found to exist between the parties, then the Assembly may record a date which is the beginning of the year of patience. During the ensuing year, it is highly desirable that, if opportunity arises, further efforts at reconciliation should be made. The Assembly also has the duty to see that just arrangements are made for the support of dependants during the year of patience. If, at the end of the year, no reconciliation is possible, then the Assembly may grant the Bahá'í divorce.'[2]

According to the *Kitáb-i-Aqdas*, 'if at any time during the waiting period affection should recur, the marriage tie is valid'.[3]

years In His Writings revealed in Arabic, the Báb divided the years following the date of His Revelation into cycles of nineteen years each. The names of the years in each cycle are:

years

1	Alif	A	11	Bahháj	Delightful
2	Bá’	B	12	Javáb	Answer
3	Ab	Father	13	Aḥad	Single
4	Dál	D	14	Vahháb	Bountiful
5	Báb	Gate	15	Vidád	Affection
6	Váv	V	16	Badí‘	Beginning
7	Abad	Eternity	17	Bahí	Luminous
8	Jád	Generosity	18	Abhá	Most Luminous
9	Bahá	Splendour	19	Váḥid	Unity
10	Ḥubb	Love			

Each cycle of nineteen years is called a Váḥid; nineteen cycles constitute a period called ‘Kull-i-Shay’ ’.

See also calendar, Bahá’í.

youth, Bahá’í Specifically, Bahá’ís over the age of fifteen who have taken on the spiritual obligations of maturity, but under the age set for voting in Bahá’í elections, presently twenty-one. Generally, any Bahá’í from the early teens to the late twenties may be considered a Bahá’í youth.

The Universal House of Justice has written many letters to the youth, beginning with a letter dated 10 June 1966 which outlined the three fields of service open to youth: the ‘study of the teachings, the spiritualization of their lives and the forming of their characters in accordance with the standards of Bahá’u’lláh’; teaching the Faith; and preparation for their later years.[4]

Zillu’s-Sulṭán with his son

Left An idealised portrait of Zaynáb

Z

zádih [Pers] Child, offspring. It is used in combination with other words, often to form a name or title, e.g. Imám-Zádih, a descendant of an Imám.

Zanján City in northwestern Iran in which the fiercest and most devastating of the three military campaigns against the Bábís took place in May 1850. When Ḥujjat returned to Zanján after his detention in Ṭihrán, he was the object of hostility on the part of the authorities. The city was split into two opposing camps, and Ḥujjat and his companions were forced to seek safety in the nearby fort of ‘Alí-Mardán Khán, about three thousand in all. They held the fort against repeated attack and siege for nearly nine months. Ḥujjat was wounded, his wife and baby killed, and then he himself died. In a fierce attack the remaining Bábís were struck down. The survivors were tortured, killed and their bodies mutilated.
See also Ḥujjat.

Zarrín-Táj *See* Ṭáhirih.

Zaynab A girl from a village near Zanján who disguised herself as a man to join the besieged Bábís, led by Ḥujjat, in the fort at Zanján. She showed such audacity and courage that the enemy were routed before her. Ḥujjat recognized her but was persuaded not to reveal her secret. He gave her the name Rustam-‘Alí. For some five months she remained as one of the defenders of the fort until at last she was killed defending the barricades.

Ẓillu's-Sulṭán Shadow of the King, Prince Mas‘úd Mírzá, ‘Náṣiri'd-Dín's eldest son and ruler over more than two fifths of his kingdom, stigmatized by Bahá'u'lláh as "the infernal Tree"'.

Zoroaster Also, Zarathustra. Founder of the Zoroastrian religion and accepted by Bahá'ís as a Manifestation of God. Zoroaster was born around 660 BC in Persia and died around 583 BC. According to Shoghi Effendi, Zoroaster's prophecy of the coming of a World-Saviour, Sháh-Bahrám, who would triumph over evil and usher in an era of blessedness and peace, refers to the coming of Bahá'u'lláh.[1] Bahá'u'lláh was a descendant of Zoroaster.

References

A

1 Balyuzi, *King of Glory*, p. 412.
2 Shoghi Effendi, *God Passes By*, p. 242.
3 Balyuzi, *King of Glory*, pp. 94–8.
4 Ruhe, *Door of Hope*, p. 205.
5 ibid. p. 206.
6 From a letter written on behalf of Shoghi Effendi, 19 February 1932. *Lights*, no. 828.
7 *Synopsis*, pp. 36–7.
8 Ruhe, *Door of Hope*, pp. 103–4.
9 Taherzadeh, *Revelation 4*, p. 425.
10 'Abdu'l-Bahá, *Some Answered Questions*, pp. 140–44.
11 Shoghi Effendi, *World Order*, p. 144.
12 ibid. p. 150.
13 ibid. p. 9.
14 Shoghi Effendi, *God Passes By*, p. 171.
15 Shoghi Effendi, *Advent*, p. 17.
16 ibid. p. 28.
17 Taherzadeh, *Revelation 2*, p. 115.
18 *Bahá'í Prayers*, p. 212.
19 Taherzadeh, *Revelation 2*, pp. 137–8.
20 ibid. p. 138. See *Gleanings* CLII and CLIII for text.
21 Shoghi Effendi, *God Passes By*, pp. 191–2.
22 Rabbani, *Pearl*, p. 152.
23 Shoghi Effendi, *God Passes By*, p. 238.
24 Ruhe, *Door of Hope*, pp. 126–9.
25 Bahá'u'lláh, *Gleanings*, XI.
26 Letter from the Universal House of Justice, August 1987.
27 Taherzadeh, *Revelation 4*, p. 361.
28 Bahá'u'lláh, *Gleanings*, XI.
29 Taherzadeh, *Revelation 4*, p. 361.
30 Ruhe, *Door of Hope*, p. 171.
31 Smith, *Bahá'í Religion*, p. 14.
32 ibid.

B

1 'Abdu'l-Bahá, *Tablets*, pp. 149–50. *Lights*, no. 322.
2 Letter from the Universal House of Justice, 7 September 1966. *Lights*, no. 321.
3 Bahá'u'lláh, *Íqán*, p. 193.
4 'Abdu'l-Baha, *Selections*, pp. 230–31.
5 ibid.
6 Shoghi Effendi, *God Passes By*, p. 31.

7 Balyuzi, *Báb*, p. 169.
8 Shoghi Effendi, *World Order*, p. 102.
9 Bahá'í International Community, 'Focus Statement'.
10 *Bahíyyih Khánum*, pp. 42–3.
11 Shoghi Effendi, *God Passes By*, p. 216.
12 ibid. pp. 24–5.
13 ibid. p. 25.
14 ibid.
15 ibid.
16 ibid.
17 Balyuzi, *Báb*, p. 171.
18 Balyuzi, *'Abdu'l-Bahá*, p. 76.
19 ibid. p. 78.
20 ibid. p. 80.
21 Balyuzi, *King of Glory*, p. 372.
22 Momen, *E. G. Browne,* p. 407.
23 *Oxford Magazine*, 25 May 1892, p. 394.
24 *Synopsis*, pp. 62–3.
25 Balyuzi, *King of Glory*, p. 35.

C

1 Shoghi Effendi, *Promised Day*, p. 127.
2 ibid. p. 99.
3 Shoghi Effendi, *World Order*, p. 178.
4 Bahá'u'lláh, *Íqán*, p. 193.
5 'Abdu'l-Bahá, *Selections*, p. 32.
6 *Star of the West*, vol. III, no. 13, p. 15.
7 Shoghi Effendi, *Advent*, pp. 24–5.
8 ibid. p. 28.
9 Shoghi Effendi, *World Order*, p. 16.
10 ibid. p. 163.
11 From a letter written on behalf of Shoghi Effendi, 5 July 1957. *Gift*, p. 35.
12 Kolstoe, *Consultation*, p. 9.
13 Bahá'u'lláh cited in *Heaven*, no. 1.
14 Universal House of Justice, *Wellspring*, p. 96.
15 ibid. p. 140.
16 ibid. p. 141.
17 From a postscript to a letter dated 13 April 1927, written by Shoghi Effendi. *Lights*, no. 391.
18 From a letter written on behalf of Shoghi Effendi, 21 October 1932. *Lights*, no. 403.
19 Shoghi Effendi, *God Passes By*, p. 237.
20 Bahá'u'lláh, *Tablets*, p. 221.
21 'Abdu'l-Bahá, *Selections*, p. 209.
22 'Abdu'l-Bahá, *Promulgation*, p. 455.
23 ibid. pp. 445–6.
24 Shoghi Effendi, *God Passes By*, p. 238.
25 ibid.
26 *Star of the West*, vol. XII, no. 14, p. 233.

27 From a letter written on behalf of Shoghi Effendi, 30 November 1944. *Lights*, no. 410.
28 Shoghi Effendi, *God Passes By*, p. 329.
29 Balyuzi, *King of Glory*, p. 364.
30 Shoghi Effendi, *God Passes By*, p. 100.

D

1 Shoghi Effendi, *God Passes By*, p. 26.
2 Balyuzi, *Báb*, p. 162.
3 Shoghi Effendi cited in *Deepening*, p. 29.
4 Taherzadeh, *Revelation 3*, p. 144.
5 Shoghi Effendi, *Advent*, p. 65.
6 Shoghi Effendi, *World Order*, 107.
7 ibid.
8 Universal House of Justice, *Messages*, pp. 32–3.
9 Bahá'u'lláh, *Gleanings*, LXXX.
10 *'Abdu'l-Bahá in London*, pp. 95–6.
11 Bahá'u'lláh, *Hidden Words*, (Arabic) no. 32.
12 ibid.
13 Taherzadeh, *Revelation 1*, pp. 123–4.
14 Universal House of Justice, *Wellspring*, p. 32.
15 Balyuzi, *Báb*, p. 20.
16 Bahá'u'lláh, *Hidden Words*, (Persian) no. 5.
17 Universal House of Justice, *Wellspring*, pp. 88–9.
18 Shoghi Effendi cited in *Deepening*, p. 20.
19 Universal House of Justice, *Wellspring*, pp. 114–15.
20 Bahá'u'lláh, *Gleanings*, XCVI.
21 Shoghi Effendi, *Advent*, p. 28.
22 Bahá'u'lláh, *Seven Valleys,*, pp. 32–3.
23 Bahá'u'lláh, *Tablets*, pp. 187–8.
24 From a letter written on behalf of Shoghi Effendi, 16 May 1925. *Lights*, no. 1051.
25 Shoghi Effendi, *Advent*, p. 27.
26 From the Universal House of Justice, 11 November 1967. *Lights*, no. 718.
27 'Abdu'l-Bahá, *Selections*, p. 149.
28 ibid.

E

1 'Abdu'l-Bahá, *Promulgation*, p. 132.
2 From a letter written on behalf of Shoghi Effendi, 11 January 1933. *Lights*, no. 253.
3 'Abdu'l-Bahá, *Promulgation*, p. 216.
4 Bahá'u'lláh, *Gleanings,* LXXI.
5 ibid. XCVIII.
6 ibid. CXXII.
7 Bahá'u'lláh cited in *Education*, p. 3.

8 ibid. p. 5.
9 'Abdu'l-Bahá, *Promulgation*, p. 300.
10 ibid. p. 182.
11 ibid. p. 175.
12 ibid. pp. 133–4.
13 Letter from Shoghi Effendi, 5 June 1947.
14 Shoghi Effendi, *Citadel*, p. 5.
15 ibid. p. 6.
16 Letter from the Research Department of the Universal House of Justice to National Spiritual Assemblies, February 1986.
17 ibid.
18 ibid.
19 Bahá'u'lláh cited in *Women*, p. 1.
20 'Abdu'l-Bahá, *Promulgation*, pp. 133–4.
21 'Abdu'l-Bahá, *Some Answered Questions*, p. 301.
22 From a letter written on behalf of Shoghi Effendi, 4 October 1950. *Lights*, no. 1047.
23 'Abdu'l-Bahá, *Some Answered Questions*, pp. 270–71.
24 ibid.
25 ibid. pp. 225–6.

F

1 Bahá'u'lláh, *Tablets*, p. 50.
2 'Abdu'l-Bahá, *Bahá'í World Faith*, p. 382.
3 'Abdu'l-Bahá, *Promulgation*, p. 199.
4 'Abdu'l-Bahá, *Bahá'í World Faith*, p. 364.
5 Bahá'u'lláh, *Gleanings*, LXXIV.
6 Bahá'u'lláh, *Tablets*, p. 156.
7 From a letter written on behalf of Shoghi Effendi, 10 January 1936. *Lights*, no. 487.
8 From a letter written on behalf of Shoghi Effendi, 18 February 1954. *Lights*, no. 526.
9 Shoghi Effendi cited in *Gift*, p. 30.
10 ibid. p. 33.
11 Shoghi Effendi, *God Passes By*, p. xiv.
12 ibid. p. xiii.
13 'Abdu'l-Bahá, *Some Answered Questions*, p. 189.
14 ibid. p. 287.
15 Bahá'u'lláh, *Bahá'í Prayers*, p. 245.
16 From a letter of Shoghi Effendi, 12 March 1923. *Lights*, no. 57.
17 Universal House of Justice, *Wellspring*, pp. 19–20.
18 Letter of the Universal House of Justice, Naw-Rúz 1974. *Lights*, no. 542.

G

1 Shoghi Effendi, *World Order*, pp. 168–9.

2 Smith, *Bahá'í Religion*, p. 13.
3 Bahá'u'lláh, *Gleanings*, XIX.
4 Smith, *Bahá'í Religion*, pp. 13–14.
5 Shoghi Effendi, *God Passes By*, pp. 411–12.
6 'Abdu'l-Bahá, *Will*, p. 8.
7 'Abdu'l-Bahá, *Selections*, p. 293.
8 ibid. p. 319.
9 From a letter of Shoghi Effendi, 3 July 1948. *Lights*, no. 874.
10 Shoghi Effendi, *Divine Guidance*, pp. 54–5.
11 Shoghi Effendi, *Advent*, p. 61.
12 Universal House of Justice, *Wellspring*, p. 133.
13 'Abdu'l-Bahá, *Will*, p. 11.
14 Universal House of Justice, *Wellspring*, p. 11.
15 'Abdu'l-Bahá, *Will*, p. 11.
16 ibid. pp. 11, 12.
17 From a letter of the Universal House of Justice, 5 May 1977. *Lights*, no. 629.

H

1 Shoghi Effendi, *God Passes By*, p. 194.
2 Esslemont, *New Era*, pp. 252–3.
3 'Abdu'l-Bahá, *Will*, pp. 12–13.
4 ibid. p. 12.
5 ibid.
6 Shoghi Effendi, *Messages*, p. 127.
7 Universal House of Justice, *Wellspring*, p. 41.
8 Taherzadeh, *Revelation 4*, pp. 312–13.
9 Shoghi Effendi, *God Passes By*, p. 339.
10 ibid. pp. 339–40.
11 'Abdu'l-Bahá, *Some Answered Questions*, pp. 296–8.
12 'Abdu'l-Bahá, *Selections*, pp. 161–2.
13 'Abdu'l-Bahá, *'Abdu'l-Bahá in London,* pp. 59–60.
14 From a letter written on behalf of Shoghi Effendi, 23 May 1935. *Lights*, no. 591.
15 From a letter written on behalf of Shoghi Effendi, 12 March 1934. *Lights*, no. 588.
16 Bahá'u'lláh, *Hidden Words*, (Arabic) no. 59.
17 ibid. (Arabic) no. 1.
18 ibid. (Persian) no. 3.
19 'Abdu'l-Bahá, *Some Answered Questions*, p. 259.
20 Bahá'u'lláh, *Epistle*, p. 132.
21 Shoghi Effendi, *God Passes By*, p. 140.
22 ibid.
23 ibid. p. 183.
24 ibid.
25 ibid. p. 140.
26 ibid. p. 147.
27 *Synopsis*, p. 61.
28 Taherzadeh, *Revelation 3*, p. 144.
29 ibid.

30 Shoghi Effendi, *God Passes By*, p. 300.
31 Shoghi Effendi, *World Order*, pp. 5–7.
32 Bahá'u'lláh cited in *Local Spiritual Assemblies*, p. 3.
33 Taherzadeh, *Revelation 4*, p. 425.
34 Balyuzi, *Báb*, p. 100.
35 ibid. pp. 185–7.
36 Universal House of Justice cited in *Ḥuqúqu'lláh*, no. 100.
37 Bahá'u'lláh cited in ibid no. 10.
38 Universal House of Justice cited in ibid. no. 96.
39 *Synopsis*, p. 60.
40 Bahá'u'lláh cited in *Ḥuqúqu'lláh*, no. 4.
41 ibid.
42 ibid. no. 11.
43 Universal House of Justice cited in ibid. no. 106.
44 Taherzadeh in *Bahá'í News*, June 1988, p. 14.
45 'Abdu'l-Bahá cited in *Ḥuqúqu'lláh*, no. 62.
46 Shoghi Effendi cited in ibid. no. 94.
47 Taherzadeh in *Bahá'í News*, June 1988, p. 14.
48 Nabíl, *Dawn-Breakers*, p. 383.

I

1 'Abdu'l-Bahá, *Promulgation*, p. 291.
2 ibid. p. 313.
3 'Abdu'l-Bahá, *Paris*, p. 129.
4 'Abdu'l-Bahá, *Will*, p. 14.
5 From a letter written on behalf of Shoghi Effendi, 17 October 1944. *Lights*, no. 625.
6 'Abdu'l-Bahá, *Paris*, p. 69.
7 'Abdu'l-Bahá, *Some Answered Questions*, p. 212.
8 'Abdu'l-Bahá, *Bahá'í Prayers*, p. 65.
9 'Abdu'l-Bahá, *Some Answered Questions*, p. 232.
10 ibid. p. 240.
11 *Bahá'í World*, vol. IV, p. 261.
12 From a letter of the Universal House of Justice, 8 June 1973. *Lights*, no. 647.
13 Shoghi Effendi, *World Order*, p. 134.
14 Bahá'u'lláh, *Tablets*, p. 221.
15 'Abdu'l-Bahá, *Will*, p. 11.
16 From a letter of the Universal House of Justice, 5 May 1977. *Lights*, no. 629.
17 From a letter written on behalf of Shoghi Effendi, 17 November 1933. *Lights*, no. 88.
18 Shoghi Effendi, *World Order*, p. 136.
19 ibid. p. 133.
20 Shoghi Effendi, *God Passes By*, p. 300.

J

1 Bahá'u'lláh, *Hidden Words*, (Arabic) no. 2.

2 Bahá'u'lláh, *Epistle*, p. 32.
3 ibid. p. 30.
4 Bahá'u'lláh, *Tablets*, p. 164.
5 ibid. pp. 128–9.
6 ibid. p. 64.
7 Bahá'u'lláh, *Gleanings*, CXXVIII.
8 ibid. CLXIII.
9 Shoghi Effendi cited in *Local Spiritual Assemblies*, pp. 14–15.

K

1 Bahá'u'lláh, *Tablets*, p. 68.
2 ibid. p. 67.
3 Nabíl, *Dawn-Breakers*, p. 27.
4 ibid. pp. 191–2.
5 Ruhe, *Door of Hope*, p. 107.
6 Taherzadeh, *Revelation 4*, p. 74.
7 ibid. p. 75.
8 'Abdu'l-Bahá, *Some Answered Questions*, p. 280.
9 Bahá'u'lláh, *Íqán*, pp. 100–101.
10 'Abdu'l-Bahá, *Promulgation*, pp. 172–3.
11 Bahá'u'lláh, *Tablets*, p. 28.
12 Shoghi Effendi, *Promised Day*, p. 72.
13 ibid. p. 73.
14 Shoghi Effendi, *God Passes By*, p. 239.
15 ibid. p. 213.
16 ibid. p. 214.
17 *Principles*, pp. 6–7.
18 Shoghi Effendi, *God Passes By*, p. 138.
19 ibid. p. 139.
20 ibid.
21 Shoghi Effendi, *Messages*, p. 60.
22 ibid. p. 69.
23 The Báb, *Selections*, p. 89.
24 Bahá'u'lláh, *Bahá'í Prayers*, p. 4.
25 Bahá'u'lláh, *Gleanings*, I.
26 ibid. CLIII.
27 Bahá'u'lláh, *Tablets*, p. 39.
28 ibid. pp. 51–2.
29 'Abdu'l-Bahá, *Promulgation*, p. 346.

L

1 Shoghi Effendi, *World Order*, pp. 203, 206.
2 Bahá'u'lláh, *Tablets*, p. 127.
3 ibid. p. 221.
4 *Synopsis*, pp. 24–5.
5 Bahá'u'lláh cited in *Local Spiritual Assemblies*, p. 3.

6 Shoghi Effendi, *World Order*, p. 6.
7 ibid.
8 Shoghi Effendi, *God Passes By*, p. 331.
9 'Abdu'l-Bahá, *Divine Plan*, p. 47.
10 Bahá'u'lláh, *Hidden Words*, (Arabic) no. 3.
11 ibid. (Arabic) no. 4.
12 'Abdu'l-Bahá, *Promulgation*, p. 297.
13 ibid. p. 268.
14 ibid. p. 379.
15 ibid. p. 40.
16 Bahá'u'lláh, *Hidden Words*, (Arabic) no. 5.
17 ibid. (Persian) no. 3.
18 'Abdu'l-Bahá, *Promulgation*, p. 267.
19 'Abdu'l-Bahá, *Paris*, p. 181.

M

1 Shoghi Effendi, *God Passes By*, pp. 16, 18.
2 ibid. pp. 101–2.
3 Shoghi Effendi, *World Order*, pp. 113–14.
4 ibid.
5 ibid. p. 115.
6 ibid.
7 From a letter written on behalf of Shoghi Effendi, 4 October 1950. *Lights*, no. 1033.
8 *Synopsis*, p. 39.
9 ibid. p. 59.
10 From a letter written on behalf of the Universal House of Justice, 31 July 1979. *Lights*, no. 1410 (18).
11 Bahá'u'lláh, *Bahá'í Prayers*, pp. 104–5.
12 'Abdu'l-Bahá, *Some Answered Questions*, p. 118.
13 Taherzadeh, *Revelation 4*, pp. 302–3.
14 ibid. p. 305.
15 *Synopsis*, p. 62.
16 'Abdu'l-Bahá, *Selections*, pp. 93–5.
17 *Star of the West*, vol. V, no. 16, p. 250.
18 'Abdu'l-Bahá, *Selections*, p. 100.
19 Shoghi Effendi, *God Passes By*, p. 340.
20 Shoghi Effendi, *Advent*, p. 39.
21 From a letter written on behalf of Shoghi Effendi, 8 December 1935. *Lights*, no. 279.
22 Shoghi Effendi, *Citadel*, p. 125.
23 Bahá'u'lláh, *Gleanings*, LXXIX.
24 'Abdu'l-Bahá cited in *Importance of Prayer*, p. 11.
25 ibid. p. 12.
26 Shoghi Effendi cited in ibid. p. 20.
27 ibid. p. 18.
28 Shoghi Effendi, *God Passes By*, p. 188.
29 *Bahá'í World*, vol. VIII, pp. 249–51.
30 'Abdu'l-Bahá, *Some Answered Questions*, pp. 243–4.

31 Universal House of Justice, *Wellspring*, p. 134.
32 'Abdu'l-Bahá, *Some Answered Questions*, p. 44.
33 ibid. p. 117.
34 Shoghi Effendi, *Advent*, p. 28.
35 ibid.
36 Shoghi Effendi, *God Passes By*, p. 185.
37 ibid. pp. 324–5.
38 Nabíl, *Dawn-Breakers,* pp. 149–50 (UK).
39 Shoghi Effendi, *World Order*, p. 134.

N

1 'Abdu'l-Bahá. *Will*, p. 14.
2 Shoghi Effendi, *God Passes By*, pp. 332–3.
3 Shoghi Effendi, *World Order*, p. 65.
4 ibid. p. 41.
5 ibid. pp. 41–2.
6 Shoghi Effendi, *God Passes By*, p. 108.
7 Shoghi Effendi, *World Order*, p. 25.
8 Shoghi Effendi, *Advent*, p. 26.
9 ibid. p. 14.

O

1 Shoghi Effendi, *World Order*, p. 42.
2 ibid. p. 43.

P

1 Bahá'u'lláh, *Tablets*, p. 118.
2 ibid. p. 189.
3 'Abdu'l-Bahá, *Selections*, p. 275.
4 Bahá'u'lláh, *Gleanings*, CXIX.
5 Shoghi Effendi, *World Order*, p. 162.
6 *Synopsis*, p. 61.
7 ibid.
8 From a letter of the Universal House of Justice, 30 March 1971. *Lights*, no. 1191.
9 From a letter of the Universal House of Justice, 2 July 1965. *Lights*, no. 1194.
10 Rabbani, *Pearl*, p. 412.
11 Shoghi Effendi, *World Order*, p. 198.
12 ibid. p. 64.
13 *Bahá'í World*, vol. VIII, p. 536.
14 Shoghi Effendi, *World Order*, pp. 64–5.
15 ibid. p. 65.

16 Bahá'u'lláh, *Hidden Words*, (Persian) no. 53.
17 ibid. (Persian) no. 51.
18 ibid. (Persian) no. 55.
19 ibid. (Arabic) no. 25.
20 ibid. (Persian) no. 54.
21 ibid. (Arabic) no. 57.
22 ibid. (Persian) no. 49.
23 Bahá'u'lláh, *Gleanings*, CXXX.
24 *Synopsis*, p. 13.
25 Bahá'u'lláh cited in *Importance of Prayer*, p. 3.
26 ibid.
27 From a letter of the Universal House of Justice, Naw-Rúz 1974. *Lights*, no. 895.
28 From a letter of the Universal House of Justice, 6 April 1967. *Lights*, no. 914.
29 'Abdu'l-Bahá, *Promulgation*, p. 455.
30 'Abdu'l-Bahá, *Selections*, p. 249.
31 'Abdu'l-Bahá, *Promulgation*, p. 68.
32 Shoghi Effendi, *God Passes By*, p. 4.
33 'Abdu'l-Bahá, *Promulgation*, p. 440.
34 ibid.
35 Bahá'u'lláh, *Gleanings*, XXXVIII.
36 Shoghi Effendi, *World Order*, p. 114.
37 ibid. p. 111.
38 Universal House of Justice, *Promise*, p. 1.
39 'Abdu'l-Bahá, *Some Answered Questions*, p. 188.
40 Bahá'u'lláh, *Íqán*, p. 220.
41 'Abdu'l-Bahá, *Some Answered Questions*, p. 188.
42 Shoghi Effendi, *World Order*, p. 111.
43 'Abdu'l-Bahá cited in *Gift*, p. 13.
44 ibid. p. 14.

Q

1 Bahá'u'lláh, *Epistle*, p. 77.
2 Nabíl, *Dawn-Breakers*, pp. 41–2.
3 Shoghi Effendi, *God Passes By*, p. 23.
4 ibid.
5 ibid. pp. 23–4.
6 Balyuzi, *Báb*, p. 150.
7 From a letter written on behalf of Shoghi Effendi, 2 December 1935. *Lights*, no. 1165.

R

1 Rabbani, *Pearl*, p. 17.
2 Universal House of Justice, *Promise*, pp. 11–12.
3 Shoghi Effendi, *Advent*, p. 19.
4 'Abdu'l-Bahá, *Promulgation*, p. 140.
5 'Abdu'l-Bahá, *Selections*, pp. 52–3.

6 From a letter written on behalf of Shoghi Effendi, 6 September 1946. *Lights*, no. 1136.
7 Bahá'u'lláh, *Tablets*, pp. 63–4.
8 ibid. pp. 129–30.
9 ibid. p. 125.
10 'Abdu'l-Bahá, *Promulgation*, pp. 454–5.
11 'Abdu'l-Bahá, *Selections*, p. 52.
12 Shoghi Effendi, *World Order*, p. 40.
13 'Abdu'l-Bahá, *Some Answered Questions*, pp. 120–21.
14 Taherzadeh, *Revelation 1*, p. 21.
15 Shoghi Effendi, *God Passes By*, pp. 153–4.
16 ibid. p. 153.
17 Ruhe, *Door of Hope*, p. 95.
18 Shoghi Effendi, *God Passes By*, p. 193.
19 ibid.
20 Bahá'u'lláh, *Tablets*, pp. 37–8.
21 Blomfield, *Chosen Highway*, p. 96.
22 Faizi, *Greatest Name*, pp. 3–20.
23 From a letter written on behalf of Shoghi Effendi, 24 June 1949. *Lights*, no. 890.
24 Shoghi Effendi, *God Passes By*, p. 386.
25 ibid.
26 ibid. p. 388.

S

1 'Abdu'l-Bahá, *Selections*, pp. 64–5.
2 Taherzadeh, *Revelation 3*, p. 211.
3 From a letter written on behalf of Shoghi Effendi, 10 December 1947. *Lights*, no. 1149.
4 Shoghi Effendi, *God Passes By*, p. 94.
5 Bahá'u'lláh, *Íqán*, p. 69.
6 Bahá'u'lláh, *Tablets*, pp. 51–2.
7 ibid. p. 26.
8 'Abdu'l-Bahá, *Promulgation*, p. 63.
9 Taherzadeh, *Revelation 1*, p. 66.
10 *Bahá'í World*, vol. XVI, pp. 397–8.
11 Ruhe, *Door of Hope*, p. 174.
12 Bahá'u'lláh, *Tablets*, p. 167.
13 Taherzadeh, *Revelation 4*, p. 133.
14 From a letter written on behalf of Shoghi Effendi, 5 September 1938. *Lights*, nos. 681, 682.
15 From a letter written on behalf of Shoghi Effendi, 21 May 1954. *Lights*, no. 723.
16 'Abdu'l-Bahá, *Will*, p. 11.
17 Shoghi Effendi, *Citadel*, pp. 95–6.
18 ibid. p. 96.
19 Bahá'u'lláh, *Epistle*, pp. 20–21.
20 'Abdu'l-Bahá, *Selections*, pp. 147–8.
21 Shoghi Effendi, *God Passes By*, p. 260.
22 Shoghi Effendi cited in *Deepening*, p. 27.

T

1 Bahá'u'lláh cited in Shoghi Effendi, *World Order*, p. 135.
2 Shoghi Effendi cited in 'Abdu'l-Bahá, *Divine Plan*, p. vii.
3 'Abdu'l-Bahá, *Divine Plan*, p. 38.
4 Shoghi Effendi, *God Passes By*, p. 73.
5 ibid. p. 75.
6 Bahá'u'lláh, *Tablets*, p. 52.
7 ibid. p. 35.
8 Ruhe, *Door of Hope*, pp. 225–6.
9 Bahá'u'lláh cited in *Gift*, p. 7.
10 'Abdu'l-Bahá cited in ibid. p. 3.
11 Bahá'u'lláh cited in ibid. p. 7.
12 'Abdu'l-Bahá cited in ibid. p. 10.
13 Rabbani, *Pearl*, p. 412.
14 Taherzadeh, *Revelation 4*, p. 426.
15 Shoghi Effendi, *Bahá'í Administration*, p. 56.
16 Bahá'u'lláh, *Íqán*, p. 195.
17 ibid. pp. 193–4.
18 Bahá'u'lláh cited in *Trustworthiness*, p. iii.

U

1 Bahá'u'lláh, *Tablets*, p. 129.
2 Bahá'u'lláh, *Gleanings*, CXXII.
3 Bahá'u'lláh, *Tablets*, p. 67.
4 'Abdu'l-Bahá, *Paris*, p. 139.
5 From a letter written on behalf of Shoghi Effendi, 20 October 1945. *Lights*, no. 816.
6 'Abdu'l-Bahá, *Selections*, p. 32.
7 Shoghi Effendi, *Advent*, p. 32.
8 'Abdu'l-Bahá, *Selections*, pp. 290–2.
9 Bahá'u'lláh, *Tablets*, p. 124.
10 Bahá'u'lláh, *Gleanings*, LXXXIV.
11 'Abdu'l-Bahá, *Foundations*, p. 54.
12 Ruhe, *Door of Hope*, p. 171.
13 'Abdu'l-Bahá, *Will*, p. 11.
14 ibid. p. 14.
15 ibid. p. 19.
16 ibid. p. 20.
17 'Abdu'l-Bahá, *Foundations*, p. 54.
18 Universal House of Justice, *Wellspring*, p. 25.
19 ibid. pp. 38–9.
20 Shoghi Effendi, *God Passes By*, p. 238.
21 ibid. p. 58.

V

1 Bahá'u'lláh, *Prayers and Meditations*, CLXXX.
2 'Abdu'l-Bahá, *Bahá'í Prayers*, p. 234.

W

1 From a letter written on behalf of Shoghi Effendi, 25 January 1936. *Lights*. no. 255.
2 'Abdu'l-Bahá, *Promulgation*, p. 216.
3 Shoghi Effendi, *God Passes By*, p. 328.
4 Bahá'u'lláh, *Gleanings*, IX.
5 Bahá'u'lláh, *Tablets*, p. 66.
6 'Abdu'l-Bahá, *Promulgation*, p. 166.
7 'Abdu'l-Bahá cited in *Women*, p. 18.
8 ibid. p. 20.
9 'Abdu'l-Bahá, *Promulgation*, p. 109.
10 Universal House of Justice cited in *Women*, pp. 14–15.
11 Bahá'u'lláh, *Tablets*, p. 26.
12 'Abdu'l-Bahá, *Paris*, pp. 176–7.
13 Shoghi Effendi, *World Order*, p. 203.
14 ibid. pp. 40–41.
15 Shoghi Effendi, *Messages*, p. 43.
16 Shoghi Effendi, *World Order*, pp. 3–4.
17 ibid. p. 19.
18 ibid. p. 43.
19 Shoghi Effendi, *God Passes By*, p. 256.

Y

1 From a letter of the Universal House of Justice, 27 January 1969. *Lights*, no. 811.
2 From a letter of the Universal House of Justice, 29 March 1966. *Lights*, no. 804.
3 *Synopsis*, p. 42.
4 Universal House of Justice, *Wellspring*, pp. 94–5.

Z

1 Shoghi Effendi, *God Passes By*, p. 95.

Bibliography

'Abdu'l-Bahá. *'Abdu'l-Bahá in London*. Reprinted. Oakham: Bahá'í Publishing Trust, 1982.

——— *Foundations of World Unity*. Wilmette, Illinois: Bahá'í Publishing Trust, 1979.

——— *Paris Talks*. London: Bahá'í Publishing Trust, 10th ed. 1961.

——— *The Promulgation of Universal Peace*. Compiled by Howard MacNutt. Wilmette, Illinois: Bahá'í Publishing Trust, 2nd ed. 1982.

——— *Selections from the Writings of 'Abdu'l-Bahá*. Compiled by the Research Department of the Universal House of Justice. Translated by a Committee at the Bahá'í World Centre and by Marzieh Gail. Haifa: Bahá'í World Centre, 1978.

——— *Some Answered Questions*. Collected and Translated from the Persian by Laura Clifford Barney. Wilmette, Illinois: Bahá'í Publishing Trust, 1964.

——— *Tablets of the Divine Plan*. Wilmette, Illinois: Bahá'í Publishing Trust, rev. ed. 1977.

——— *Will and Testament of 'Abdu'l-Bahá*. Wilmette, Illinois: Bahá'í Publishing Committee, 1944.

Bahá'í Education. Compilation issued by the Universal House of Justice. Oakham: Bahá'í Publishing Trust, 1976.

Bahá'í International Community. 'Focus Statement', 1986.

Bahá'í News. A magazine published by the National Spiritual Assembly of the United States. Wilmette, Illinois. ed. June 1988.

Bahá'í Prayers. Wilmette, Illinois: Bahá'í Publishing Trust, 1982.

Bahá'í World, The. vols. IV, VIII, XVI. Reprinted. Wilmette, Illinois: Bahá'í Publishing Trust, 1980.

Bahá'í World Faith. Wilmette, Illinois: Bahá'í Publishing Trust, rev. ed. 1976.

Bahá'u'lláh. *Epistle to the Son of the Wolf*. Wilmette, Illinois: Bahá'í Publishing Trust, 1962.

——— *Gleanings from the Writings of Bahá'u'lláh*. Translated by Shoghi Effendi. Wilmette, Illinois: Bahá'í Publishing Trust, 1963.

——— *The Hidden Words of Bahá'u'lláh*. Wilmette, Illinois: Bahá'í Publishing Committee, 1954.

——— *Kitáb-i-Íqán: The Book of Certitude*. Wilmette, Illinois: Bahá'í Publishing Trust, 1960.

——— *Prayers and Meditations*. Wilmette, Illinois: Bahá'í Publishing Trust, 1979.

——— *The Seven Valleys and The Four Valleys*. Translated by Marzieh Gail (with Ali-Kuli Khan). Wilmette, Illinois: Bahá'í Publishing Trust, rev. ed. 1978.

——— *Tablets of Bahá'u'lláh revealed after the Kitáb-i-Aqdas*. Compiled by the Research Department of the Universal House of Justice and translated by Habib Taherzadeh with the assistance of a Committee at the Bahá'í World Centre. Haifa: Bahá'í World Centre, 1978.

Bahíyyih Khánum, The Greatest Holy Leaf. A compilation from Bahá'í sacred texts and writings of the Guardian of the Faith and Bahíyyih Khánum's own letters made by the Research Department at the Bahá'í World Centre. Haifa: Bahá'í World Centre, 1982.

Balyuzi, H. M. *'Abdu'l-Bahá*. Oxford: George Ronald, 1971.

——— *The Báb*. Oxford: George Ronald, 1973.

——— *Bahá'u'lláh, King of Glory*. Oxford: George Ronald, 1980.

Bibliography

Deepening. Compilation issued by the Universal House of Justice. Oakham: Bahá'í Publishing Trust, 1983.

Esslemont, J. E. *Bahá'u'lláh and the New Era*. Wilmette, Illinois: Bahá'í Publishing Trust, 4th rev. ed. 1976.

Gift of Teaching, The. Compilation issued by the Universal House of Justice. Oakham: Bahá'í Publishing Trust, 1977.

Heaven of Divine Wisdom, The. Compilation issued by the Universal House of Justice. Oakham: Bahá'í Publishing Trust, 1978.

Ḥuqúqu'lláh. Compiled by the Research Department of the Universal House of Justice. Oakham: Bahá'í Publishing Trust, 1986.

Importance of Prayer, Meditation and the Devotional Attitude, The. Compiled by the Research Department of the Universal House of Justice. Oakham: Bahá'í Publishing Trust, 1980.

Kolstoe, John E. *Consultation: A Universal Lamp of Guidance*. Oxford: George Ronald, 1985.

Lights of Guidance. Compiled by Helen Hornby. New Delhi: Bahá'í Publishing Trust, 1983.

Local Spiritual Assemblies. Compilation issued by the Universal House of Justice. Oakham: Bahá'í Publishing Trust, 1970.

Momen, Moojan, ed. *Selections from the Writings of E. G. Browne on the Bábí and Bahá'í Religions*. Oxford: George Ronald, 1987.

Nabíl-i-A'ẓam. *The Dawn-Breakers: Nabíl's Narrative of the Early Days of the Bahá'í Revelation*. Wilmette, Illinois: Bahá'í Publishing Trust, 1962.

Principles of Bahá'í Administration. London: Bahá'í Publishing Trust, 1973.

Rabbani, Ruhiyyih. *The Priceless Pearl*. London: Bahá'í Publishing Trust, 1969.

Ruhe, David S. *Door of Hope*. Oxford: George Ronald, 1983.

Shoghi Effendi. *The Advent of Divine Justice*. Wilmette, Illinois: Bahá'í Publishing Trust, rev. ed. 1963.

——— *Bahá'í Administration: Selected Messages 1922–1932*. Wilmette, Illinois: Bahá'í Publishing Trust, 1974.

——— *Citadel of Faith: Messages to America 1947–1957*. Wilmette, Illinois: Bahá'í Publishing Trust, 1965.

——— *God Passes By*. Wilmette, Illinois: Bahá'í Publishing Trust, 1944.

——— *The Light of Divine Guidance: The Messages from the Guardian of the Bahá'í Faith to the Bahá'ís of Germany and Austria*. Hofheim-Langenhain: Bahá'í-Verlag, 1982.

——— *Messages to the Bahá'í World 1950–1957*. Wilmette, Illinois: Bahá'í Publishing Trust, 1958.

——— *The Promised Day is Come*. Wilmette, Illinois: Bahá'í Publishing Trust, 1967.

——— *The World Order of Bahá'u'lláh*. Wilmette, Illinois: Bahá'í Publishing Trust, 1955.

Smith, Peter. *The Bahá'í Religion: A Short Introduction to its History and Teachings*. Oxford, George Ronald, 1988.

Star of the West. Reprinted. Oxford: George Ronald, 1984.

Synopsis and Codification of The Kitáb-i-Aqdas, the Most Holy Book of Bahá'u'lláh, A. Haifa: Bahá'í World Centre, 1973.

Taherzadeh, Adib. *The Revelation of Bahá'u'lláh*. Vol. 1. Oxford: George Ronald, 1974.

——— *The Revelation of Bahá'u'lláh*. Vol. 2. Oxford: George Ronald, 1977.

——— *The Revelation of Bahá'u'lláh*. Vol. 3. Oxford: George Ronald, 1983.

——— *The Revelation of Bahá'u'lláh*. Vol. 4. Oxford: George Ronald, 1987.

Trustworthiness. Compiled by the Research Department of the Universal House of Justice. Oakham: Bahá'í Publishing Trust, 1987.
Universal House of Justice. *Messages from the Universal House of Justice 1968–1973*. Wilmette, Illinois: Bahá'í Publishing Trust, 1976.
——— *The Promise of the World Peace*. Haifa: Bahá'í World Centre, 1985.
——— *Wellspring of Guidance*. Wilmette, Illinois: Bahá'í Publishing Trust, 1969.
Women. Compiled by the Research Department of the Universal House of Justice. Oakham: Bahá'í Publishing Trust, 1986.

AN INTRODUCTION TO THE BAHÁ'Í FAITH AND TO BAHÁ'Í LITERATURE . . .

A BASIC BAHÁ'Í DICTIONARY gives you

- Definitions of words found in Bahá'í literature
- Explanations of Bahá'í concepts
- An introduction to figures from Bahá'í history
- Descriptions of significant events
- A glossary of Persian and Arabic terms
- 800 entries and 200 illustrations

ISBN 0-85398-231-7
9 780853 982319

Also available in a hardcover edition

£9.95 net or
US $16.40 (recommended)

ISBN 0-85398-231-7

GEORGE RONALD • OXFORD